D0402215

Hearts of Iron, Feet of Clay

By
Gary Inrig

MOODY PRESS
CHICAGO

TO
Elizabeth,
God's gift of love,
who has constantly strengthened
my hand in God.

Library of Congress Cataloging in Publication Data

Inrig, Gary.
  Hearts of iron, feet of clay.

  Includes bibliographical references.
  1. Bible. O.T. Judges—Commentaries. I. Title.
BS1305.3.I57 222'32'06 79-148
ISBN 0-8024-3487-8

Moody Paperback Edition, 1981

4 5 6 7 Printing/GB/Year 87 86 85 84 83

Printed in the United States of America

Contents

Preface

Hoof-and-mouth disease is the scourge of the cattle industry, and an outbreak can decimate herds very quickly. Therefore, when the disease hit one cattle area a few years ago, authorities clamped on a strict quarantine to isolate and control the problem. There was one rancher who was determined to save his animals. He carefully sprayed every building on his farm, every room of his house, and every vehicle on his property. He then moved all his animals into a carefully scrubbed and disinfected building, padlocked the door and restricted all contact with the outside world. No visitors were allowed on his property, and he even went to the point of picking up his newspaper at the front gate with sterile gloves, then baking it in the oven to kill any bacteria. Yet, despite his desperate efforts, within three weeks some of his cows became ill, and the entire herd had to be liquidated. As one health officer noted, "The virus is transmitted through the air, and you can't quarantine the wind."

In our time, the winds of the "me generation" are blowing a strong and deadly virus. "Doing your own thing" has been enshrined as the national life-style, and the virus of relativism has infected every area of life, especially our concepts of spiritual truth and moral absolutes. Our society is increasingly secular, increasingly pagan, and vigorously anti-Christian. If ever a verse of the Bible has the ring of the twentieth century about it, it is the motto of the times of the judges: "Everyone did what was right in his own eyes."

The implication of this for us as believers in the Lord Jesus is obvious. We Christians cannot hermetically seal ourselves from the spirit of the age, so that we live in splendid isolation from it. First of all, the Lord Jesus calls us to live in the world for His glory, and monasticism is not a biblical alternative. Our mandate from the risen Christ prohibits isolation. But equally significant is the fact that isolation is unrealistic. Every area of modern society, from our school system through our entertainment media to the world of business, has been penetrated by secularism, and it meets us in the most unexpected places. In fact, we often see it in its most dangerous form within the Christian community, and often Christians live, act, and choose as if God's Word had never been written.

How do we live in a society without fixed standards, a society daily becoming more secular and pagan? God's call is clear: "Prove yourselves to be blameless and innocent, children of God above reproach in the midst of a crooked and perverse generation, among whom you appear as lights in the world, holding fast the word of life" (Phil. 2:15-16). These are important verses. They remind us that we are not simply to survive the moral confusion and spiritual anarchy which surround us, somehow staying unpolluted by the world. We are also to shine, reflecting the glory of the Lord Jesus to a world which desperately needs to see Him. In other words, we are not just to be good in the midst of evil. We are not even just to be good for something, serving our fellowman. We are to be good for Someone, the Lord Jesus Christ, as we bear witness to Him in the world.

But still the question remains: When everyone around us is doing right in his own eyes, how do Christians keep on track, doing what is right in their Lord's eyes? Solid answers to that question are found in a book written about another time of moral and spiritual anarchy. It lies neglected on the pages of the Old Testament, but I am convinced that God has something very practical and contemporary to say to us in the book of Judges.

Few periods of history are so much like our own—at one moment scaling the peaks of glory and at the next plunging headlong into the swamp of sin. In its pages are some of the most exciting events in biblical history, and on their heels march some of the saddest accounts of sinful

failure and disobedience. But through it all, there is found
the hand of God working in, through, and despite His
people.

The book of Judges is filled with people very much like
us—people with God-given potential for greatness and unfailing capacity for catastrophe. When they dared to trust
God and depend upon Him, they were indeed people with
hearts of iron, who made a positive, godly impact on their
times. But when even the greatest heroes depended upon
the flesh, they were revealed as people with feet of clay,
who not only experienced but caused spiritual catastrophe.
As we study their lives and discover the great principles
God reveals about His work in His people, we can learn
what it is to live a powerful, productive life in the middle of
a society which is increasingly hostile to the disciples of the
Lord Jesus.

I want to take this opportunity to express my apprecia-
tion to the believers at Bethany Chapel, Calgary, for their
encouragement and insightful contributions to my life and
ministry. A special word of thanks is due to Miss Pat
Johnson, who has labored hard and long in preparing the
manuscript. Also to Elizabeth, Janice, Stephen, and Heather
go profound love for their patience, support, and love.

ONE_

The Consequences of Compromise

The cartoon said it all. A sophisticated college student was speaking to a missionary unmistakably identified by his proverbial pith helmet and shorts. Bewildered, the student asked, "But what do you do when you can't take the superstition and violence and immorality any longer?"

"Simple," came the reply. "We get on a plane and go back to the mission field."

Ouch! But every day the media shouts the message that we would rather not hear. The lights go out in a great city and an orgy of lawlessness results. The concrete canyons of our cities are filled with people living in fear, often barricaded within secure fortresses. A national magazine chronicles the awesome power of organized crime and follows it a few weeks later with the startling story of youthful crime and violence, carried out with a terrifying, cold-eyed amorality. A major Canadian church issues a preliminary report which seriously considers putting to death severely retarded children, and a chief architect of the report suggests that such children are not genuine human beings. Homosexuality has become so widely accepted that one-quarter of the population of a major American city is said to practice it, while biblical morality is ridiculed or dismissed as irrelevent by our most popular television programs. Divorce rates soar while the phenomenon of "living together" becomes standard operating procedure among a great part of the population.

The list could be lengthened indefinitely. No serious observers can doubt that the Western world is experiencing an enormous moral crisis. Ours is a cut-flower civilization. While a sign of life remains, we have cut ourselves off from our biblical roots, and the petals are beginning to droop and fall. It is not an exaggeration to say that we are a society without standards. The youthful rock star who told an interviewer, "I believe absolutely nothing," is, unfortunately, speaking for a good part of his generation.

One thing seems obvious. There has never been a time like our time when God's people were overwhelmed by such a flood of immorality and amorality. It is perhaps more like a tidal wave than a flood, because it threatens to carry everything away before it, leaving only destruction in its wake.

But is it really unprecedented? We do not minimize the present crisis by recognizing that significant parallels to our time are found in the past, and some of the most relevant are found in a neglected Old Testament book, the book of Judges. It is a part of Scripture which describes a time of moral, spiritual, and ethical anarchy, a society without standards whose life-style is captured in a thoroughly modern phrase, found at the back door of the book: "Everyone did what was right in his own eyes" (Judg. 21:25).

Judges is a book which speaks to our time because it presents us with living examples of people who served God in such a time and not only survived spiritually but flourished. At the same time, it presents us with people who did not survive, but who succumbed to the wave of sin. Judges vividly demonstrates to us the consequences of spiritual compromise and disobedience to God, as the world tries to squeeze believers into its mold. No other part of Scripture so emphatically declares that spiritual disaster occurs when a group of people draw back from a wholehearted commitment to the Lord Jesus.

Our time is a dangerous and exciting one in which to serve the Lord Jesus Christ. The challenges and opportunities He has given to His Body in the last quarter of the twentieth century are unique and exhilarating. But Satan is on the march as well, and unless we grab hold of the great principles of spiritual living presented in the book of Judges, we may find ourselves to be spiritual dropouts, mere spectators at the climax of the invisible war between God and Satan.

Judges begins by giving us a graphic reminder of the consequences of compromise and partial obedience in a time of spiritual anarchy. It is the fundamental principle that the Holy Spirit communicates about spiritual survival in a society without standards. Partial defense is no defense at all. As D. L. Moody once said, "The place for the ship is in the sea, but God help the ship if the sea gets into it!" When God's people begin to take on the water of the world, they go down fast, and in the opening verses of this great book we see that process vividly portrayed.

AFTER THE DEATH OF JOSHUA—1:1

Now it came about after the death of Joshua that the sons of Israel inquired to the LORD, saying, "Who shall go up first for us against the Canaanites, to fight against them?"

The first few words of the book of Judges may at first glance seem to be only a helpful historical notation. "After the death of Joshua," however, is a statement of drastic change in the spiritual health of the nation of Israel. Although the books of Joshua and Judges stand side by side on the pages of Scripture, they are poles apart in what they record of Israel's obedience to God. Joshua is the record of the exploits of Israel as they trusted their Lord and obeyed God. God brought His people into Canaan and gave them victory after victory over their foes. Joshua is a book of conquest, but Judges is a long, sad story of defeat. Joshua is a book of faith, Judges of unbelief and disobedience. Joshua depicts a people united in following God's man, but Judges is a book of division and anarchy, as every man "did what was right in his own eyes." In Joshua, God's Word is central and men submit to His authority, while in Judges, Scripture is neglected and rejected.

There are two verses which clearly indicate the difference between the time of Joshua and the period of the judges. As Joshua was about to die, he issued his famous challenge to the people to "choose this day whom you will serve." With one voice the people answered, *"Far be it from us that we should forsake the LORD to serve other gods"* (Josh. 24:16, itals. added). Under Joshua's leadership, there was a strong vocal commitment to the authority of the Lord in Israel. But early in Judges we have God's description of the time of the judges: "And the sons of Israel did what was evil in the sight of the LORD, and *forgot the LORD their God, and served the Baals and the Asheroth"* (Judg. 3:7, itals. added). In Joshua, "we will not forget the LORD." In Judges, "the people forgot the LORD." Why did that happen? How did a people who knew continuous victory by faith sink to be a nation experiencing constant failure due to compromise? And how can we guard against the same thing in our lives? We sing,

> Prone to wander, Lord, I feel it,
> Prone to leave the God I love.

What happened in the time of Judges is sad, but it is not unique. Perhaps by seeing where the sons of Israel failed, we can guard against leaving the fount of blessing today.

That is one important question the book of Judges answers, but it also confronts us on another level. This is not simply a dreary desert of defeat. There is failure, but there is also faith. Few other books give us such insight into the grace and long-suffering of our God. Side by side with compromise and apostasy runs the story of men and women who knew what it was to live for God by faith in difficult times. Many of the great heroes of faith enrolled in Hebrews 11 come from the book of Judges, and when their peers were being swallowed up by the temptations of the times, they were making a positive impact for their Lord. From a study of their successes and failures, and more significantly, from a recognition of God's gracious work in their lives, we can learn some great lessons of spiritual survival in a society without standards.

We may be surprised to discover that the book of Judges covers about one-quarter of the historical period described in the Old Testament. About 300 to 350 years pass between Judges 1 and Judges 21, yet it remains one of the most neglected books in the Bible. Except for the stories of Gideon and Samson, most Christians know very little about the book, and even those stories are known only in the most superficial way. But to neglect it is to rob ourselves of significant truths the Holy Spirit wants to teach us.

The outline of Judges is a very simple one, as the book falls naturally into three sections:

THE PREVIEW OF THE JUDGES 1:1—3:6—The Cycle of Sin
THE PERIOD OF THE JUDGES 3:7—16:31—The Downward
    Spiral
THE PICTURE OF THE JUDGES 17:1—21:25—Spiritual Anarchy

Who wrote Judges we are not told. Jewish tradition, which may be reliable, suggests that it was Samuel, and internal evidence points to a composition in the early monarchy. However, the message of the book is not dependent on either its date of writing or its authorship, and the questions may be safely set aside.

THE COVENANT-KEEPING GOD—2:1

The message of Judges is not difficult to discern. It revolves around two great themes—the faithfulness of the covenant-keeping God and the unfaithfulness of His covenant-breaking people. It is a message declared by the direct intervention of God in an encounter which provides a preview to the entire period. It is recorded in the first verse of Judges 2 in connection with a highly symbolic act: "Now the angel of the LORD came up from Gilgal to Bochim. And he said, 'I brought you up out of Egypt and led you into the land which I have sworn to your fathers; and I said, 'I will never break My covenant with you.' "

We must pay careful attention when we read that "the angel of the LORD went up from Gilgal to Bochim." The exact nature of the angelic appearance is not indicated, but this was much more than an ordinary angelic appearance, remarkable as that would be. The clue is found in the words the angel spoke. He did not say, "God brought you up from Egypt." He used the first person throughout: "I brought you up ... I swore ... I said ... I will never break My covenant." In other words, the Angel of the Lord was God Himself appearing in human form to His people. To be more specific, we must recognize that the Angel of the Lord is the Lord Jesus. This was not the first such appearance, nor would it be the last.

No event in which the Lord Jesus temporarily takes human form to appear to men can fail to be very important, and that is certainly true in Judges 2. Before the sad story of Judges unfolded, the Lord of grace personally warned men of the consequences of their actions. The first way He did that was by moving from Gilgal to Bochim. It is a symbolic act of great significance.

Gilgal is a place of great importance in the book of Joshua. When the people had miraculously crossed the Jordan River, they came to Gilgal. It was there that they obeyed God by renewing the practice of circumcision and by keeping the Passover. It was at Gilgal that God Himself appeared to Joshua and gave him the promise that He was the commander in chief of the Lord's army and that He would lead Israel into victory. Gilgal was the place of victory and blessing. In contrast, *Bochim* means "weeping," and when the Lord moved from Gilgal, He was spelling out for Israel the cost of carnality. "At Gilgal, you trusted Me and you knew victory. Now you have turned from Me. Your home will be Bochim, the place of weeping and judgment."

The tragedy of that shift of location is that God had committed Himself unconditionally to His people, and their defeat was completely unnecessary. "I will never break My covenant with you." That was a pledge made on the basis of God's eternal covenant with Abraham. When He called

Abraham, He promised him three things: that he would have descendants, a seed; that his seed would possess a land that He would give them; and that from Abraham would flow blessing to the world, for "in you all the families of the earth shall be blessed" (Gen. 12:3). It is a promise God repeated over and over to Abraham, Isaac, and Jacob, and the great Abrahamic covenant became the foundation of God's dealings in history with Israel, through Israel, and supremely, in the Lord Jesus.

On the basis of that covenant, God reached into Egypt and delivered His people from slavery. Under Joshua, He brought them into the promised land of Canaan. God is a covenant-keeping God. He had kept the patriarchs in the land, had preserved Israel for 400 years in Egypt, had guided and supplied a rebellious people for 40 years in the wilderness, and had given them victory in the promised land over their enemies. "I will never break My covenant." He had not and He would not. In fact, He could not. He is a faithful God who cannot deny Himself.

The Abrahamic covenant is extremely important. First, it is the key to God's program in history. God must keep His promise to Abraham. He is not done with the people of Israel. There is coming a time when the Lord Jesus, the seed of Abraham, will come back to earth and set up His Kingdom to fulfill the Abrahamic covenant. Second, it gives us great assurance. God keeps His promises. He doesn't add on all kinds of hidden conditions and "ifs" and "maybes." He does what He says. "I will never break My covenant, My promise." How do we know our sins are forgiven? He *said so.* How do we know we have eternal life? He *said so.* How do we know we are part of His family? He *said so,* and He never goes back on His Word. That is a foundation block for life. We can trust the Word of God because the God of the Word stands behind it.

THE COVENANT-BREAKING NATION—2:2

But God did not stop there. He continued to speak in Judges 2:2: "And as for you, you shall make no covenant with the inhabitants of this land; you shall tear down their altars. *But you have not obeyed Me; what is this you have done?*" (itals. added).

Having reminded the people of His unconditional promise, the Lord reminded them of the responsibility He had given to them. At Mount Sinai the people had committed themselves to following the sovereign God. To worship Him as their God meant first of all that they were to make no covenant or treaty alliance with the people of Canaan. The only covenant permitted to them was their covenant with God. The enemy was the enemy, and there could be no relationship with him. "You shall make no covenant with the inhabitants of this land."

The second demand flowed from the first. The fact that they were to make no treaties did not mean that they could live in a state of strained coexistence. "You shall tear down their altars." The sin of the Canaanites was a deadly cancer, and the Lord called upon His people to remove it surgically from the land, before it infected them. They were to destroy the idols and altars of the Canaanites and drive them from the land.

The Lord was echoing the command He had given at Mount Sinai: "You shall make no covenant with them or with their gods. They shall not live in your land, *lest they make you sin against Me;* for *if* you serve their gods, it will surely be a snare to you" (Exod. 23:32-33, itals. added). The truth of that prophecy is revealed on every page of the book of Judges.

But we must not misunderstand the command. God had not given the Israelites a challenge and left them to do the best they could. That is never His method. When He gives a responsibility, He gives a resource to do it, and He had committed Himself to giving His people victory. Their job was to trust Him and obey Him. "And all these blessings shall come upon you and overtake you, if you will obey the LORD your God. The LORD will cause your enemies who rise up against you to be defeated before you; they shall come out against you one way and shall flee before you seven ways. The LORD will command the blessing upon you in your barns and in all that you put your hand to, and He will bless you in the land which the LORD your God gives you" (Deut. 28:2, 7-8). So with the responsibility of unwavering obedience to the Lord came a resource of unlimited power through the Lord.

THE FAILURE OF ISRAEL

But what happened? The Angel of the Lord put it very simply: "But you have not listened to My voice. Why have you done this?" The record of that disobedience is the subject of Judges 1. At first, it appears to be a long list of names and places, a catalog of Israel's warfares. It is a dull list of unfamiliar names and places which could not possbily have any relevance in the present. Or could it? In fact, Judges 1 diagnoses the problem which is the key to the entire period of the judges and perhaps points a finger at a problem area in our own lives.

The chapter opens with a record of the victories of the tribe of Judah. And it is a very impressive record. In verses 4, 8-9, 17-18, Judah went up against all kinds of Canaanite strongholds. But there are two disturbing notes.

The first is found in verse 6. Judah conquered Bezek, and they captured the king. Then they cut off his thumbs and his big toes. That was a very effective way of ending his military career; there was no way he could handle a bow or sword again. But mutilation was a pagan practice. They were drawing their standards from people around them. And besides, God wanted these men put to death, not mutilated. The obedience of Judah was only partial.

The second disturbing note is found in verse 19. Judah did not drive out the Canaanites in the valley because the Canaanites had iron chariots. Now that seems logical— Judah was outgunned. But in fact, that was not the reason at all. God had promised that He would drive out the enemy. Later, in chapter 4, Deborah led Israel into victory against an army with 900 iron chariots. Furthermore, the greatest victories Israel would have would come under David, and he never used iron chariots. The real reason Judah did not have victory was that they did not trust God. *Diminished power is always the result of diminished faith.*

The rest of the chapter catalogs the partial weakness of other tribes. Benjamin failed to drive out the Jebusites (v.21), while Manasseh did not drive out the pagan inhabitants of its area. Even when they did possess power to drive out the Canaanites, they preferred to use them as forced labor, a cheap source of energy (vv. 27-28). Their problem was not a lack of power but a lack of obedience. The same record is given of Ephraim (v. 29), Zebulun (v. 30), and Asher (vv. 31-32). With monotonous regularity the clause recurs, "They did not drive out the inhabitants."

In two cases, the results of incomplete obedience are more obvious. Naphtali did not drive the Canaanites from its area (v. 33) but chose to live in a position of compromise. It was Dan that knew the most bitter results of disobedience (v. 34). They were pressed into the hill country, because the Amorites wouldn't allow them to come down to the plain. They became subject to forced labor, reduced to servitude when God had promised them victory.

The lesson of Judges 1 is very clear. The people of Israel chose deliberately to obey God only partly. Rather than following the Lord wholeheartedly, they compromised. They went partway, and that compromise meant inevitable catastrophe. The Angel of the Lord spelled out the consequences.

THE CONSEQUENCES OF COMPROMISE—2:3-5

Therefore I also said, "I will not drive them out before you; but they shall become as thorns in your sides, and their gods shall be a snare to you." And it came about when the angel of the LORD spoke these words to all the sons of Israel, that the people lifted up their voices and wept. So they named that place Bochim; and there they sacrificed to the LORD.

Despite their sin and unbelief, God did not turn His back on His people. The Angel did not appear to announce that, in frustration, He was breaking His covenant. The purpose of His coming was a purpose of grace, designed to bring the nation to radical repentance.

The Lord spelled out the consequences of compromise: "All right. You would not obey and drive out the Canaanites. That was your decision, and you will have to live with it. I am not going to drive them out. I am going to leave them, and you are going to experience the natural consequences of compromise. Those people are going to drag you down, and they are going to be a constant nuisance and snare to you."

When the people realized what God was saying, they began to weep. One of the most certain facts of spiritual experience is that the path of partial obedience leads to Bochim. There is no joy in halfhearted spiritual experience. A young man came to see me and, after a short time, he began to spit out his bitterness and anger. Above all, he was angry at God because his profession of faith had brought him no joy or peace or satisfaction. Other people talked about the joy of the Lord, but his life had turned to ashes in his mouth. But as we talked, he also began to describe his involvement in sin and his lack of time in God's Word and in fellowship with the Lord and with other Christians. He was living at Bochim, the place of weeping.

The most miserable people in the world are professing believers who will not commit themselves to the Lord Jesus. They do not have the best of both worlds but the worst. That was true in the time of Judges, and it is true today. If as Christians we try to walk the tightrope of compromise and partial obedience, we will not know spiritual victory and God's blessing. We will know the bitterness of defeat and frustration in our Christian lives.

But even there the grace of God is not through. He does not just leave His people to suffer the consequences of sin. In His grace, He sends to call them back to wholehearted obedience and commitment to Him. The book of Judges is not simply a record of man's sin and God's judgment, it is a record of God's love, which seeks men even in their sin.

Do you know spiritual victory in your life? Do you know God's blessing in your life? If you don't maybe you need to check out the pattern of obedience in your life. Remember: Halfhearted obedience is the path of misery.

TWO

The Second-Generation Syndrome

Once upon a time there was a foolish old man who lived in northern China. His house faced toward the south with two great mountains, Taihang and Wangwu, in his backyard. Those two mountains frustrated him; so, armed with his hoe and great determination, he decided to remove them.

One day, as he and his sons were hoeing away at the mountains, a man of the region, known for his great wisdom, drew near to watch. Finally, the wise old man said, "How silly! It is impossible for you to dig up those two huge mountains with your hoes."

The foolish old man looked at him and said, "When I die, my sons will carry on. When they die, there will be my grandsons. And then their sons and grandsons, and so on to infinity. High as they are, those mountains can not grow any higher; and with every bit we dig, they will be that much lower. Why can't we clear them away?"

So the foolish old man went on digging, undeterred by the skepticism of the wise old man. When God saw how determined the foolish old man was, He sent two angels to carry away the mountains on their backs.

This children's tale embodies the most revolutionary political philosophy of the twentieth century. In 1945, Mao Tse-tung used the story to illustrate how China was going to rid itself of the two mountains of feudalism and imperialism. When he seized power in China, in 1949, Mao attacked those mountains with all the determination of the foolish old man, plus his own violent ruthlessness. He did not ignore "wise old men," he butchered them by the score.

21

His hands also were stained with the blood of countless Christians.

In time, however, Mao Tse-tung became concerned. The story would come true only if the sons kept digging away at the mountains. What if the next generation, who had never experienced the revolution, lost its zest for the job? In 1966, when he saw China becoming bourgeois and lazy, he developed the Maoist theory of revolution. To eliminate any possibility of antirevolutionary, reactionary, revisionist cliques, China must be kept in constant ferment—then every generation will have a firsthand experience of a revolution.

I am no admirer of Mao Tse-tung. His satanic philosophy has kept hundreds of millions of people from the opportunity of hearing the good news of salvation. At the same time, I recognize Mao's keen insight into human nature, regarding a pattern I call the second-generation syndrome.

The second generation has a natural tendency to accept the status quo and to lose the vision of the first generation. Too often the second-generation experience is a second-hand experience.

That syndrome operates in the spiritual realm as well as in the political. Church history is filled with examples of it, and, sadly, so are many churches. The parents' fervor for the Lord Jesus Christ becomes the children's formalism and the grandchildren's apathy. We meet this syndrome most vividly in the book of Judges. Perhaps as we examine Scripture and see this syndrome in action, we will be better able to guard against it in our own lives and in the lives of our second generation.

> When Joshua had dismissed the people, the sons of Israel went each to his inheritance to possess the land. And the people served the LORD all the days of Joshua, and all the days of the elders who survived Joshua, who had seen all the great work of the LORD which He had done for Israel. Then Joshua the son of Nun, the servant of the LORD, died at the

age of one hundred and ten. And they buried him in the territory of his inheritance in Timnath-heres, in the hill country of Ephraim, north of Mount Gaash. And all that generation also were gathered to their fathers; and there arose another generation after them who did not know the LORD, nor yet the work which He had done for Israel. Then the sons of Israel did evil in the sight of the LORD, and served the Baals, and they forsook the LORD, the God of their fathers, who had brought them out of the land of Egypt, and followed other gods, from among the gods of the peoples who were around them, and bowed themselves down to them; thus they provoked the LORD to anger (Judg. 2:6-12).

Now these are the nations which the LORD left, to test Israel by them (that is, all who had not experienced any of the wars of Canaan; only in order that the generations of the sons of Israel might be taught war, those who had not experienced it formerly). These nations are: the five lords of the Philistines and all the Canaanites and the Sidonians and the Hivites who lived in Mount Lebanon, from Mount Baal-hermon as far as Lebo-hamath. And they were for testing Israel, to find out if they would obey the commandments of the LORD, which He had commanded their fathers through Moses. And the sons of Israel lived among the Canaanites, the Hittites, the Amorites, the Perizzites, the Hivites, and the Jebusites; and they took their daughters for themselves as wives, and gave their own daughters to their sons, and served their gods (3:1-6).

In my university days, I had some friends who were almost a cult in their interest in Walt Kelly's comic strip, *Pogo*. I must confess that the satire was beyond my intellectual capacity—Snoopy and the *Peanuts'* gang turned me on—but I do remember one strip vividly. Pogo and the others had marched off to battle in the swamp, and Pogo returned with the sardonic report, "We have met the enemy—and he is us."

How true that is! The greatest battle we fight is with ourselves. Though not a very flattering insight, it is an important one, as illustrated in the passage we have just read. Israel failed to defeat their own worst instincts. But before we examine their failure, let us reflect briefly on the impact of Joshua and his generation. They are the first generation, the standard by which we can judge the condition of the second generation.

THE IMPACT OF JOSHUA—2:6-9

Joshua was one of the great figures of the Old Testament. He was a great soldier, brilliant organizer, charismatic leader, and a gifted administrator. But merely to list those characteristics is to be very superficial, because none of them reveals the heart of the man. Two characteristics stand out above all others in his life and account for the way in which God worked through him.

The first characteristic is Joshua's responsiveness to the Word of God. At the beginning of his leadership, as he faced the awesome task of succeeding Moses, God came to him with a promise and a challenge:

> Only be strong and very courageous; be careful to do according to all the law which Moses My servant commanded you; do not turn from it to the right or to the left, so that you may have success wherever you go. This book of the law shall not depart from your mouth, but you shall meditate on it day and night, so that you may be careful to do according to all that is written in it; for then you will make your way prosperous, and then you will have success (Josh. 1:7-8).

God promised Joshua prosperity and wisdom through obeying, reading, and proclaiming His Word. Throughout his life, Joshua acted on that promise, and God honored his obedience.

Joshua's second outstanding characteristic was his active faith. "Just as I have been with Moses, I will be with you; I will not fail you or forsake you" (Josh. 1:5). Trusting that promise, Joshua guided two million people toward a river in flood, and God cut off the waters so the people crossed on dry ground. In obedience to God's orders, he marched the nation around the city of Jericho, and the walls of the city crumbled. By faith, he commanded the sun and moon to stand still in the valley of Aijalon, and they did. Believing God's victory-promise, he attacked an overwhelming military alliance at Merom and led his people to defeat their enemies.

Joshua was not a perfect man, and Scripture is honest enough to record his failures. But God used him, not because of his gifts and abilities, but because he trusted God and orderd his life by the Word of God. As a result, God did great deeds for His people through Joshua. That is the thrust of Judges 2:7. Johsua kept Israel in the place of God's blessing. "And the people served the LORD all the days of Joshua, and all the days of the elders who survived Joshua, who had seen all the great work of the LORD which He had done for Israel."

This verse teaches an important lesson. One man, committed unreservedly to God and His Word, can make an enormous difference for good in the lives of God's people. One woman, living her life for Jesus Christ, can bring blessing to a whole group of people. If you will trust God and build your life on His Word, you can have a godly influence on your family, student group, or local church. That truth is written many times on the pages of Scripture.

But Joshua died, as verse 8 reminds us. Shortly after, "All that generation also were gathered to their fathers." It had been a generation who knew victory, blessing, and forward movement. Then, abruptly in the middle of verse 10, we meet the second generation; and, with them, the situation entirely changes.

THE FAILURE OF THE SECOND GENERATION—2:10

"There arose another generation after them who did not know the LORD, nor yet the work which He had done for Israel." That statement cries out with questions. How did they fail? How could they fail? What produced this result when their parents had seen and experienced so much of God's hand of blessing?

THE NATURE OF THEIR FAILURE

The first questions we must ask are: "In what way did they fail? What was the nature of their failure?" When we read in verse 10 that the second generation "did not know the LORD, not yet the work which He had done for Israel," that is not a reference to intellectual ignorance. They were not uninformed of the events of the Exodus or of the conquest. Theologically, they had a great deal of information about the Lord. What they had not seen with their eyes (and many of them had witnessed through children's eyes, the crossing of the Jordan River and the fall of Jericho), they had heard with their ears. It was not facts they lacked.

They knew about the Lord. They knew about His deeds. But they did not know Him or acknowledge Him. They had become complacent about the living God and had forgotten how to walk in fellowship with Him. They had lost touch with God. Instead of being filled with wonder that God had reached into Egypt and delivered His people from the hand of Pharaoh, or being moved to praise God when they heard the history of Mount Sinai or Gilgal or Jericho or the Canaanite conquests, they simply yawned with boredom. "Aw, we've heard all that before."

Here we come to the heart of the second-generation syndrome. It is a lukewarmness, a complacency, an apathy about amazing biblical truths that we have heard from our childhood, or from our teachers. Whether we like it or not, it is a syndrome which is very much a part of twentieth-century Christian experience. It operates on a personal or a family level, as we begin to leave our first love for the Lord Jesus. It is a pattern which challenges churches and even nations, and nowhere does it work with more devastating effect than in Bible colleges and theological seminaries where, day after day, we come in contact with God's truth. If we are not careful, the syndrome begins, as it does in Joshua and Judges, in the midst of a beautiful display of God's grace and power. History tells us that not even the most vivid display of the life-transforming power of the Holy Spirit will prevent this problem.

But why? Why did it happen then, and why does it happen to us? Some of us have been brought up in fine Christian homes; we know all about the truths of the Word of God, and yet there is a complacency about spiritual things in our lives that cripples us spiritually. We must realize two things about this kind of complacency. The first is something Erich Fromm once pointed out, when he said, "Hate is not the opposite of love. Apathy is." To be complacent in the face of Calvary is the greatest possible rejection of God. The second is that complacency grows like a cancer.

I don't quite know why, but a yawn is one of Satan's most effective weapons, and the thing that really troubles me about the second-generation syndrome is the effect it has on new believers. I am convinced that one of the greatest stumbling blocks young Christians must confront is not the opposition of the world, but the apathy of so-called established Christians.

So then, we need to examine carefully the cause of this second-generation syndrome in the lives of the people of Israel; and, perhaps as we realize the cause of their failure, we can guard against it in our lives. Maybe part of the problem lay with the first generation. Interestingly, however, the book of Judges puts none of the blame there. The second generation was held responsible for their failure, and God would not allow them to shift the blame.

THE CAUSE OF THEIR FAILURE

Three factors stand out, above others, as we analyze what happened to the second generation.

1. *They were satisfied with the status quo.* After Joshua had led the people in some victorious assaults on the land of Canaan, God came to him and said, "Joshua, you are old and advanced in years, and very much of the land remains to be possessed." Then, through Joshua, God gave orders to each of the tribes to take their territory from the Canaanites. The first generation did conquer parts of Canaan, but they left pockets of the enemy untouched.

Then the second generation came along. Their reaction was, "Why bother? We have all the land we need. Those Canaanites are not so bad. We can get along with them." God had given them a command to move out and take the land, but they refused to move out in faith. They were content and comfortable with the status quo.

There has never been a first generation, no matter how great it is, that conquered all the land, that has been all God wants it to be. But the great temptations are to believe that their experience is either the standard for our experiences or that their ideals are beyond our expectations, and we should settle for something less. That is wrong. God did not plan for the experiences of previous generations to be a diving board from which we go down, but to be a foundation on which we are to build.

It is Satan's lie to make us believe that the status quo is all there is. His strategy allows us to say that it does not matter that the Canaanites have the valleys, as long as we have the high country.

I thank God for godly Christian parents, but I want to take what they have given me and build on it and have an even richer experience than they had. I pray that my children will go one step beyond me, and so on. I thank God for what went on in churches in times past. I thank God for what He revealed and what men learned. But I will not, I cannot, be satisfied with simply reliving and reproducing the past. God has more country for Christians to take, and I want to move out for Him.

The first sign, then, of the second-generation syndrome is complacency about the status quo. Watch out for it! The second cause of the syndrome is equally dangerous, one God warned about years before it happened.

2. *They took God's blessings for granted and did not acknowledge Him.* In Deuteronomy 6:10-12, God issued a warning to His people that still speaks to us, especially in the affluent West.

Then it shall come about when the LORD your God brings you into the land which He swore to your fathers, Abraham,

Isaac and Jacob, to give you, great and splendid cities which you did not build, and houses full of all good things which you did not fill, and hewn cisterns which you did not dig, vineyards and olive trees which you did not plant, and you shall eat and be satisfied, *then watch yourself, lest you forget the LORD* who brought you from the land of Egypt, out of the house of slavery (itals. added).

God the Holy Spirit considered this message so important that He had Moses reinforce it in Deuteronomy 8:11-18. The great danger is that the enjoyment of God's blessings makes us blessing-centered rather than God-centered.

The Lord God does not command us to give thanks because it makes Him feel good, but because it does us good. Praise, worship, thanksgiving, and acknowledgement of God's blessings are the greatest protections against the second-generation syndrome. The solution to the problem is not a joyless asceticism which turns its back on God's blessings. As Paul reminds us, "For everything created by God is good, and nothing is to be rejected, *if it is received with gratitude*" (1 Tim. 4:4, itals. added). Our attitude toward our blessings and possessions is one of the most determinative factors in our spiritual health. To be ungrateful about grace is not only foolish, it is dangerous.

We need to recognize the subtlety of our sinful hearts. In our desperation, we call upon God to meet our needs, and, in His infinite grace, He does. Then, with a characteristic display of spiritual amnesia, we begin to take the credit for God's blessing. Israel looked at the land they possessed and said, "Look at what we did!" They became man-centered in their view of life, and, by their attitude of self-congratulation, they sowed the seeds of self-destruction.

That is why the Word of God commands us to give thanks in everything. (1 Thess. 5:18). This is God's expressed will for every Christian. As believer-priests we are to "continually offer up a sacrifice of praise to God, that is, the fruit of lips that give thanks to His name" (Heb. 13:15). It is essential then, in our personal lives, in our families, and in our fellowship in the Body to cultivate and nourish a spirit of praise and thanksgiving. Apathy dies where praise flourishes.

3. *They neglected God's Word.* The third cause of the second-generation syndrome is painfully obvious in Judges. It is astonishing to discover almost no reference to the study of Scripture in this book. What was so central in Joshua is peripheral in Judges. The people possessed Scripture but chose to ignore it. It is almost as if it were not written at all. Ritually, the people did many of the things the Law required, but their obedience was based on tradition, not on personal biblical conviction.

There is an enormous difference between a direct and an indirect relationship to Scripture. An issue comes up in conversation, and two people give exactly the same answer. But on the lips of one, the answer is hollow. He is peddling secondhand convictions, something he has heard from parents or preachers or friends. The other person says the same thing, but his answer rings with the authority of personal conviction. He has been in the Word himself, studied and prayed about the matter, and heard the Shepherd's voice. That Christian knows the fresh dynamic experience of walking with Jesus Christ. Beware of secondhand convictions and secondhand experiences. Don't neglect the Word of God!

God's Strategy Against Complacency—3:1-6

It is important to recognize that God did not leave the second generation to wallow in their apathy. His strategy for moving them forward is spelled out in verses 1-2. The Lord allowed unconquered nations, pockets of resistance, to remain "to test Israel by them . . . only in order that the generations of the sons of Israel might be taught war, those who had not experienced it formerly." Was God interested in giving Israel some kind of technical instruction in military strategy? Obviously not. God desired a group of people who knew how to trust Him in battle. Early in Joshua's career, he had learned that the Lord is the Banner of His people, the One who leads into battle and brings victory (Exod. 17:8-16). Victory does not come from man's courage or wisdom or skill; it comes from a faithful God. That is the lesson God wanted those inexperienced soldiers to learn.

Have you ever wondered why God did not take away your sinful nature when you trusted Him? Why are there so many areas of weakness in your life and such difficult problems and obstacles for you to overcome? Why are there so many needs around for you to fill? Are you ever puzzled because there are no perfect churches, but unsolved problems exist in even the most biblically faithful fellowships?

At least part of the answer is found in Judges 3:2. The Lord uses those difficulties to teach us how to wage spiritual war. He wants to shake us out of our apathy and teach us to trust Him. Often it is only when the enemy has run all over us, and our resources are gone, that we develop a teachable spirit. There are times in our lives when the roof gets blown off, and everything seems to fall to pieces. Those times of failure and crisis become teaching times as the Lord shows us how to make war—how to trust Him.

The implication of this strategy of God in our lives is clear. We cannot stand still in our Christian experience. There are enemies to be faced. There is ground to be gained. If we try to stand still, we can be sure that the principalities and powers, against which we contend, do not. Either we advance, or we perish. There are areas of need in our lives. There is ground to be won in our families and churches. And as long as we live in a world of more than 4 billion people, more than half of whom have never heard of the Lord Jesus, we cannot stand still. We cannot stand by while men and women rush toward hell.

An old man was traveling on an ocean liner, when a huge storm blew up without warning. One woman lost her balance and fell overboard. People stood frozen with horror. Suddenly, a man plunged into the waves, grabbed her, and held her until a rescue boat came. When they were pulled out, everyone was astonished and embarrassed to discover that the hero was the oldest man on the boat—a man in his eighties.

That evening they held a party to honor him. When they called on him to make a speech, the old man rose slowly. He looked around at the people, then said, "I would like to know just one thing." There was an embarrassed silence. "Who pushed me?"

Sometimes that is the only way we start moving. The Lord will keep pushing us out of our complacency, out of the second-generation syndrome, into a fresh, vital experience of walking with the Lord Jesus.

Are you already moving, or do you need a push?

In 1963, John Gardner wrote a challenging little book, *Self-Renewal*. His words are addressed to motivate the renewal of societies and organizations, and he is not writing as a Christian. But he too is concerned with the second-generation syndrome, and his words deserve to be weighed carefully:

> The renewal of societies and organizations can go forward only if someone cares. Apathy and lowered motivation are the most widely noted characteristics of a civilization on the downward path. Apathetic men accomplish nothing. Men who believe in nothing change nothing for the better. They renew nothing and heal no one, least of all themselves. Anyone who understands our situation at all knows that we are in little danger of failing through lack of material strength. If we falter it will be a failure of heart and spirit.[1]

That applies with even greater force to spiritual things. The challenge of the second generation is dynamic renewal and growth. The danger is apathy and spiritual rigor mortis. Which way are you going? Are you a spectator or a soldier?

THREE

The Downward Spiral

In 1745, Charles Edward Stuart suddenly appeared at Glenfinnan in the Scottish Highlands. He was a tall, good-looking, young man and an exciting, dynamic leader. The heir of the Scottish kings and queens, Stuart had returned to Scotland to recapture the throne. George II, the British king, was an arrogant, cruel man, who spoke only German; and the Scots hated him. The Highlanders loved their Prince Charles and committed themselves to follow him and dethrone the foreigner.

At first they were successful in battle. But, suddenly, at the Battle of Culloden, their dreams came to an abrupt end. The Scots were crushed by the English army, and, although Charles escaped, his troops were slaughtered. The prince found his way to France to plan and dream about the day he would return to take his ancestral throne.

He never did. In fact, to meet Charles twenty years later was to confront a tragedy. He had become a hopeless alcoholic, his body and health broken. His life had become a record of disgrace and shame, a long trail of broken marriages, discarded mistresses, and public scandals. His former friends wanted nothing to do with him. The Scots may still sing about their "Bonnie Prince Charlie," but there was very little that was "bonnie" about Charles at the end of his life.

The life of Charles Stuart is the story of a great beginning followed by a tragic downward spiral into the slavery of sin. His life seemed to be one cycle of sin after another, taking him lower and lower and lower. Sin, unchecked in our lives, has a way of doing that to us. It is possible to begin brilliantly and end ignominiously. Some Christians are like the Russian satellite that went up on the back of a rocket, but came down like a rock and required a team of searchers in northern Canada to find the fragments. A good start does not assure a successful conclusion.

However, the downward spiral of sin does not function only in the lives of individuals. It also operates in groups and nations, and is vividly illustrated in the life of the nation of Israel during the time of the judges. Here were a people who had experienced a great beginning as God worked in a mighty way in their midst, but, as time went on, they moved further and further away from the living God into the quicksand of sin. Finally, they bore almost no resemblance to the people God had liberated from Egypt, kept in the desert, and led through Canaan in triumph.

At the beginning of the book of Judges, God gives us a preview of that period of time. A pattern is repeated seven times in that 350-year period which gives the key to understanding God's dealing with His people. The pattern is revealed in Judges 2:11-23, and it points out a principle of sowing and reaping that will be reproduced in our lives, if we do not guard against it.

> Then the sons of Israel did evil in the sight of the LORD, and served the Baals, and they forsook the LORD, the God of their fathers, who had brought them out of the land of Egypt, and followed other gods from among the gods of the peoples who were around them, and bowed themselves down to them; thus they provoked the LORD to anger. So they forsook the LORD and served Baal and the Ashtaroth. And the anger of the LORD burned against Israel, and He gave them into the hands of plunderers who plundered them; and He sold them into the hands of their enemies around them, so that they could no longer stand before their enemies. Wherever they went, the hand of the LORD was against them for evil, as the LORD had spoken and as the LORD had sworn to them, so that they were severely distressed. Then the LORD raised up judges who delivered them from the hands of those who plundered

them. And yet they did not listen to their judges, for they played the harlot after other gods and bowed themselves down to them. They turned aside quickly from the way in which their fathers had walked in obeying the commandments of the LORD; they did not do as their fathers. And when the LORD raised up judges for them, the LORD was with the judge and delivered them from the hand of their enemies all the days of the judge; for the LORD was moved to pity by their groaning because of those who oppressed and afflicted them. But it came about when the judge died, that they would turn back and act more corruptly than their fathers, in following other gods to serve them and bow down to them; they did not abandon their practices or their stubborn ways. So the anger of the LORD burned against Israel, and He said, "Because this nation has transgressed My covenant which I commanded their fathers, and has not listened to My voice, I also will no longer drive out before them any of the nations which Joshua left when he died, in order to test Israel by them, whether they will keep the way of the LORD to walk in it as their fathers did, or not." So the LORD allowed those nations to remain, not driving them out quickly; and He did not give them into the hand of Joshua (Judg. 2:11-23).

Five terms, simply but succinctly, capture the pattern of these verses. They also summarize the period of the judges because they describe the repeated cycle of 350 years. The terms are: *sin, servitude, supplication, salvation,* and *spiral downward.* It is as if the children of Israel refused to acknowledge the truth that God was teaching them, and, because they would not learn from the past, they were forced to relive it.

THE SIN OF ISRAEL—2:11-13

THE LAVISH GRACE OF GOD

In verses 11-13, we have the first part of the pattern, and to evaluate it properly, we must remember all that God had already done for the people of Israel. The nature of Israel's sin can be measured only against the abundance of the grace of God toward her. Verse 12 points back to the

Exodus, God's supernatural deliverance from hopeless bondage in Egypt. But God's grace is not only a saving grace, it is also a preserving grace. Despite Israel's rebellion, God had kept and cared for them. He had led them in the wilderness, protected them from their enemies, persevered with them through their murmurings, and provided for their needs until the death of Moses. Then, in grace, He had raised up Joshua and brought Israel into the land of Canaan, where He had driven out their enemies and given them the land.

The Israelites had known victory over every enemy and victory in every battle (except the first battle at Ai) because, as Joshua recognized, "The LORD your God is He who has been fighting for you" (Josh. 23:3). The book of Joshua summarizes God's grace in one simple statement. "Not one of the good promises which the LORD had made to the house of Israel failed; all came to pass" (21:45).

Israel had experienced another side to the grace of God. At Mount Sinai, the nation had entered into a solemn covenant with God. They had acknowledged Him as their great King and accepted the straightforward conditions of the covenant He made with them. They were to be faithful to Him, obey His laws, do His will, and reject all alliances with the false gods of Canaan. The King had established Israel's foreign policy, clearly spelling it out in passages such as Deuteronomy 7:1-5 and 20:16-18. There was to be no peaceful coexistence with the Canaanites—no peace treaties, no intermarriages, and no religious syncretism. Israel's marching orders were to destroy the Canaanites and demolish their pagan worship. At Mount Sinai, the people enthusiastically accepted God's demands.

THE APOSTASY OF ISRAEL

It was another matter when the land was theirs. With the death of Joshua and the following generation, the last living link with Mount Sinai was gone, and the result was gross sin. As Judges 2:11 reads, "Then the sons of Israel did evil in the sight of the LORD." The Hebrew text is more strongly worded, "Then the sons of Israel did *the* evil in the sight of the LORD." Israel did not merely fall into sin and break some of God's laws. They threw themselves into the sin, the supreme sin, the sin of all sins. "They served the Baals and they forsook the LORD." Note it well. The greatest sin a human being can commit is not murder or rape or other despicable acts of atrocity. It is to turn his back on the living God to serve man-made gods. Verse 12 captures the seriousness of Israel's sin. "They forsook the LORD ... followed other gods ... bowed themselves down to them; thus they provoked the LORD to anger."

It was bad enough that they turned away from the living God. What they chose to put in His place is almost beyond belief. They turned their back on the beauty and perfection of God and chose instead the sewer of Baal worship. "They forsook the LORD and served Baal and the Ashtaroth."

The Canaanites did not believe in one true God. Instead, they believed in a number of local gods, The chief god was named El, but a younger god, named Baal, had risen up to take his place. A "Baal" was a god in charge of a special place. He was the god of the storm and rains, and the god of fertility, who controlled all forms of reproduction. Ashtaroth was a female deity—goddess of sensual love, fertility, and maternity. In her, violence and sexual depravity mingled together, and she became the patron of sex and war.

The Canaanite religion was based on the concept of sympathetic worship. That is, you worship your god by behaving as he does. The result was that Baalism was perhaps the most degraded and degrading form of worship ever practiced on earth. The Canaanites engaged in temple prostitution, fertility rites, drunken sexual orgies of the most debased variety, idolatry, snake-worship, homosexuality, and even human sacrifice. Baal worship was bad wherever it existed, but in Canaan it existed in its rawest form. Everything about it—its view of God, moral standards, ethics and values, rituals—stood in absolute and total contradiction to everything God had revealed about Himself to His people.

However, the Israelites did the unthinkable. They did not stop speaking of Yahweh or forget Him entirely. Rather, they borrowed the rites, practices, and idols of Canaanite paganism and grafted them onto their existing worship, in a new syncretistic religion. They were tolerant of that which God commanded them to destroy. They accepted what God called them to hate, and they compromised when God called them to wholehearted obedience.

Why? How could a people who had seen so much of the power of God drift so far from Him? It did not happen all at once. It never does.

1. *They lost fellowship with God by incomplete obedience.* When Israel did not drive out the people as God commanded, they were sowing the seeds of their own spiritual failure.

2. *They did not consciously remind themselves of the grace of God.* They forsook God, when they forgot all that He had done for them. That is the reason we have the Lord's Supper in the New Testament. "Keep on doing this in remembrance of Me," the Lord said; and every time we come to the Lord's table, we confront ourselves afresh with the great truths of what He has done for us.

3. *They rejected the Word of God.* Israel began to look at life the way the Canaanites did. Instead of being controlled by the truths of Scripture, they were controlled by the opinions and impulses of their sinful natures.

We will be exempt from none of the results Israel experienced if we follow in the path of their spiritual neglect. But sin is not the end of the process. Galatians 6:8 reminds us, that when we sow to the flesh, we reap from the flesh; and the harvest of the flesh is corruption and decay. For Israel, the harvest was political bondage.

THE SERVITUDE OF ISRAEL—2:14-15

Some time ago a friend told me about a friend of hers who had had an outstanding academic career that promised her a brilliant future. Then she met a young man, who wanted to become a doctor, and fell deeply in love with him. They decided to marry, and she gave up her personal hopes and dreams to put him through medical school. Year after year she worked unselfishly at a very menial job and put up with all the frustrations and inconveniences of his schedule. Finally he finished all his training and specialty. On that glad day, he told her that he was leaving her. He had found someone else.

It is not hard to realize why that woman felt used and abused. To take all the gifts of love, then to turn around and despise that love to take up with a cheap substitute, is the most devasting insult possible. Yet that is exactly what Israel did with the grace of God. They chose the cheap, immoral gods of Canaan and rejected the eternal God of love.

That is why we read what we do in verse 14: "And the anger of the LORD burned against Israel." This is not the petty anger of hurt feelings, but the holy anger of a righteous God against sin. It is the revulsion of a perfect God against evil, wickedness, and sinful rebellion.

As Christians, we must not forget that God and evil cannot coexist. Because of the Lord Jesus, we know that God's anger blazed out at Calvary, and we will never come under His wrath. We have been saved from wrath through Christ. But it is impossible for us to live in sin and have fellowship with God. The disciplining hand of God will work in our lives if we choose sin in deliberate disobedience to Him. Sin that is not confessed to the Lord brings servitude and bondage in our lives. The joy fades, and the frustration builds.

One of my favorite hymns is "Come, Thou Fount of Every Blessing." It is a great hymn of praise to God, but there is a sad story related to it. Two strangers were riding in a coach—a miserable-looking man and a happy-faced woman, who was reading the hymn. She showed the hymn to her unknown companion and told him how much the words meant to her. The man looked at it and suddenly broke into tears. Sobbing, he said to her, "Madam, I am the poor, unhappy man who wrote that hymn many years ago, and I would give a thousand worlds, if I had them, to enjoy the feeling I had then." Robert Robinson had drifted out of fellowship with God, and he knew the awful bondage that sin brings.

God promised victory to Israel if they would trust Him. But when they turned away from God, they inevitably condemned themselves to defeat and bondage. They were plundered; they were enslaved; they were oppressed. Probably when they first began to get involved with Canaanite sin, they said, "This is liberating. We are not under those old laws of Moses anymore." But that false freedom led them straight into slavery. Six different times, for a total of 114 years, they knew foreign bondage. In addition to external oppression, they were afflicted with inner decay. Sin produces servitude. That is the fact of Judges.

But God's grace is triumphant over man's sin. Although He allowed His people to experience servitude, He did not abandon them to it, and so we come to the third part of the cycle. Following sin and servitude, there comes supplication.

THE SUPPLICATION OF ISRAEL

In chapter 2, there is no direct reference to the fact that Israel, in its distress, called out to God. Verse 18 does tell us that "The LORD was moved to pity by their groaning because of those who oppressed and afflicted them," but that is not an explicit reference to prayer. However, five times within the book, the people cry out to the Lord in their servitude, and each time that supplication marks the beginning of the end of their servitude.

How often we live in our weakness, leaving God out of

account, until, finally, all the threads begin to unravel. Then, in our desperation, we call out to God. Our need of God is not any greater in that situation than it always is, but we sense our need more. So we pray. We beg God to intervene and to put the pieces back together again. That kind of prayer can be a life-changing experience which turns everything around. Or it can be a shallow, superficial call for help, which we forget as soon as things improve. The amazing fact is that, no matter how deep our sin or how shallow our prayer, God hears us. In Judges, each time His people call, God hears and intervenes. Not once does He refuse or turn His back. He does not condition His help on their improvement or on their past record, but on their need. The throne we approach in prayer is a throne of grace, where we receive mercy and find grace to help in time of need (Heb. 4:16).

THE SALVATION OF ISRAEL

God does not simply hear our prayers, He answers them. When Israel turned to Him in servitude, He intervened to bring about their deliverance, their salvation; and He did so by raising up twelve men and one woman who are called judges. The term immediately conjures up the image of very dignified officials wearing stately robes, presiding over solemn courtrooms. The judges God raised up bear absolutely no resemblance to that picture. These judges had no courtroom, wore no robes, received no salary. In fact, these people were probably more like Matt Dillon or Wyatt Earp than a dignified Supreme Court judge. They resembled western sheriffs, men, with forceful personalities, who led the people and enforced justice. Verse 16 calls them deliverers, and that was often their function. They led the people against the enemy; then they provided civil justice and leadership, settled disputes, and trusted God to deal with problems. God also intended them to be spiritual leaders within the nation.

Three significant facts about the judges are stated in

verse 18. First, God raised them up. They were not appointed by men or elected. They were divinely appointed. Second, God was with them. The ministry of the Holy Spirit in the lives of the judges is one of the major concepts of the book. God empowered them to carry out the task He gave them. Third, God worked through the judges. They were the channels of His presence. As long as the individual judge was alive, God brought freedom and victory to His people. During this period of time, then, Israel was a theocracy. There was a minimum of formal government, and the major leaders of the nation were directly raised up by God, empowered by God, and answerable to God. He was King in Israel.

There are judges who can be designated "major judges" because they served as political liberators and civil leaders. Into this category fall Othniel, Ehud, Deborah and Barak, Gideon, Jephthah, and Samson. Other judges served as local leaders or as preservers of the peace, and they received only passing mention. There are six minor judges—Shamgar, Tola, Jair, Ibzan, Elon, and Abdon. Another important fact is that the judges were not always national leaders. Often God raised them up to deal with a specific enemy, which was troubling one group of tribes. Thus Jephthah and Samson were probably serving at about the same time. This raises interesting problems of geography and chronology within the book, but these questions do not affect its central message.

Why did God raise up the judges? It would have been much easier to discard a people with a record of consistent failure. But God is not a man. He does not break His covenants, and He does not desert His people. In fact, as the people experience their richly deserved judgment, we read, "The LORD was moved to pity by their groaning." What a beautiful insight into the heart of God! His people sin against Him. They rebel, reject Him, and spurn His love. If God said, "That's enough," justice would have no complaint. But as God saw Israel wallowing in their bondage of sin, His heart was moved with pity and love. Judges is full of the grace of God, the same grace and love which ultimately sent the Lord Jesus to the cross. If God allowed men to be destroyed in their sin, the angels would keep on singing their eternal song: "Holy, holy, holy is the Lord of hosts." But God's love keeps reaching out and reaching out and reaching out, even to the uttermost cost of Calvary.

THE SPIRAL INTO DEEPER SIN—2:19-23

Sadly, the cycle does not end with the love of God. That love is accepted and used, then discarded like a worn-out shoe. The judge dies, but the people have not learned their lesson. So, "They would turn back and act more corruptly than their fathers, in following other gods to serve them and bow down to them; they did not abandon their practices or their stubborn ways" (v.19). Once again the whole dreary pattern repeats itself. That is the incessant pattern of Judges—*sin, servitude, supplication, salvation, spiral downward.*

What is the great lesson in all this? It is an eloquent reminder that sin is always a serious matter to the children of God. If we do not deal decisively with sin in our lives, we will never experience the fullness of God's blessing. There can be no compromise, no peaceful coexistence with sin. If we try to go partway in our commitment to the Lord Jesus, we will find ourselves bound up in a spiral that is taking us quickly downhill.

The antidote to the Judges complex is the constant application of 1 John 1:9 to our lives. "If we confess our sins, He is faithful and righteous to forgive us our sins and to cleanse us from all unrighteousness." That is God's provision for fellowship, and our opportunity for abundant, victorious living.

FOUR

God's Place for You

With tears streaming down her face, she looked at me and said, "I want more than anything else to make my life count for the Lord Jesus. When you were talking about what He has done for us and our position in Him, that really got through to me. But how can He use somebody like me?" Then she talked about Christians she respected and their qualities, which she admired and envied. They inspired her, but they also discouraged her because she lacked their personalities or gifts or talents. So how could God have anything significant for her to do?

I have had that discussion, in one form or another, scores of times. Sincere Christians share their despair because they do not fit their concept of what a Christian must be before God can or will use them. The reasons are as diverse as the people who come. Some are consumed with guilt over sin and failure. Others feel inadequate due to a lack of education. Many suffer with the scars of their family history or personal background. Several have physical problems and limitations. A number have difficulty accepting themselves and bear the burden of a poor self-image.

We could extend the list indefinitely, but the point is that many Christians are paralyzed by the belief that they do not fit the mold. They have an image, often very hazy but always very idealistic, of the person God uses, and invariably, they see themselves as being a long way from fitting that image. The conclusion is inevitable: I am not what God requires, so the Lord cannot use me.

As with most problems, the real problem is that we are

44

not guided by Scripture in our thinking. For when we turn
to God's Word, we discover a delightful truth. God is not
stuck on one pattern. He does not have a heavenly mold
into which we must fit, or else we will be discarded.
The world produces conformity; God produces individuality. Our God is a God of infinite variety who uses people of
all kinds, shapes, and colors, and He has a wonderfully
unique purpose for each one of us. To prove this, we need
only consider the first three judges mentioned in the book
of Judges. During this period, God used eleven men and one
woman, each very different in personality and ministry.
Nowhere is the difference more obvious than in the first
three judges we meet, in Judges 3.

OTHNIEL: THE FIRST JUDGE—3:7-11

And the sons of Israel did what was evil in the sight of the
LORD, and forgot the LORD their God, and served the Baals
and the Asheroth. Then the anger of the LORD was kindled
against Israel, so that He sold them into the hands of
Cushan-rishathaim king of Mesopotamia; and the sons of
Israel served Cushan-rishathaim eight years. And when the
sons of Israel cried to the LORD, the LORD raised up a deliverer for the sons of Israel to deliver them, Othniel the son of
Kenaz, Caleb's younger brother. And the Spirit of the LORD
came upon him, and he judged Israel. When he went out to
war, the LORD gave Cushan-rishathaim king of Mesopotamia
into his hand, so that he prevailed over Cushan-rishathaim.
Then the land had rest forty years. And Othniel the son of
Kenaz died.

By the time we have finished Judges, we will be thoroughly
sick of the cycle of sin. In verses 7-9, we see it in action for
the first time. The people of Israel turned their backs on the
living God and threw themselves into the pagan, sensual
worship of the Canaanite gods. As a result, the loving God
allowed them to come under the rule of a king named
Cushan-rishathaim. Much about him is a mystery.
Rishathaim means "double-wickedness," which suggests
that he was a cruel and powerful man. Mesopotamia was

probably his place of origin, and Cushan was, in all likelihood, a leader of a band of people called the Habiru, who swept in from the east and became a powerful force in the Middle East. Whatever his origin, Cushan kept the Israelites in bondage for eight years, until finally they recovered their spiritual senses long enough to call upon the Lord in repentance. In response to their prayer God raised up a deliverer, the first judge, named Othniel.

Othniel first appears on the scriptural scene in Joshua 15, a story repeated in Judges 1:11-15. Caleb, the great man of faith, though eighty-five years old, had attacked the heart of Canaanite power at Kiriath-arba, or Hebron; and God had given him a great victory. But Judah had one other main center of Canaanite power, Kiriath-sepher, or Debir. Caleb issued a challenge. "The one who attacks Kiriath-sepher and captures it, I will even give him my daughter Achsah for a wife." In response to that challenge, Othniel attacked the city and captured it; now, years later, God reached out and chose Othniel to lead His people against Cushan.

THE CHARACTERISTICS OF OTHNIEL

Othniel was an extraordinary man in many ways First, he was a man with a solid family background. In verse 13, he is called "Othniel the son of Kenaz, Caleb's younger brother." That could mean that either Kenaz or Othniel was Caleb's younger brother, but, without going into details, it is more likely that Othniel was Caleb's brother, probably a half brother. Either as Caleb's brother or as his nephew, Othniel had the privilege of belonging to a family that was led by an outstanding believer. Caleb, with Joshua, was one of the two greatest men of his generation. God's witness to his life was: "He has followed the LORD fully" (Num. 14:24; Deut. 1:36). Othniel had the privilege of seeing the principles of trust and obedience demonstrated in the life of his family.

We do not know much about Othniel's parents. Because of God's judgment on the people in the wilderness, we do know that he was probably about thirty years younger than Caleb. Since his parents would have died when he was young, his half brother would have become a father to him. Therefore, he could thank God for the gift of a godly family which had taught him to love and trust God.

What a great thing it is to have a solid Christian family! Not long ago, I read the story of a young pastor who was dying of cancer. As he was lying on his deathbed, his father and his uncle, both of whom were pastors, came to see him. They visited for awhile, and then the young man asked his uncle, "Would you mind if I talk to my dad alone?" When the father came out after their visit, he said to his brother, "I want to tell you what David did when we were alone. He called me over to his bed and said, 'Can I put my arms around you?' I stooped over as best I could and let him hug me. 'Now, dad, would you put your arms around me?' I could hardly control my emotions, but I put my arms around him. Then, with his arms around me, he said, 'Dad, I just want you to know that the greatest gift God ever gave me, outside of salvation itself, was the gift of a mother and father who love God and taught me to love Him, too.' "[1]

But a godly family background, though a great privilege, does not equip a person to be used by God. Othniel was a man with some distinguished personal characteristics. Three stand out.

1. *He was a man of proven ability.* He had gone into battle and won a victory over some very powerful foes. Othniel was a skillful, proven leader.

2. *He was a man of demonstrated courage.* Cushan was a powerful enemy, and Othniel required courage to face him. Kiriath-sepher was a stronghold of giants, but Othniel moved against them.

3. *He was a man of personal faith.* Judges 3:10 indicates that Othniel did not have only a family faith. He knew what it was to be led and directed personally by the Lord.

Othniel was a man of quality, the kind of person who stands out in any crowd. In modern terms, he had a lot going for him. In fact, the Jewish rabbis were so impressed by him that they ranked him first among the judges and applied to him the words of the Song of Solomon 4:7, "You are altogether fair, my love; there is no flaw in you."

But those outstanding characteristics do not explain why God used Othniel. The key to his character is found in the statement that "the Spirit of the LORD came upon him." Othniel did not derive his strength from his godly family background or his sterling personal character, but from the enablement of God the Holy Spirit. The Holy Spirit worked through Othniel, and God's people had relief for forty years. They were kept from apostasy for that period because of the impact of this godly man.

A man may change his generation as Othniel did, but he cannot guarantee the spirituality of the next generation. After forty years, the cycle of sin revolved again, and this time God raised up a judge of a very different character.

EHUD, THE SECOND JUDGE—3:12-30

Now the sons of Israel again did evil in the sight of the LORD. So the LORD strengthened Eglon the king of Moab against Israel, because they had done evil in the sight of the LORD. And he gathered to himself the sons of Ammon and Amalek; and he went and defeated Israel, and they possessed the city of the palm trees. And the sons of Israel served Eglon the king of Moab eighteen years. But when the sons of Israel cried to the LORD, the LORD raised up a deliverer for them, Ehud the son of Gera, the Benjamite, a left-handed man. And the sons of Israel sent tribute by him to Eglon the king of Moab. And Ehud made himself a sword which had two edges, a cubit in length; and he bound it on his right thigh under his cloak. And he presented the tribute to Eglon king of Moab. Now Eglon was a very fat man. And it came about when he had finished presenting the tribute, that he sent away the people who had carried the tribute. But he himself turned back from the idols which were at Gilgal, and said, "I have a secret message for you, O king." And he said, "Keep silence." And all who attended him left him. And Ehud came to him while he was sitting alone in his cool roof chamber. And Ehud said, "I have a message from God for you." And he arose from his seat. And Ehud stretched out his left hand, took the sword from his right thigh and thrust it into his belly. The handle also went in after the blade, and the fat closed over the blade, for he did not draw the sword out of his belly; and the refuse came out. Then Ehud went out into the vestibule and shut the doors of the roof chamber behind him, and locked them. When he had gone out, his servants came and looked, and behold, the doors of the roof chamber were locked; and they said, "He is only relieving himself in the cool room." And they waited until they became anxious; but behold, he did not open the doors of the roof chamber. Therefore they took the key and opened them, and behold, their master had fallen to the floor dead. Now Ehud escaped while they were delaying, and he passed by the idols and escaped to Seirah. And it came about when he had arrived, that he blew the horn in the hill country of Ephraim; and the sons of Israel went down with him from the hill country, and he was in front of them. And he said to them, "Pursue them, for the LORD has given your enemies the Moabites into your hands." So they went down after him and seized the fords of the Jordan opposite Moab, and did not allow anyone to cross. And they struck down at that time about ten thousand Moabites, all robust and valiant men; and no one escaped. So Moab was subdued that day under the hand of Israel. And the land was undisturbed for eighty years.

This time the servitude of the people was under the hands of Eglon, the king of Moab. It was a bondage brought about directly by God. In verse 8, we read, "God sold them into the hands of Cushan." Then, in verse 12, "The LORD strengthened Eglon . . . because they had done evil in the sight of the LORD." These were not just the movements and accidents of history; they were the hand of God in judgment upon the sin of His people.

Eglon, who apparently was a very coarse man, gathered together his people, linked the Ammonites and the Amalekites with him, and swept through the Transjordan where the tribes of Reuben, Gad, and the half-tribe of Manasseh were. Then they crossed the Jordan, established their capital at Jericho, and began to spread their influence through the areas of Benjamin and Ephraim. With a force of about 10,000 men, they crushed the Israelites for eighteen years.

Finally, in desperation, the Israelites called to the Lord, and the Lord raised up a deliverer, a man named Ehud. We will not go over the details of how Ehud delivered the people except to notice some of his characteristics.

1. *He was a prominent man.* Ehud was in charge of taking the tribute up to Eglon. This was a form of taxation, and the person who brought it was normally a man of prominence who could be trusted with a great deal of money, a leader within his tribe.

2. *He was a man with a limitation.* At first glance, it does not seem very significant that Ehud was left-handed. The text actually says that he was "hindered in the right hand," an ironic situation in a man from the tribe of *Benjamin*, which means "son of my right hand."

I have often wondered why the left-handers of the world have not united to form "lefty lib." After all, we have liberation movements for almost every other minority group. Maybe the first glimmerings are on the way. A left-hander recently complained to a minority rights department that file cabinets were designed for the benefit of right-handers. Here is a great opportunity for someone looking for a cause! A man who is awkward is called *gauche,* a French word meaning left-handed. Something that is wicked or evil we call *sinister,* the Latin word for the left hand. But someone with skill and ability is *dexterous,* which means right-handed in Latin. We have attacked racist and sexist language. Perhaps next we will challenge "dexterous language."

We do not take this discussion seriously, of course, because we know that at worst being left-handed is a nuisance, an inconvenience at certain times. But in Ehud's time, it was considered to be a defect. In fact, in some cultures, the place of honor was the left side; you were allowing a person to stand on your weak side, your unprotected side. Ehud could have been devastated by this problem. "Why am I left-handed in a world of right-handers? Why am I different?"

Many of us are defeated by things in our lives which may be no more significant than left-handedness. But if we do not accept our limitations, they can keep us from being usable. When we accept ourselves with our weaknesses and limitations, God can use us.

That is exactly what Ehud did. He not only accepted his left-handedness, he used it. What others thought was a defect, he turned into a tool to be used for God. Ehud's whole story is about how a left-handed man uses his left-handedness to kill the enemy. In the same way, if you will accept your so-called limitations of whatever sort, you will find God opening up whole new areas of ministry.

I have been profoundly impressed recently by reading the life story of Joni Eareckson. As a young woman, she became a quadriplegic in a diving accident. For years, Joni struggled with the terrifying fact that she would never again be able to walk or use her arms. Then, as God worked in her life, she developed her skill. God began to use her in a beautiful way to share His love with other people. When she accepted what she was, the Lord began to use her as she was.[2]

3. *He was a courageous man.* Apparently it was impossible for Ehud to arouse an army to join him; so, absolutely alone, at the risk of his own life, he walked into the palace to deal with Eglon. That was an act of undeniable bravery.

4. *He was a careful, organized man.* Ehud had thought through carefully exactly what he was going to do. God used him, both when he killed Eglon, and later, when he raised an army, strategically took the fords of the Jordan and, having cut off their escape route, attacked the enemy.

5. *He was a spiritually committed man.* It was God who raised up Ehud, and, as verse 28 shows, Ehud was very conscious that the battle was the Lord's. "The LORD has given your enemies the Moabites into your hands." Ehud

recognized what Othniel had known, that it was not his cleverness or his competence which produced the victory, but the power of God.

All we know about the third judge is described in only one verse, but it introduces us to some significant facts about a unique man.

SHAMGAR—3:31

> And after him came Shamgar the son of Anath, who struck down six hundred Philistines with an oxgoad; and he also saved Israel.

Shamgar lived at a time when the Philistines were beginning to exert their power in the southwest corner of the land. Later they became a major force, but in Shamgar's time, they were already causing trouble. To meet the need, God raised up Shamgar as a judge. He was not an Othniel or an Ehud, but he was a man used by God to strike down the Philistines.

First, Shamgar was a man with a very confused family background. Shamgar was not a Hebrew name. It was Canaanite. His father's name, Anath, is the name of the Canaanite god of sex and war. On that basis, some have doubted whether Shamgar was even an Israelite. The truth is that his family had completely capitulated to the paganism all around them. They certainly did not prepare Shamgar to be a judge and deliverer of God's people.

Second, Shamgar was a peasant. We know that from his weapon, an oxgoad. An oxgoad was a long wooden stick tipped with metal at one end, and a blade on the other for cleaning the plow. Peasants used the tool to keep their oxen plowing together in the fields.

Third, Shamgar was a man of courage. Only a very brave person, when armed only with an oxgoad would take on at least 600 men. In this context, Shamgar's courage was born of his faith in God.

The Men God Uses

At this point, we need to draw together the threads of Judges 3. Three great principles stand out.

1. *God uses completely different kinds of men.* If you were trying to find in Judges 3 a stereotype of the kind of person God uses, you would end up very confused.

You would look at Othniel and say, "Well, obviously God uses a man of proven ability, superior character, and spiritual depth from the finest kind of background."

But God worked through Ehud too, a man other people thought had a serious limitation. Prominent, courageous, capable—but with a defect. Yet God used Ehud's limitation for His glory.

But you say, "I cannot even identify with Ehud. After all, he was a pretty important man." Therefore, God chose Shamgar, a peasant from a paganized family, and He worked through him.

Now I don't know what you see when you look at yourself. You may see a Shamgar or an Ehud. You are not an Othniel, and you know it. But God uses Ehuds, and God uses Shamgars, and He will use you if you only will trust Him.

2. *God uses people who draw their strength from Him.* Even Othniel with all His abilities and talents was successful only because of what the Holy Spirit did through him. Let me remind you of Isaiah 40:29-31:

> He gives strength to the weary, and to him who lacks might He increases power. Though youths grow weary and tired, and vigorous young men stumble badly, yet those who wait for the LORD will gain new strength. They will mount up with wings like eagles, they will run and not get tired, they will walk and not become weary.

There is a beautiful word in verse 31. It is the word to *exchange* or to replace. Those who wait for the Lord will exchange their strength. That is what God calls us to do—to come to Him and exchange our weakness for His strength.

3. *God uses people who step out in faith and trust Him.* Shamgar, Ehud, and Othniel were different in many ways, but they had one thing in common. They had the courage to take a risk, to step out in faith for God. They were bold enough to take God at His word and confront the enemy.

This summer someone said to me, "Gary, do you remember when you said that faith means that we take risks for God? That met a real need in my life because there was an area I needed to do that in. So I have begun to step out and risk myself for God and trust Him to look after the consequences. I cannot believe the difference it has made in my life."

Whoever you are, God has a place for you. Your limitations are not a problem for Him. He can deal with them. Accept yourself—not your sins, but your limitations. God does. Then step out in faith to see Him take you as a unique individual and work through you for His glory. Hudson Taylor, as he looked back over thirty years during which he had seen 600 missionaries respond to his vision to reach China through the China Inland Mission summarized what he had learned: "God is sufficient for God's work . . . God chose me because I was weak enough. God does not do His great works by large committees. He trains someone to be quiet enough and little enough, and then He uses him."

By that standard, which is God's standard, all of us qualify. The issue is not whether He can or will use us, to His glory. The great question is whether or not we will trust Him to use us.

FIVE

Deborah: God's Exceptional Leader

Someone has said there are only three kinds of people in the world—those who watch what is happening; those who make things happen; and those who scratch their heads and ask, "Hey, what's happening?"

The ability to make things happen is the gift of leadership. Perhaps Harry Truman defined it best. "Leadership," he said, "is the ability to get men to do what they don't want to do and to like it." That ability is a precious commodity in the modern world. In the past decade, the Western world has had its faith in existing leadership shaken badly, and few Western democracies have escaped major political scandals. Arnold Toynbee once observed that the rise and fall of societies has a one-to-one correlation with the quality of its leadership, a concept that is hardly encouraging for Western society. The German philosopher Karl Jaspers once wrote, "The power of leadership appears to be declining everywhere. More and more of the men we see coming to the top seem to be merely drifting. The result is a helplessness in a leadership that hides from the public."[1]

It is not only in the political realm that leadership is a crucial issue. Our local church life is directly affected by the quality of its leaders. One group of churches in the Northwest did a study of growth patterns in sixty churches. They studied statistics for attendance, age, and income, and then surveyed the attitudes and thinking of various leaders. They discovered that whether a church was static or growing depended directly on the attitudes of leaders. Where the church leaders were positive, flexible, confident, cheerful, and goal-oriented, the church was growing. But where the leaders had little vision or creativity and no clear goals, the church was standing still.

On an even more basic level, there is a critical need for leadership in our family life. Too many homes, even Christian homes, are simply drifting, because there is no one exercising decisive leadership. The power vacuum is filled quickly by the children, and, as a result, a kind of anarchy pervades our school system and society. When parents abdicate their God-given responsibilities, disaster is inevitable.

As I read the Word of God, I become convinced that God has called every Christian to exercise a leadership responsibility. Some types are obvious—such as elders and deacons in local churches or executives in Christian groups and organizations. There are also God-given responsibilities in the home. On a more personal basis, the Lord Jesus has called every believer to be a disciple, and that involves me as I build into another person's life. If you aren't involved in leadership, you soon will be. Leadership is a spiritual issue of great importance, and, therefore, we need to acquire a clear, biblical concept of God's standards for leaders.

We want to do that by looking at an exceptional leader. She is the only woman in biblical history who has a major, God-given leadership role. That immediately marks her out as an uniquely gifted individual, a leader of distinction from whom we can learn a great deal. That person, of course, is Deborah. We meet her in Judges 4.

To understand Deborah, we need to understand the times in which she served God. As we have seen, the book of Judges is a kind of spiritual merry-go-round, in which the same things happened again and again. In Deborah's time, that cycle went around for the third time.

THE SITUATION OF THE PEOPLE—4:1-3

Then the sons of Israel again did evil in the sight of the LORD, after Ehud died. And the LORD sold them into the hand of

Jabin king of Canaan, who reigned in Hazor; and the commander of his army was Sisera, who lived in Harosheth-hagoyim. And the sons of Israel cried to the LORD; for he had nine hundred iron chariots, and he oppressed the sons of Israel severely for twenty years.

The first time God's people went into sin, God raised up Othniel as the judge, to deliver them from the hand of Cushan-rishathaim, and for forty years the people had rest. But when Othniel died, the people turned to paganism and idolatry all over again, and God brought in Eglon, the king of Moab, to punish them. For eighteen years, Eglon ground the Israelites under his heel, until finally, the Israelites cried out to God and He sent Ehud to be their political liberator and judge.

By this time, you would think the people would be starting to get the point. "Hey, have you noticed? Every time we start getting mixed up with Baal and this Canaanite religion and all these sexual orgies, some foreign king comes along and jumps all over us. But when we turn to God, we get delivered. Maybe we should just stick with the Lord."

The Master Teacher had made the lesson painfully clear, but, unfortunately, people usually do not learn obvious lessons quickly. So, in Judges 4:1, the cycle started all over again. "The sons of Israel *again* did evil in the sight of the LORD, after Ehud died" (itals. added). It was not just that they did evil. They did *the evil*—they turned from God and threw themselves into pagan religion—the sensual, corrupt, depraved worship of the Canaanites.

THE SERVITUDE OF ISRAEL

Once again the people of Israel were forced to learn the principle the Savior taught, in John 8:34: "Everyone who commits sin is the slave of sin." One of Satan's great lies is that sin is liberating. "Come on. Try it—you'll like it. Why are you tied up in knots with all those old-fashioned ideas of morality? Live a little. Cut loose! Be Free!" But the truth is that sin enslaves. When the Israelites turned to Baal worship, the Lord "sold" them into the bondage of a Baal-worshiping king. This time it was a king who headed up an alliance of northern kings, from the area around the Sea of Galilee. Under Joshua, 150 years earlier, when the people trusted God, they had burned the city of Hazor and killed its king, Jabin. But now another king named Jabin, aided by a brilliant general named Sisera, swept down to dominate the northern tribes of Israel.

It is helpful to have a concept of Jabin's complete dominance of Israel. He pushed down from Hazor, to the north of the Sea of Galilee, down through Galilee and into the strategic central plains of Esdraelon, also known as the Valley of Megiddo. He also controlled down into Ephraim. Thus, for twenty years, the northern tribes were oppressed severely by Jabin and Sisera, from Sisera's strategic headquarters at Harosheth-hagoyim, on the plain of Esdraelon. Militarily, Israel was confronted by two awesome facts. First, Jabin had 900 iron chariots, as well as a large infantry. Nine hundred iron chariots do not sound impressive in a world spending 400 billion dollars annually on armaments, but they represented the very latest in military technology then. The chariots made it impossible for Israel to defend the valleys and plains. Their military position was nothing less than appalling. Israel was outmanned, outgunned, and out-positioned. They not only lacked iron chariots, they lacked virtually all iron weapons. Deborah described their position before the battle in her famous song, in Judges 5:8:

> Then war was in the gates.
> Not a shield or a spear was seen
> Among forty thousand in Israel.

Humanly speaking, it was a hopeless situation. A nation without arms was helpless before a nation armed to the teeth. But despite external appearances, Israel's real problem was not military, but spiritual. Their real need was not an iron smelter but a living faith in God. If Israel would trust

Him, He would deliver them from even the most impossible situation. To teach them that, God did a very unusual thing. He did not raise up a great warrior, an Othniel or a Shamgar or an Ehud. Instead, in this militarily hopeless situation, He chose a woman to be the deliverer of His people. Naturally speaking, it was the last place Israel would look for help. But she was God's answer to their need.

DEBORAH THE JUDGE—4:4-9

Now Deborah, a prophetess, the wife of Lappidoth, was judging Israel at that time. And she used to sit under the palm tree of Deborah between Ramah and Bethel in the hill country of Ephraim; and the sons of Israel came up to her for judgment. Now she sent and summoned Barak the son of Abinoam from Kedesh-naphtali, and said to him, "Behold, the LORD, the God of Israel, has commanded, 'Go, and march to Mount Tabor, and take with you ten thousand men from the sons of Naphtali and from the sons of Zebulun. And I will draw out to you Sisera, the commander of Jabin's army, with his chariots and his many troops to the river Kishon; and I will give him into your hand.'" Then Barak said to her, "If you will go with me, then I will go; but if you will not go with me, I will not go." And she said, "I will surely go with you; nevertheless, the honor shall not be yours on the journey that you are about to take, for the LORD will sell Sisera into the hands of a woman." Then Deborah arose and went with Barak to Kedesh.

HER POSITION

We do not know many things about Deborah. For example, we are told nothing of her family or her ancestry or even what tribe she was from. Her husband was a man named Lappidoth, but, beyond that, Scripture is silent about him.

We do know two things about Deborah. She was a prophetess. A prophetess or prophet spoke on the basis of a revelation from God. Sometimes it was a revelation about the future. Other times God revealed His will for the present. A prophet could do that because he was filled with the Holy Spirit, and God was revealing truth to him. It was God, and only God, who made a prophet.

In the entire Old Testament only three women are said to have the gift of a prophetess. There was Miriam, the sister of Moses (Exod. 15:20); Huldah, a woman who spoke for God in the time of Josiah (2 Kings 22:14-20); and the third, of course, was Deborah. In the New Testament, we meet some women with this gift. Anna, the old woman who saw the baby Jesus in the Temple (Luke 2:36), and the four daughters of Philip (Acts 21:8-9).

The second fact we learn about Deborah is that she was a judge. Verse 5 depicts individuals from the whole nation streaming up to the hill country of Ephraim, so that Deborah could hear cases and render judgments. Because of the obvious gift of God in her life, she had become the political and judicial center of the nation.

Those two facts make Deborah absolutely unique. There was never another time in the nation of Israel's history when God chose a woman to be their leader. Wicked Queen Athaliah murdered her family to seize the throne, but that is something very different. Deborah was chosen by God, called by God, raised up by God, and empowered by God. She was God's leader.

Deborah was obviously an exceptional woman—one of only three prophetesses in the Old Testament—and the only woman ever called by God to be the national leader of His people. So it is hardly surprising to discover that this unique woman had some outstanding gifts as a leader. In this chapter, we see some significant principles of leadership embodied in her life.

HER PRINCIPLES OF LEADERSHIP

1. *She saw a need and was committed to do something about it (5:6-7).* Deborah was a woman who refused to accept the status quo. She saw a desperate need in the life of her people and set out to do something about it. Obviously, Deborah was not the only one to see the problem, but she

was the only one who was determined to do something about it. Notice what she says in chapter 5:6-7:

> In the days of Shamgar the son of Anath,
> In the days of Jael, the highways were deserted,
> And travelers went by roundabout ways.
> The peasantry ceased, they ceased in Israel,
> Until I, Deborah, arose,
> Until I arose, a mother in Israel.

Two things went into Deborah's action. First, she was critically realistic about the situation. It is right here that many of us get fogged out in our leadership responsibilities. I am amazed at how often people who talk to me about the crisis in their marriage say with tears, "Why didn't I see it before? Now it is too late." This applies in other areas as well. Often parents or church leaders seem to be almost blind to what is really happening until the time bomb has exploded and only the rubble remains.

John Gardner, former Cabinet minister under John Kennedy and later the head of Common Cause, has made a very perceptive observation. He noticed that twentieth-century institutions are caught in a savage crossfire between uncritical lovers and unloving critics. As he points out, love without criticism brings stagnation, but criticism without love brings destruction. What is needed is a loving criticism of our society and its institutions. That certainly applies to Christians. We need a loving realism about our churches, organizations, and families.

Next, Deborah went beyond critical evaluation to goal-setting. She had a clear goal, the immediate and obvious one of political liberty. Two marks of a leader are that he or she is future-oriented and goal-oriented.

What are my goals for my life? For my family? For my Bible study group? For my church? A leader knows where he is going.

2. *She enlisted help (4:6a)*. Deborah was a very realistic woman. Israel had a military problem, and she needed a

military helper. So she sent up north for the best person she could find, a man named Barak. We are not told how she knew about Barak or what she knew about him, but apparently he had already distinguished himself as a soldier. Everything that follows shows that he was a gifted man militarily.

Deborah was wise enough to know the value of a team and perceptive enough to recognize both her own limitations and Barak's strengths. Campbell Morgan puts it like this:

> Deborah was a woman of poetry and flame, and with a fine scorn (she) laid a whip of scorpions round the men who skulked, when they ought to have been fighting. Barak was a strategist and adviser. Deborah without Barak would have kindled enthusiasm, but would have accomplished nothing.[2]

One mark of a leader is that he or she is aware of personal talents and abilities, but equally realistic about his or her limitations. So a leader recruits help and builds a team.

3. *She motivated help (4:6b-9)*. Barak may have been gifted, but apparently he was wrapped up in fear and uncertainty. Deborah deliberately set out to encourage and motivate him. She did three things.

First, she confronted him with God's command. "Behold, the LORD, the God of Israel, has commanded." She spoke up boldly, "Barak, this is God's will, not mine. It is not an option, it is a requirement of God."

Second, she strengthened him with God's promise. Notice verse 7. That was God speaking, "I will draw Sisera out to you . . . and I will give him into your hand." What a great lesson this is. It is one thing to challenge someone to do a job. It is another to remind him of the great promises of God—that God will enable and empower him for the job God is calling him to do.

Third, Deborah encouraged Barak with her presence. There are many reasons why Barak may have said what he did, in verse 8: "If you will go with me, then I will go; but if you will not go with me, I will not go." Some have thought it was because he lacked faith to trust God on his own, or because he was fearful. Probably it was because he knew the people would rally around him if Deborah was with him. But whatever the reason, Deborah immediately said, "I will surely go with you."

4. *She developed a plan (4:6b-7).* Almost anyone can see a need, but it is another thing to come up with a plan to deal with it. Note how specific Deborah was. Barak was to recruit ten thousand men from the tribes of Naphtali and Zebulun, and they were to march to Mount Tabor. Tabor was on the Plains of Esdraelon, not far from Sisera's head-quarters. The plan was to meet the enemy at his strongest point, in a pitched battle near the Kishon River, as verse 7 says. The Kishon was a major river, but at the place where Deborah was indicating, it was only seasonal. During the dry season it dried up, and this was the dry season.

In all these ways, Deborah demonstrated outstanding talents as a leader. But having said all that, I do not think we have come to the heart of this unusual woman. We cannot really understand her until we consider her faith.

HER FAITH

Only by faith in God could Deborah have carried out her plans and reached her goal. Her faith shone through her challenge to Barak, in verses 6-7, and motivated him in verse 14, "Arise! For this is the day in which the LORD has given Sisera into your hands; behold, the LORD has gone out before you." Then, she reveals very clearly the quality of her faith in her song, in Judges 5.

The most important characteristic of a Christian leader, in whatever area of life, is a dynamic, bold faith in God. I may have all the leadership principles down pat; I may be a management expert; I may be an organizer with a systems flow chart that General Motors would envy. But if I do not trust God, if I do not live in a personal fellowship with the Lord Jesus, I will be a failure as an elder or a teacher or a parent or a disciple maker or in whatever area I serve as a leader. What the people I lead need more than anything else is not a great system or a great organization, but a person who knows his God.

God's Victory over Jabin and Sisera—4:10-24

And Barak called Zebulun and Naphtali together to Kedesh, and ten thousand men went up with him; Deborah also went up with him. Now Heber the Kenite had separated himself from the Kenites, from the sons of Hobab the father-in-law of Moses, and had pitched his tent as far away as the oak in Zaanannim, which is near Kedesh. Then they told Sisera that Barak the son of Abinoam had gone up to Mount Tabor. And Sisera called together all his chariots, nine hundred iron chariots, and all the people who were with him, from Harosheth-hagoyim to the river Kishon. And Deborah said to Barak, "Arise! For this is the day in which the LORD has given Sisera into your hands; behold, the LORD has gone out before you." So Barak went down from Mount Tabor with ten thousand men following him. And the LORD routed Sisera and all his chariots and all his army, with the edge of the sword before Barak; and Sisera alighted from his chariot and fled away on foot. But Barak pursued the chariots and the army as far as Harosheth-hagoyim, and all the army of Sisera fell by the edge of the sword; not even one was left. Now Sisera fled away on foot to the tent of Jael the wife of Heber the Kenite, for there was peace between Jabin the king of Hazor and the house of Heber the Kenite. And Jael went out to meet Sisera, and said to him, "Turn aside, my master, turn aside to me! Do not be afraid." And he turned aside to her into the tent, and she covered him with a rug. And he said to her, "Please give me a little water to drink, for I am thirsty." So she opened a bottle of milk and gave him a drink; then she covered him. And he said to her, "Stand in the doorway of the tent, and it shall be if anyone comes and inquires of you, and says, 'Is there anyone here?' that you shall say, 'No.'" But Jael, Heber's wife, took a tent peg and seized a hammer in her hand, and went secretly to him and drove the peg into his temple, and it went through into the ground; for he was sound asleep and exhausted. So he died. And behold, as Barak pursued Sisera, Jael came out to meet him and said to him, "Come, and I will show you the man whom you are seeking." And he entered with her, and behold Sisera was lying dead with the tent peg in his temple. So God subdued on that day Jabin the king of Canaan before the sons of Israel. And the hand of the sons of Israel pressed heavier and heavier upon Jabin the king of Canaan, until they had destroyed Jabin the king of Canaan.

God used Deborah to prepare Barak. Then she stepped into the background and Barak moved into the foreground. The victory was acted out in three stages.

THE MILITARY SITUATION (4:10-14)

The first thing to notice is the ordering of the troops. Barak went to Zebulun and Naphtali and recruited an army of ten thousand men. Then they marched out to Mount Tabor. In response, Sisera moved out to meet him with his 900 iron chariots and a huge army. Now let us see the situation clearly:

First, Israel was outmanned. We are not told how many men Sisera had, but apparently there were considerably more than ten thousand. Usually only a very small percentage of an army would be in chariots.

Second, they were totally outsupplied. Sisera had 900 iron chariots; Israel did not even have spears and shields.

Third, they were apparently out-positioned. For ill-equippped men on foot to march against the best of Sisera's army on a flat plain amounted to mass suicide. In A.D. 67 the Jews tried this kind of attack against the Romans in exactly the same place, and they were slaughtered.

Yet that is exactly what God commanded His people to do, as we read in verse 14. It was not really Barak's strategy or Deborah's plan at all. It was God's. He wanted to teach His people that it was not chariots or troop numbers that really made the difference; it was He. Because Barak had learned to trust God, he led his ten thousand men into battle, and, for that reason, his name appears in Hebrews 11 as a man of faith.

THE INTERVENTION OF GOD (4:15-16)

What happened? Verse 15 does not really tell us. Here was Sisera, licking his lips in anticipation of a great slaughter as he saw those ten thousand men streaming down at him. His chariots would make quick work of them. But suddenly defeat was snatched out of the jaws of victory. The Lord threw Sisera and all his chariots and army into confusion. How did such a result occur? Judges 5:21 gives us the clue. "The torrent of Kishon swept them away, the ancient torrent, the torrent Kishon." At this time of year, Kishon was a dried-up creek bed.[3] How could it be called a torrent? The answer is that, suddenly, at exactly the right time, in the middle of the dry season, God caused a violent storm to sweep through the area. The downpour turned the ground into a muddy quagmire, and the chariots bogged down. Sisera's major weapon had become a handicap, and, as a result, Sisera's armies panicked and broke ranks, and the Israelites pursued and defeated them.

THE DEATH OF SISERA (4:17-24)

Then God intervened in another way. Sisera, running away from God's people, stumbled into the tent of a non-Israelite named Jael, where he expected to find safety. We are not told why Jael acted as she did. Her motive is never given, and the Bible certainly does not defend the manner in which she acted. But the irony is that it was not a valiant warrior like Barak who conquered the great general Sisera. It was a pagan woman. Surely God was saying something to His people by that strange twist of events. "You were terrified and enslaved by Sisera. Because you turned away from Me, you had absolutely no power. But if you will trust in Me, I will look after the Siseras in your life, and I do not need a great man to do it. I can use a Jael. I do not need you! But you need Me!"

When Israel trusted God, their enemy was defeated. Humanly speaking, that victory came because two people, a man and a woman, trusted God. That is the great lesson of

Judges 4. Deborah's leadership qualities deserve our study and imitation. But above all, our eyes need to be directed to the God of Deborah. The essence of godly leadership in an unswerving commitment to be His servant. Good leaders are loyal, believing followers.

SIX

No Hesitation, No Excuses

The first time I remember watching television was to see the coronation of Queen Elizabeth in June 1953. A group of families, including mine, descended on the home of a mutual friend who had a television set—they were not very common then. Frankly, it was one of the most boring days I had ever spent. The pageantry and the ritual were not very interesting to a ten-year-old boy, and, after a few hours, I wanted desperately to see if Howdy Doody was on another channel. However, despite my bad attitude, I knew that something very important was going on, and that it would be a great honor to be invited to sit in Westminster Abbey and see the coronation in person.

Prior to her coronation, the queen had sent out invitations to her friends and various Commonwealth dignitaries which read like this:

> We greet you well. Whereas we have appointed the second day of June 1953 for the solemnity of our coronation, these are therefore to will and to command, all excuses set apart, that you make your personal attendance upon us, at the time above mentioned, there to do and to perform such services as shall be required of you.

A queen does not request attendance, she commands it. The striking phrase in that invitation occurs in the very middle: "All excuses set apart." When a monarch expresses her will and issues her command, her subjects respond without hesitation or excuses.

Queen Elizabeth is held in esteem by all her subjects, but she is only a constitutional monarch. The believer serves One who is far greater—the Lord Jesus Christ, King of kings and Lord of lords. Compared to Him, Queen Elizabeth is a nobody. Were the queen or the President to summon us, we would instantly obey. Yet King Jesus has expressed His will and issued His commands, and all our excuses must be set apart. He deserves our willing, eager, loyal, and faithful service, without hesitation or excuses.

There are times in our lives when we need to stand back and look at the way we are responding to the commission of our Lord Jesus. It is only too easy for our service to fall into the pattern of grudging duty. Then we begin to suffer from a great performance gap. We may make resolutions, pledges, and commitments, but somehow they are never translated into actions. Then rationalizations and excuses set in until finally, paralyzed by inactivity, we become completely lethargic.

Judges 5 gives us a good opportunity to engage in accurate analyses of this side of our spiritual lives. It is the song of Deborah, the hymn of praise which she sang to God on the day He gave the miraculous victory over Jabin and Sisera. Judges 5 is a great piece of Hebrew poetry, but it is much more than that. It is a profound insight into the spiritual warfare in which we, as believers in the Lord Jesus, are engaged.

Before we read Judges 5, there is one thing we should notice. This is one of those chapters in the Bible where there are some rather big differences between the King James Version and modern versions. There is a simple reason for this. Judges 5 is a difficult passage to translate. It uses some very symbolic and archaic language, and, although it is beautiful, it is hard to interpret accurately. Therefore, a more modern translation, based on a fuller knowledge of the Hebrew language than the King James Version translators had, is helpful. As usual, we will follow the *New American Standard Bible*.

Then Deborah and Barak the son of Abinoam sang on that
    day, saying,
"That the leaders led in Israel,
That the people volunteered,
Bless the LORD!
Hear, O kings; give ear, O rulers!
I—to the LORD, I will sing,
I will sing praise to the LORD, the God of Israel.
LORD, when Thou didst go out from Seir,
When Thou didst march from the field of Edom,
The earth quaked, the heavens also dripped,
Even the clouds dripped water.
The mountains quaked at the presence of the LORD,
This Sinai, at the presence of the LORD, the God of Israel.

"In the days of Shamgar the son of Anath,
In the days of Jael, the highways were deserted,
And travelers went by roundabout ways.
The peasantry ceased, they ceased in Israel,
Until I, Deborah, arose,
Until I arose, a mother in Israel.
New gods were chosen;
Then war was in the gates.
Not a shield or a spear was seen
Among forty thousand in Israel.
My heart goes out to the commanders of Israel,
The volunteers among the people;
Bless the LORD!
You who ride on white donkeys,
You who sit on rich carpets,
And you who travel on the road—sing!
At the sound of those who divide flocks among the
    watering places,
There they shall recount the righteous deeds of the LORD,
The righteous deeds for His peasantry in Israel.
Then the people of the LORD went down to the gates.

"Awake, awake, Deborah;
Awake, awake, sing a song!
Arise, Barak, and take away your captives, O son of
    Abinoam.

Then survivors came down to the nobles;
The people of the LORD came down to me as warriors.
From Ephraim those whose root is in Amalek came down,
Following you, Benjamin, with your peoples;
From Machir commanders came down,
And from Zebulun those who wield the staff of office.
And the princes of Issachar were with Deborah;
As was Issachar, so was Barak;
Into the valley they rushed at his heels;
Among the divisions of Reuben
There were great resolves of heart.
Why did you sit among the sheepfolds,
To hear the piping for the flocks?
Among the divisions of Reuben
There were great searchings of heart.
Gilead remained across the Jordan;
And why did Dan stay in ships?
Asher sat at the seashore,
And remained by its landings.
Zebulun was a people who despised their lives even to
    death,
And Naphtali also, on the high places of the field.

"The kings came and fought;
Then fought the kings of Canaan
At Taanach near the waters of Megiddo;
They took no plunder in silver.
The stars fought from heaven,
From their courses they fought against Sisera.
The torrent of Kishon swept them away,
The ancient torrent, the torrent Kishon.
O my soul, march on with strength.
Then the horses' hoofs beat
From the dashing, the dashing of his valiant steeds.
'Curse Meroz,' said the angel of the LORD,
'Utterly curse its inhabitants;
Because they did not come to the help of the LORD,
To the help of the LORD against the warriors.'

"Most blessed of women is Jael,
The wife of Heber the Kenite;

Most blessed is she of women in the tent.
He asked for water and she gave him milk;
In a magnificent bowl she brought him curds.
She reached out her hand for the tent peg,
And her right hand for the workmen's hammer.
Then she struck Sisera, she smashed his head;
And she shattered and pierced his temple.
Between her feet he bowed, he fell, he lay;
Between her feet he bowed, he fell;
Where he bowed, there he fell dead.

"Out of the window she looked and lamented,
The mother of Sisera through the lattice,
'Why does his chariot delay in coming?
Why do the hoofbeats of his chariot tarry?'
Her wise princesses would answer her,
Indeed she repeats her words to herself,
'Are they not finding, are they not dividing the spoil?
A maiden, two maidens for every warrior;
To Sisera a spoil of dyed work,
A spoil of dyed work embroidered,
Dyed work of double embroidery on the neck of the
    spoiler?'
Thus let all Thine enemies perish, O LORD;
But let those who love Him be like the rising of the sun in
    its might."
And the land was undisturbed for forty years.

It is important to notice that Deborah sang this song of praise on the same day God gave His people victory. She was in some very good company. Back in Exodus 15, the first thing Moses did, when the people escaped through the Red Sea, was to sing a psalm of praise to God, and Miriam led in song as well. When God brought the people through the Jordan River, the first thing Joshua did was to erect two monuments in praise and acknowledgment to God. We ought to learn, as we observe these people, the priority of praise in believers' lives. When God does something for us, the natural response of our hearts should be to praise Him, and to acknowledge publicly what He has done. That is what David meant when he said in Psalm 40:1-3,

> I waited patiently for the LORD;
> and He inclined to me, and heard my cry.
> He brought me up out of the pit of destruction,
> out of the miry clay;
> And He set my feet upon a rock, making my
> footsteps firm.
> And He put a new song in my mouth, a song of
> praise to our God;
> Man will see and fear, and will trust in the LORD.

Deborah's "new song" falls rather naturally into five parts.

Verses 1-5 are an introduction, praising God for the way He displayed His glory in Israel's history.

Verses 6-11 contrast what Israel was before God's deliverance through Deborah with their present prosperity.

Verses 12-18 give the response of God's people to the battle call of Deborah and Barak.

Verses 19-23 describe God's victory.

Verses 24-31 celebrate the death of the man who had oppressed and crushed the people of God.

Two themes run through the psalm and we meet both of them in the first verse. "That the leaders led in Israel, that the people volunteered, bless the LORD!" The first theme is the greatness of God displayed in the victory He accomplished. What happened in the battle was not ultimately due to the skill of the soldiers or the strategy of Barak or the charisma of Deborah. It was the triumph of God, and so the psalm recounts "the righteous deeds of the LORD, the righteous deeds for His peasantry in Israel" (v. 11).

But God does not work in a vacuum. He uses men and women, and in this case He used a group of people who responded to Him willingly, eagerly, and unhesitatingly. That is the second theme of the psalm—the response of God's people to God's challenge, and it is that theme we want to focus upon as we study the song of Deborah.

ISRAEL'S DESPERATE SITUATION

We can thank God that we live in a free country. We do not know what it is to be occupied by an enemy nation, held as prisoners in our own homes. But that is exactly what Israel experienced under Jabin and Sisera.

- The highways were empty; when you wanted to travel to see your friends or do business, you had to sneak around by the back way.
- The people who lived in the open country and the villages, the peasants as they are called in verse 7, had to leave their homes and move into walled cities.
- Even the cities were not safe. As verse 8 says, "There was war in the gates." The cities were under seige, and the people were totally unequipped. "Not a shield or a spear was found among forty thousand in Israel." They had to make their own weapons.
- The army had been reduced, until there were only about forty thousand available men.

Why had Israel come to this place? Verse 8 gives us the reason in four simple words: "New gods were chosen." The people had turned away from God to the Baals and the other gods of Canaan and, as a result, the power of God had gone from them.

THE VOLUNTEER SPIRIT

But then, in His grace, when He would have had every reason to abandon them, God reached out in love to Israel and raised up Deborah. She describes herself in verse 7, as a mother in Israel, who brought loving guidance, concern, and direction to the people of God. Under the leading of the Holy Spirit and the revelation of God, she recruited Barak to be the military leader, motivated him with the promises of God, and then gave him God's plan for the military campaign. The heart of that plan was to recruit ten thousand men from Naphtali and Zebulun to go with Barak to attack Sisera.

That sounds simple, but it was not. Sisera was enormously powerful, with 900 iron chariots. The Israelites were virtually unarmed, and the plan was to attack Sisera head on, on the Plains of Esdraelon, where Israel would be weakest and Sisera would be at his very strongest. How do you recruit ten thousand men to march against hopeless odds, to an almost certain death?

THE RESPONSE TO THE CHALLENGE

The astonishing thing is that there was no problem. The people responded eagerly and enthusiastically. That fact stirred Deborah's heart, and she celebrated it in her song. Three features stand out.

1. *There was a spontaneous response (vv. 2, 9).* "That the leaders led in Israel, that the people volunteered, bless the LORD!" The word "volunteered" is an interesting one. It indicates something done freely, voluntarily, and eagerly. For example, it is used of a spontaneous freewill offering, given because a man loves God. More profoundly, it is used in Hosea 14:4 to describe the way God's love flows out to men freely and spontaneously.

Barak did not have to twist arms or plead or trick men into a commitment. There was no draft or a series of TV ads saying how wonderful life in the army was. There was a challenge from the heart of God and a free, spontaneous, unhesitating response to that challenge. That response to God impressed Deborah so much that she repeats it in verse 9:

> My heart goes out to the commanders of Israel,
> The volunteers among the people;
> Bless the LORD!

2. *There was a practical response (v. 13).* The people were not just moved emotionally. They acted. That is the message of verse 13. It is one thing to say in the safety of home, "Yeah, I'll go." It is another thing to actually face the front lines. They were only a remnant. They were not a powerful

military force, but they went as warriors, ready to do battle for God.

3. *There was an individual response.* The leaders did not stand back and say, "OK you peasants, fight. We will stay here and plan." The peasants did not stand back and say, "Let the leaders do it." But individually, each man faced up to his responsibility before God. The leaders led, the people followed, but the choice and the response was an individual one.

THE ROLL CALL OF THE TRIBES (13-18)

However, Deborah was not content simply to record the general principles of the response. In precise detail, she listed the tribes that came and characterized their response. The roll call included Ephraim, Benjamin, Machir (the half-tribe of Manasseh living west of the Jordan), Zebulun, Issachar, and Naphtali. Three tribes deserve special attention. In verse 15 the men of Issachar are pictured as they rushed into battle at Barak's heels, not a step behind their leader. Zebulun (v. 18) is called a people who "despised their lives even to death." No sideliners there. And Naphtali stood on the high places of the field. That is to say, they deliberately chose the hottest and most difficult part of the battle. It is a graphic picture of courage and valor.

All of this has a direct application to my life as a believer in Jesus Christ. I must not read a chapter like Judges 5 without measuring myself against the kind of commitment that I read of here—wholehearted, spontaneous, enthusiastic, risk-taking commitment—which obeys the command of God and marches into the teeth of the enemy to do battle for God.

The Lord Jesus has called me to be His disciple. He has challenged me to engage in spiritual warfare, not against men, but the hosts of Satan. He has commissioned me to live for Him in the world. He has given me the privilege of serving Him, in all kinds of different ways.

I can respond to that call in a number of ways.

I can give the grudging reply of duty, "Well, if I'm drafted, I guess I'll have to serve!"

I can answer as a reluctant volunteer, "Hey, maybe if I enlist early enough, I can get a good, soft office job."

I can have the spirit of the mercenary, "How much're ya gonna pay me? What's in it for me?"

I can exhibit the attitude of the glory-seeker, "If I'm not a general, I'm not interested."

Or I can have the same commitment as Zebulun, Issachar, and Naphtali, and eagerly volunteer to be in the center of the battle for God.

When Israel built the tabernacle, Exodus 36 tells us it was built by "everyone whose heart stirred him" to do the work and to give contributions willingly. Finally, the workmen came to Moses with a problem, "Moses, they are bringing much more than enough. Tell them to stop." And they had to restrain the people from giving!

One of the sad things about the evangelical church is that we see so little of that kind of enthusiastic response to God's call. So many of us are willing to give only the spare parts of our lives to the Lord Jesus. There is so much duty and so little love in our service for the King. But what a beautiful thing it is to see a willing heart, rushing into battle at the heels of King Jesus, despising life to the point of death to bring glory to Him!

THE MOTIVE FOR VOLUNTEER SERVICE

What moved these men to spontaneous volunteer service for the Lord God? Why did they risk so much? According to Deborah there were two reasons.

1. *Their attitude toward God (v. 31).* "Let those who love Him." These volunteers were the righteous part of the nation who, in a day of apostasy, knew what it was to love God. When God possesses our hearts, we begin to serve Him enthusiastically, spontaneously, and freely.

Maybe that is where our problem really lies. It is not the quantity of our service that is really decisive, it is the quality of our relationship with the Lord Jesus. That is why the Lord Jesus comes to us and says, as He did to Peter,

"Peter, do you love Me?"

"Lord, you know I do!"

"Feed My lambs."

That is the order. "Do you love Me? Serve Me."

Then we get like Peter and look at someone else and say, "What about this man? What will he do?" And the Lord says, "What is that to you? You follow Me." Love for Jesus Christ produces service befitting the King, but if we do not love Him, everything else will be out of shape in our lives.

We find a second factor in their motivation, in verse 23.

2. *Their attitude toward service (v. 23).* There was a small town in Israel, whose location is unknown. Somehow, in that battle they could have stopped the Canaanites, but they chose not to. They were conscientious objectors in God's battles. As a result, in verse 23, Meroz is cursed "because they did not come *to the help of the Lord,* to *the help of the Lord* against the warriors" (itals. added). You see, it was not a matter of helping Deborah or Barak or Israel or even themselves. It was helping the Lord. That was what the volunteering tribes knew. They were serving the Lord.

I cannot tell you how often that has helped me—when I feel frustration or bitterness or complacency settling in—to stop myself and say, "But, Gary, you are not doing it for them. You are doing it for your Savior—for the Lord Jesus." Have you seen your service like that—as an act of love done for the Lord Jesus? Do you see opportunities of service as a way you can serve the Son of God? When you take that perspective on service, it has a revolutionary impact on your life.

The delightful thing is that the giving volunteer spirit produces a joyful heart. Deborah was singing, and these volunteers were singing because they knew the joy of giving to the Lord. That is a truth expressed beautifully in 1 Chronicles 29. There we read of the free gifts of the Israelites in preparation for building the Temple. Read the result:

"Then the people rejoiced because they had offered so willingly, for they had made their offering to the LORD with a whole heart" (1 Chron. 29:9). Joy in believers' lives is never simply a product of receiving. It is the result of giving themselves to the Lord and knowing the overflow of His love in their lives.

But not all the tribes responded with a volunteer spirit. Side by side with that spirit, just as in our churches today, there lived the reluctant spirit, which Deborah also described.

THE RELUCTANT SPIRIT—5:15-17

Four and one-half tribes are absent from the roster of the tribes who marched into battle. Interestingly, Judah and Simeon are never mentioned at all, probably because they were so far to the south. But four and one-half did not come because they would not, and Deborah gives us an insight into the attitudes of those tribes. They represent to us four different forms of the reluctant spirit which paralyzes our Christian service.

REUBEN: THE TRIBE WHO WOULD NOT ACT (vv. 15b-16).

You could draw a picture from Deborah's words in verses 15b and 16b. "Among the divisions of Reuben there were great resolves of heart. . . . great searchings of heart." You can almost see the people meeting together, holding debates, passing resolutions, drilling the army. But it never went any further than that. They were emotionally stirred, their hearts were moved, but their feet never went. They stayed at home, listening to the shepherds piping their sheep, but they never heard the blast of the war trumpets. They were moved by sentiment, but not to sacrifice.

I think that this is a constant danger for Christians. It is easy to be moved emotionally, to have great searchings of heart, but never to translate that into action, to leave the sheepfolds and head for battle.

GILEAD: THE TRIBES WHICH LACKED FELLOWSHIP (V. 17)

Gilead isn't the name of one tribe but two—Gad and the half tribe of Manasseh which had never crossed the Jordan River. The two and one-half tribes (including Reuben) that chose not to cross also chose not to march with Deborah and Barak. "Gilead remained across the Jordan." I cannot help but think that one of the major reasons was that they were cut off from active fellowship with the other tribes. You can mark it down: A voluntary lack of fellowship with other believers will inevitably produce a lack of enthusiasm for God's work.

DAN: THE TRIBE WHICH LACKED GROWTH (V. 17)

Dan was another tribe that would not join. Dan's problem was not a lack of action, or a lack of fellowship; it was a lack of growth. "Why did Dan stay in ships?" Deborah asked. The answer is that Dan had never realized its potential under God. Back in 1:34-36 we learned that the Amorites forced them up to the mountain country. In fact, because they would not obey God, they became so utterly weak that they had to leave the territory God had given to them. As we shall see, they moved to another area, far to the north. Dan had never developed spiritual growth. All they could see was their own situation; so they just stayed where they were. One of the saddest stories among all the sad stories in Judges concerns Dan in Judges 18. It was the first tribe to go into apostasy. Again, there is an important spiritual truth. A Christian who does not have a growing Christian life will not have a volunteering, eager spiritual experience.

ASHER: THE TRIBE WHICH LACKED VISION (V. 17b)

Asher lived on the Phoenician coast, and they were focused entirely on their work—on their ships, and docks, and trading. "Asher sat at the seashore and remained by its landings." They had no vision for God's work, no sense of the significance of the position they had in God's program, no understanding of the mission God had called them to in the world. As a result, they had no volunteers.

It is so important that we have a biblical vision of life. We need to see ourselves as God sees us; we need to see our mission in God's terms; we need to see our service in God's way. And when we grab hold of a biblical understanding of life, we will begin to develop volunteers' hearts for God.

There is one thing we should notice about these four and one-half tribes who did not respond to God's call. None ever again made a significant contribution to the cause of God. Asher virtually vanished except for a brief involvement with Gideon. Dan nosedived into apostasy; the two and one-half tribes on the east of the Jordan were overrun repeatedly. The chief victims of the reluctant spirit were the possessors of that spirit. They lived for themselves, refusing to risk what they had, and, as a result, they lost what they had.

It is always that way in the Christian life. If I do not have an eager, giving heart for God, my reluctant spirit will affect my fellow believers. But above all, it will injure me as I shrivel up within my own shell.

The children of Israel had one of the most unusual rules of war that any nation has ever had. It is given in Deuteronomy 20:8:

> The officers shall speak further to the people, and they shall say, "Who is the man that is afraid and fainthearted? Let him return and depart to his house, so that he might not make his brothers' hearts melt like his heart."

How do you think that rule would work in our society? If you do not want to go to war, you do not have to. We would get an army big enough to fill a telephone booth. But God was trying to teach His people a lesson of major importance. "I want volunteers in My army, people who will serve Me freely, eagerly, and spontaneously."

That is what He says to us today. In fact, we can capture the theme of Deborah's song by adopting the familiar words of 2 Corinthians 9:7, "Let each one do just as he has purposed in his heart; not grudgingly or under compulsion; for God loves a cheerful giver."

Does that describe your spirit in your service for the Savior? The Lord Jesus is not in the business of compulsion. He is not manipulating people into ministry. He is looking for people with the committed hearts of Issachar, Zebulun, and Naphtali. Are you rushing into battle at your Savior's heels?

SEVEN

God's Transforming Presence

In May 1855, an eighteen-year-old boy went to the deacons of a church in Boston. He had been raised in a Unitarian church, in almost total ignorance of the gospel, but when he had moved to Boston to make his fortune, he began to attend a Bible-preaching church. Then, in April of 1855, his Sunday school teacher had come into the store where he was working and simply and persuasively shared the gospel and urged the young man to trust in the Lord Jesus. He had, and now he was applying to join the church.

One fact quickly became obvious. This young man was almost totally ignorant of biblical truth. One of the deacons asked him, "Son, what has Christ done for us all—for you—which entitles Him to our love?" His response was, "I don't know. I think Christ has done a great deal for us; but I don't think of anything in particular as I know of." Hardly an impressive start. Years later his Sunday school teacher said of him:

> I can truly say that I have seen few persons whose minds were spiritually darker than was his when he came into my Sunday school class and I think the committee of the church seldom met an applicant for membership who seemed more unlikely ever to become a Christian of clear and decided views of Gospel truth, still less to fill any space of public or extended usefulness.

Nothing happened very quickly to change their minds. The deacons decided to put him on a year-long instruction program to teach him basic Christian truths. Perhaps they wanted to work on some of his other rough spots as well. Not only was he ignorant of spiritual truths, he was only barely literate, and his spoken grammar was atrocious. The year-long probation did not help very much. At his second interview, there was only a minimal improvement in the quality of his answers, but since it was obvious that he was a sincere and committed (if ignorant) Christian, they accepted him as a church member.

Over the next years, I am sure that many people looked at that young man, and convinced that God would never use a person like that, they wrote off Dwight L. Moody. But God did not. By God's infinite grace and persevering love, D. L. Moody was transformed into one of the most effective and significant servants of God in church history, a man whose impact is still with us.

One of the great truths of Scripture is that when God looks at us, He does not see us for what we are, but for what we can become, as He works in our lives. He is in the business of taking weak, insignificant people, and transforming them by His presence in their lives. He begins with us where we are, as we are. He knows our weaknesses, failures, discouragements, doubts, and inadequacies, but He does not say, "You get rid of those, and then I can use you." Rather, He comes to us in our weakness with the promise of His presence that will transform our inadequacy into His strength.

The truth of God's transforming presence is vividly portrayed in the life of one of the great heroes of the Old Testament, Gideon. At least we think of Gideon as a hero, but that is certainly not where he began, and, as we see the way God worked in his life, we can lay hold of some very encouraging truths.

We first meet Gideon in Judges 6, and to understand him properly, we need to examine carefully this first portrait. What follows only makes sense in the light of his initial appearance on the pages of God's Word.

Gideon, at this stage of his life, inevitably reminds me

of that old story of the man who came to his psychiatrist with a problem. "Doctor, you must help me. Everything's going wrong. I feel worthless. My friends tell me I have a terrible inferiority complex. Can you help me?"

So the psychiatrist told him that he would give him some tests and evaluate them. A week later, the man came back, and the psychiatrist said, "Friend, I have some good news and some bad news for you. The good news is that we have proved you do not have a complex. There is no doubt about that. But the bad news is, you are inferior."

If you had been in Ophrah and met Gideon just before the Angel did, you would have found a thoroughly discouraged man. He might have said to you, "Man, I feel lower than a flea's knees. These Midianites are turning us all into slaves, and there is not a thing we can do about it." The only honest response you could have made would have been, "I understand that, Gideon. The reason you feel that way is because you are defeated, discouraged, and helpless." To realize why Gideon felt that way, we need to understand the bondage of his people.

THE CONDITION OF ISRAEL—6:1-10

Then the sons of Israel did what was evil in the sight of the LORD; and the LORD gave them into the hands of Midian seven years. And the power of Midian prevailed against Israel. Because of Midian the sons of Israel made for themselves the dens which were in the mountains and the caves and the strongholds. For it was when Israel had sown, that the Midianites would come up with the Amalekites and the sons of the east and go against them. So they would camp against them and destroy the produce of the earth as far as Gaza, and leave no sustenance in Israel as well as no sheep, ox, or donkey. For they would come up with their livestock and their tents, they would come in like locusts for number, both they and their camels were innumerable; and they came into the land to devastate it. So Israel was brought very low because of Midian, and the sons of Israel cried to the LORD. Now it came about when the sons of Israel cried to the LORD on account of Midian, that the LORD sent a prophet to the sons of Israel, and he said to them, "Thus says the LORD, the God of Israel, 'It was I who brought you up from Egypt, and brought you out from the house of slavery. And I delivered you from the hands of the Egyptians and from the hands of all your oppressors, and dispossessed them before you and gave you their land, and I said to you, "I am the LORD your God; you shall not fear the gods of the Amorites in whose land you live. But you have not obeyed Me."'"

These verses paint a vivid portrait of the condition of Israel in the time of Gideon. Here we have the fourth go-round of the period of the judges, and, once again, it is the distressing cycle of sin, servitude, supplication, and salvation, followed by more sin and more servitude. God had given the people a wonderful deliverance through Deborah, and for forty years afterwards Israel had known freedom and peace. Then the people took their eyes off the Lord and focused their lustful gaze on the idols and evils of Baal worship, and once again God gave them over to the consequence of their sin—bondage and servitude under a foreign nation.

This time God used a group of desert people, led by the people of Midian. The Midianites had discovered a devastating new military weapon—the camel! In the twentieth century with our sophisticated instruments of death, such as neutron bombs, laser beams, satellites, and so on, it is hard for us to appreciate the military significance of camels in the twelfth century B.C. But in their time, camels gave the Midianites an enormous military advantage. They were ugly enough to strike the Israelites with fear, but their main benefit was in giving the Midianites a mobil, long-range, swift, attack-capability against the Hebrews, who were entirely dependent on foot soldiers. A camel can travel for three or four days, with a heavy load on its back, and cover about 300 miles, without food or water. The American army started an interesting experiment to use camels in the fight against the Indians, but the project was shelved when the Civil War broke out.

With their powerful new weapons, the Midianites developed a unique strategy against Israel. Rather than invading and occupying the land, they simply waited until the harvest was ready. Then, as verses 3-5 record, they would move in from the desert, cross the Jordan in huge numbers, and overwhelm the land. Their military and numerical superiority left Israel defenseless; so they would seize every bit of food they could find. Like a plague of locusts, they would swoop through the land, stripping it bare of grain, vegetables, fruit, and livestock. Finally, their camels loaded down with their spoil, they would cross back into the desert and live there until the next harvesttime. Perhaps they would leave a small force in the land, but the main host came only during the yearly invasion.

They did this for seven years and left Israel in a desperate situation, reduced to hiding food in mountain dens and caves. But nothing could stop Midian. Israel was defeated and helpless, and finally, realizing their need, they called out to God for help.

REPENTANCE NOT REGRET

Every other time in Judges when God's people called on Him for help, He immediately sent them a judge to bring deliverance. Not this time. God sent a prophet because He had a message He wanted His people to hear.

There is a great difference between a cry for help from trouble, and a cry of repentance for sin. Israel called on God, but they had not dealt with their sin. So God's prophet came in verses 7-10. He reminded them of God's faithfulness and grace—how He had delivered them from Egypt and given them the land of Canaan and set forth the terms of His covenant: "I am Yahweh your God. You shall not serve the gods of the Amorites in whose land you are dwelling."

God had done all that, in His grace for them. Yet, deliberately and defiantly, they had broken their covenant with Him. By this prophet, God was reminding them of one basic fact: They were what they were, and where they were because they had turned away from Him.

But God did not leave them there, aware of their sin and defeated by it. He was going to deliver them, and His first step was His preparation of the deliverer.

THE CALL OF GIDEON—6:11-16

Then the angel of the LORD came and sat under the oak that was in Ophrah, which belonged to Joash the Abiezrite as his son Gideon was beating out wheat in the wine press in order to save it from the Midianites. And the angel of the LORD appeared to him and said to him, "The LORD is with you, O valiant warrior." Then Gideon said to him, "Oh my lord, if the LORD is with us, why then has all this happened to us? And where are all His miracles which our fathers told us about, saying, 'Did not the LORD bring us up from Egypt?' But now the LORD has abandoned us and given us into the hand of Midian." And the LORD looked at him and said, "Go in this your strength and deliver Israel from the hand of Midian. Have I not sent you?" And he said to Him, "O LORD, how shall I deliver Israel? Behold, my family is the least in Manasseh, and I am the youngest in my father's house." But the LORD said to him, "Surely I will be with you, and you shall defeat Midian as one man."

As the eighth harvest season rolled around and with it the threat of the Midianite invasion, if you had taken a poll to discover the most likely deliverer of Israel, one name would never have appeared on your list. There was never a less likely liberator than Gideon, the son of Joash, a man from the tribe of Manasseh and the clan of Abiezer.

The first description we have of Gideon gives us a vivid portrait of his condition. The name *Gideon* means "hewer," so he was apparently a man of physical strength. But verse 11 does not picture a man of strength. His father owned land in Ophrah, which normally was a very fertile part of the country. But when we meet Gideon, he was threshing wheat by beating it with a stick in a winepress. Normally, a man would thresh wheat on a wooden threshing floor, using a threshing sledge pulled by oxen. The floor would be by a wheat field, in an exposed place, so that the wind could carry away the chaff. Only the very poorest people would have so little wheat that they would thresh it by beating. Yet that was exactly what Gideon was doing. In a hidden winepress, under a tree, beating out a few sheaves of wheat, he desperately tried to save the little bit of food that he had from the Midianites. It was the picture of a defeated, discouraged man, filled with doubts and fears. The man under the oak in Ophrah was no hero!

GOD'S TRANSFORMING PRESENCE

As Gideon was beating his few stalks of wheat, a man approached, sat down, and watched. Two things are significant about this person. First, Gideon did not know that he was an angel, so there was nothing supernatural about his appearance. He did not have wings, wear a halo, or carry a harp. As a result, it took time for Gideon to realize to whom he was speaking. Second, it was not "an angel of the LORD" who came to Gideon, but "*the* angel of the LORD" (itals. added). A careful study of references to *the* Angel of the Lord in the Old Testament reveals that He is God Himself. That truth is evident here, as we shall see, and a quick look at passages such as Genesis 22:11-19 and Exodus 3 will reinforce this idea. God Himself had come to deal with Gideon to teach him some life-transforming truths.

If I did not know God better, I might think that He was mocking Gideon in the first words He spoke, "The LORD is with you, O valiant warrior." If there was anything that Gideon was not, at that moment, it was a valiant warrior, a mighty hero. In Joshua, that expression refers to brave soldiers marching into the teeth of the enemy. Or in Judges, it refers to Jephthah, a man of great personal courage. Here, as Gideon furtively beat wheat with a stick, afraid of the Midianites, that was exactly what he was not. But that was exactly what he was going to become, because the Lord was with him.

I wonder if you have noticed how often God deals with people in this way in the Bible. He comes to a childless ninety-nine-year-old man named Abram and says, "Abram, I am going to change your name. You are going to be 'Abraham'—father of a multitude." And by God's power, Abraham has a son, Isaac. Or an impetuous, unstable emotional man is brought by his brother to the Lord Jesus, and the Savior looks at him and says, "You are Simon, the son of Jonah. You shall be called a Rock—Peter." And by God's grace and power, Peter is transformed into a pillar of the early church.

That was exactly what the Angel of the Lord was saying. "Gideon, I know what you are. I can see your circumstances. But I am much more concerned with what you are going to become, than with what you are. Gideon, I don't see you for what you are now, but for what you are going to be, because I am with you."

Other people look at us and see our flaws and failings. God looks at us and sees our possibilities, through His transforming presence. It is enormously important that we begin to realize the possibilities of our lives because of what God can do in us.

GIDEON'S PROBLEMS

But our God is not only a God of transforming power. He is also a God of infinite patience and sensitive love. Gideon was a man with two major concerns, and the Lord not only permitted Gideon to express them, He also supplied His answer to Gideon's needs.

The problem of discouragement. The first problem is uncovered in verse 13. Notice again the words Gideon used: "Oh ... if ... why ... where ... now the LORD has abandoned us." What we saw pictured in action in verse 11, we now hear spoken in words. Gideon was a discouraged, defeated man.

A little girl was listening to her mother tell some Bible stories about great people like Moses, Joshua, Samson, and Daniel. Finally, she turned to her mother and said, "Mommy, you know, God was much more exciting back then."

I think that Gideon felt like that. He loved to hear about what God had done for Israel in the past. He believed thoroughly in God's power then. But where were the miracles now? Where was God now? How could they possibly deal with the Midianites? Of all of the forms of discouragement, this is the worst. For a believer to feel that God is not interested, or to think that God has turned His back is to be reduced to a debilitating despair that crushes all the hope out of life. That is where Gideon was as God began to deal with him.

Obviously Gideon had not really come to grips with the situation. It was not God who had abandoned His people, but God's people who had turned their backs on Him. It is far easier to blame God for our problems than to recognize and deal with our sins and responsibilities. At the same time, we need to recognize that Gideon was not suffering from a "defeatist" complex. He and his people really were defeated, but as long as they responded to their defeat with doubt, they would be enchained.

When God spoke to Gideon's problem in verse 14, we notice a very small but critically significant change. The veil begins to drop away, and we read, "The LORD looked at him." As we have already said, this is one of many places in the Old Testament where the Angel of the Lord is revealed to be God Himself appearing in human form. We can go one step further. On the basis of John 1:18, we can safely say that the Angel of the Lord is, in fact, the Lord Jesus Christ, taking a human form for a brief time.

The Lord Jesus turned and fixed Gideon in His gaze; then He said, "Go in this your strength and deliver Israel from the hand of Midian. Have I not sent you?" The Lord Jesus gave Gideon the promise of His presence to overcome his defeat and discouragement.

When the Lord Jesus said, "Go in *this* your strength," He was not saying "Gideon, you can do it." Relying on his own strength made Gideon hide in a winepress. "This your strength" is the strength that God has given by His promise, "The LORD is with you....I will be with you" (vv. 12, 16). God was calling Gideon to go forward on the basis of the strength which He supplied.

Gideon had learned very well that dependence upon his strength brought defeat and discouragement. And if we look at our strength, we will always end up in defeat. But God's answer to discouragement is never positive thinking, but rather the promise of His presence.

Quite frankly, when I look at the secular world in which we are living and realize the powerful attacks of anti-Christian forces on biblical truths and values, I feel very much as Gideon did before the Midianites—puny, helpless, and insignificant. Paul was right. Christians do not contend with flesh and blood but against powerful satanic forces (Eph. 6:12). The only answer I know to that kind of satanic discouragement is to claim the promise of the presence of God and order my life around the truth that God's Holy Spirit indwells me. I do not serve Him in my own strength.

There is a clear parallel between Judges 6:14 and Matthew 28:18-20. When the Lord commissioned Gideon, it was with the promise of His strength. When He commissions us, His infinitely greater promise is, "Lo, I am with you always, even to the end of the age." Hudson Taylor once said, "All of God's great men have been weak men who did great things for God because they reckoned on His being with them; they counted on His faithfulness." That is the divine solution to discouragement—the truth of the omnipresence and adequacy of God.

The problem of adequacy. But God's promise brought out the second question that haunted Gideon. "Go!" God said, and Gideon asked, "How can I do that? The job's too big for me, and I am too small for the job. I have absolutely no qualifications, and I do not have any base of support. My father is from the smallest clan in Manasseh, and I am the youngest son." This is the complaint of verse 15.

Now in actual fact that was not quite true. Joash apparently was a fairly important man, and the family was certainly not poor. Gideon himself had ten servants, as verse 27 tells us. So Gideon was not quite as insignificant as he said.

But Gideon was filled with the sense of his total inadequacy. He had absolutely no confidence that he could do it on his own. The wonderful thing is that this is exactly where God begins with a person. Time and time again, as we read the Word of God, we see God cutting away a man's self-confidence to bring him to the place where he admits that he is totally inadequate to do or to be what God desires. In fact, I do not think there is a single major figure in the Word of God whom God did not bring to realize a deep sense of his own inadequacy. As Paul puts it in 2 Corinthians 3:5, "Not that we are adequate in ourselves to consider anything as coming from ourselves."

But God never leaves us with a sense of our own inadequacy. Paul ends verse 5 by saying: "But our adequacy is of God." Whenever we admit our inadequacy, God confronts us with the truth of His total adequacy. So in Judges 6:16, He made His promise to Gideon, "Surely I will be with you, and you shall defeat Midian as one man." Inadequate in ourselves, overwhelmingly adequate through our God— that is the lesson of Gideon's life.

I wonder to what extent you have allowed the promise of God's adequacy to minister to your life. God Himself has committed Himself to be with you and to pour His strength into your life. Is this a truth you are claiming? Your weakness does not hinder God. In fact, His pattern is to reveal His power in weakness (2 Cor. 12:9). What we most need is not self-confidence, but God-confidence.

But there was one final step before Gideon was equipped to step out for God. He needed to know that God's promises were not merely figments of his imagination. They were God's solemn word, upon which he could rest his life. Therefore, God not only commissioned Gideon, He confirmed that call to Him.

THE CONFIRMATION OF GIDEON—6:17-24

So Gideon said to Him, "If now I have found favor in Thy sight, then show me a sign that it is Thou who speakest with me. Please do not depart from here, until I come back to

Thee, and bring out my offering and lay it before Thee." And He said, "I will remain until you return." Then Gideon went in and prepared a kid and unleavened bread from an ephah of flour; he put the meat in a basket and the broth in a pot, and brought them out to him under the oak, and presented them. And the angel of God said to him, "Take the meat and the unleavened bread and lay them on this rock, and pour out the broth." And he did so. Then the angel of the LORD put out the end of the staff that was in his hand and touched the meat and the unleavened bread; and fire sprang up from the rock and consumed the meat and the unleavened bread. Then the angel of the LORD vanished from his sight. When Gideon saw that he was the angel of the LORD, he said, "Alas, O Lord GOD! For now I have seen the angel of the LORD face to face ' And the LORD said to him, "Peace to you, do not fear; you shall not die." Then Gideon built an altar there to the LORD and named it The LORD is Peace. To this day it is still in Ophrah of the Abiezrites.

By now Gideon had come to realize that there was something special about the person to whom he was talking. He was not really sure who he was, but Gideon knew that he had talked with a spokesman from God. To be sure, he both honored his guest and sought a sign that he was really God's messenger. He asked the angel to wait while he prepared a meal, as an offering.

As you read verse 19, remember that this is a time of famine. But Gideon prepared a feast. He cooked an entire kid, used about thirty-five pounds of flour to bake bread, and made some soup as well. That must have been an extremely costly offering under the circumstances, and it obviously took longer than a quick trip to MacDonalds!

Gideon brought that offering to the Lord and followed His instructions. Suddenly the meal was turned into a sacrifice. The Lord simply touched the rock with His staff, and a fire devoured the food. God often revealed His presence in that way, and, immediately, Gideon knew that he had been in the presence of God. Instantly, he was conscious of his sin and guilt, and he cried out in fear, "Alas, O Lord GOD! For now I have seen the Angel of the LORD face to face!"

God had not come to judge Gideon, but to deliver His people through him. So God, in His grace, spoke to Gideon, "Peace to you, Gideon. Do not be afraid; you will not die. I am ministering to you and showing My love to you."

In response to God's assurance, Gideon built an altar and called it Yahweh-Shalom, "the Lord is Peace," a sign of God's encounter with him. I am sure there were many times in the next few days when Gideon came back and looked at two things—the mark of fire on the rock and the pile of stones which he had built in response to God's presence. They were reminders written in rock, of God's promises, and on the basis of those promises, he marched against Midian.

In just the same way, etched in the Word of God, I find written the promises of God's presence. They are written in the indelible ink of God's faithfulness, and when I apply those promises to my life, and live in the conscious presence of my Lord, I am transformed.

On his own, Gideon was a weak, faltering, doubting man. But he had firsthand contact with the Lord Jesus, and he was never the same again. Because he had been face to face with the Lord Jesus, he was a new man. He had been transformed by the presence of God. God had taught Gideon that it was not his inadequacy but God's adequacy that really counted.

Before James Garfield became President of the U.S., he was the president of Hiram College. One day a father asked him about the curriculum. Mr. Garfield began to list the courses his son would take. The man stopped him and said, "Mr. Garfield, that is far too much for the degree he will get. Couldn't you make it easier?"

"Yes, I suppose I could," said Mr. Garfield. "But then I am reminded of the fact that when God wants to build a tall, strong oak tree, He takes a hundred years. But He only takes three months to make a squash. Which do you want your son to be?"

God is in the process of transforming men. He does not do it instantly, but He does it. He transforms us when we spend time with Him. Second Corinthians 3:18 summarizes the process like this: "But we all, with unveiled face beholding as in a mirror the glory of the Lord, are being transformed into the same image from glory to glory, just as from the Lord, the Spirit." Are you spending time looking at the Lord in the mirror of His Word?

The principle here is of central importance. We do not look for God's message to be revealed in visions. The faith has been once for all time delivered to us and recorded in God's Word (Jude 3). The Scriptures contain everything we need to be complete and equipped for *every* good work (2 Tim. 3:16-17). Through His Word, we behold the glory of the Lord Jesus. We see Him face to face, and, as we do, we are changed. It is our privilege to live consciously in His presence, and firsthand fellowship with the Lord Jesus is transforming. But we must spend time with Him. That and only that will equip us to serve Him.

EIGHT

No Turning Back

If you live in Texas, you discover very fast that Texans are people who take their history seriously. Elizabeth and I were married after my first year at Dallas Seminary. As a Canadian, Elizabeth had a visa enabling her to teach in the United States, as well as experience teaching in Canada. But we discovered that what was good enough for the rest of the U.S.A. was not necessarily good enough for Texas. She could not teach in the public schools of Dallas unless she took a history course—not American history, Texas history.

Some events in Texas history are not hard to remember, especially if you grew up when Davy Crockett was a national TV hero. The Alamo was a small mission church in San Antonio, but, in 1836, it became the scene of some very dramatic events. Texas had declared itself independent of Mexico, and Mexico responded by sending in an army led by General Santa Ana. At the Alamo, a small group of men, including Davy Crockett, found themselves facing 3,000 Mexican soldiers. They faced a critical decision—they could surrender, flee, or fight. Colonel W. B. Travis drew a line on the dirt floor with his sword and challenged those who were willing to stay and fight to certain death to step across that line. All but one did, and all died for their courageous choice.

A simple choice, but a decisive one. Once they moved across that line, there was no turning back. By their courage, they aroused an entire nation, and "Remember the Alamo!" became the great battle cry of the Texans as they fought off the Mexicans. The courage of those committed men moved other men to courage.

There was an Alamo kind of experience in the life of Gideon, a decisive turning point. It was God who drew the line, and He caused Gideon to step across and commit himself to doing God's will. In his case, Gideon's choice did not bring death, but it did mean there could be no turning back, and, because of his courage, his nation was aroused to action.

However, we must not consider this incident as simply an important event in Gideon's life. Embedded in it is a profound spiritual principle which directly affects our lives 3,000 years later. God is reminding us that it is not enough to answer God's call in the privacy of our own lives, no matter how sincere that response might be. Private commitment must produce public discipleship. God calls us to identify ourselves publicly and radically with the Lord Jesus, in a way from which there is no turning back, and once we step across that line, God pours His power into our lives.

That line-crossing experience for Gideon is described in Judges 6:25-35.

> Now the same night it came about that the LORD said to him, "Take your father's bull and a second bull seven years old, and pull down the altar of Baal which belongs to your father, and cut down the Asherah that is beside it; and build an altar to the LORD your God on the top of this stronghold in an orderly manner, and take a second bull and offer a burnt offering with the wood of the Asherah which you shall cut down." Then Gideon took ten men of his servants and did as the LORD had spoken to him; and it came about, because he was too afraid of his father's household and the men of the city to do it by day, that he did it by night. When the men of the city arose early in the morning, behold, the altar of Baal was torn down, and the Asherah which was beside it was cut down, and the second bull was offered on the altar which had been built. And they said to one another, "Who did this thing?" And when they searched about and inquired, they said, "Gideon the son of Joash did this thing." Then the men

of the city said to Joash, "Bring out your son, that he may die, for he has torn down the altar of Baal, and indeed, he has cut down the Asherah which was beside it." But Joash said to all who stood against him, "Will you contend for Baal, or will you deliver him? Whoever will plead for him shall be put to death by morning. If he is a god, let him contend for himself, because someone has torn down his altar." Therefore on that day he named him Jerubbaal, that is to say, "Let Baal contend against him," because he had torn down his altar. Then all the Midianites and the Amalekites and the sons of the east assembled themselves; and they crossed over and camped in the valley of Jezreel. So the Spirit of the LORD came upon Gideon; and he blew a trumpet, and the Abiezerites were called together to follow him. And he sent messengers throughout Manasseh, and they also were called together to follow him; and he sent messengers to Asher, Zebulun, and Naphtali, and they came up to meet them."

We will misread Gideon unless we remember him as the weak, discouraged, defeated man of verse 11, hiding from the Midianites and doubting his God. But God had begun a healing process in his life by giving him a direct encounter with the Lord Jesus. With that encounter, came God's call for his life—Gideon was to be God's man to deliver Israel from the hands of Midian.

That commission describes Gideon's general responsibilities, but God did not leave him there. He gave Gideon a specific responsibility, his first assignment in the carrying out of his divine calling. It was an assignment filled with some basic lessons which Gideon could apply to all the events that would follow. In verses 25-32, we have that assignment given and obeyed.

GIDEON'S FIRST ASSIGNMENT—6:25-32
THE ASSIGNMENT (VV. 25-26)

In Gideon's backyard was a vivid example of the reason God had allowed Midian to overwhelm and enslave Israel. Joash, Gideon's father, had apparently built an altar to Baal on his own property and with it an Asherah, a wooden pillar representing the Canaanite goddess of fertility. However, it was not only a personal idol, for the family's private use. Obviously it served as the village shrine, with Joash probably acting as the supervisor of pagan worship in the area. It is unlikely that this was a tiny shrine tucked away in a grove. A Baal altar discovered at Megiddo, not far from Ophrah, was twenty-six feet square and four and a half feet high, made of stones cemented by mud. Joash's altar was probably similar.

That backyard shrine was the object of God's command. His will was clear. Until Gideon put things right in his own backyard, God would not and could not use him to deliver his people. Gideon's orders were straightforward. He was to take a young bull, which belonged to his father, and a seven-year-old bull and use them to tear down the massive Baal altar. Then he was to cut down the wooden Asherah, and, using that wood, he was to sacrifice the seven-year-old bull on a new altar which he was to build for the Lord on a high rock.

There is a divine meaning in the two bulls which God commanded Gideon to use. The young bull belonged to Joash, and, as the local Baal shrine-keeper, he probably intended to sacrifice it to Baal. That very bull was to be used to destroy Baal's altar. The second bull was seven years old, and that was exactly the length of the Midianite oppression. But as Gideon offered that bull in faith to God on God's altar, the period of oppression ended. Seven years of bondage went up in the smoke of obedient service.

There are some profound spiritual implications in Gideon's assignment.

1. *Baal must go before Midian can go.* Before Gideon could be the deliverer of Israel, he had to be the destroyer of the false god Baal. It is the same for us. Before we can have victory in our lives over the sins or problems or habits that are defeating or discouraging us, Jesus Christ must be the unquestioned Lord of our lives. There is no victory where there is idolatry or a divided heart. There can be no compromise if we desire to know the Lord at work in our lives.

What is the Baal in your life? It may be any one of a hundred things. But whatever it is, it must be chopped down before God will deal with the Midian in your life.

2. *God's altar cannot be built until Baal's altar is destroyed.* The Lord will not allow any mixing or syncretism. The Lord's altar cannot stand alongside Baal's. The two cannot coexist. There can be no worship acceptable to God until we remove the false altars from our hearts and lives. And syncretistic worship is no worship at all. He alone must be Lord and King.

3. *The place we must start is in our own backyard.* Before Gideon could lead his whole nation to faith in God, he had to deal with the Baal in his family. That is a principle which runs all through Scripture. Scriptural victory must begin at home, and if my commitment to the lordship of Jesus Christ does not first affect my home life, it is superficial and hollow.

GIDEON'S ODEDIENCE

That night Gideon took ten of his servants and did exactly what God had commanded him to do. He was filled with fear, because he knew how much that Baal altar meant to those people, but he obeyed nevertheless.

In many ways, God was asking Gideon to fight the most difficult battle first. Often the very hardest place to represent Jesus Christ is in your own family and with your closest friends. Quite frankly, it is a great deal easier to stand up for the Lord Jesus where people do not know you than in your own home. It is much easier to share the gospel with strangers on the beach or in the airport than with your fellow workers or classmates. Midian was a lot less intimidating than Joash and Ophrah. After all, Gideon had to live with Joash every day. But that is where God called Gideon to commit himself. And I believe we can learn a great deal from that. I must not, I cannot, hide my commitment to the Lord Jesus from those closest to me. That is my first assignment as a believer—to follow Jesus Christ there.

You will notice also from verse 27 that faith is not demonstrated by fearlessness, but by obedience. As I read the verse, I see a man who obeyed God, but was afraid while he did it. God did not supernaturally remove Gideon's anxieties and fears, but Gideon obeyed God despite his fears. There are many times when I need to be reminded of that. Over and over again, I find God's call in my life stretching me to the breaking point, and I face situations full of fear and uncertainty. Still, God calls me to obey, and I discover that, when I focus on obedience, He deals with my fears. Paul learned exactly the same thing. In 1 Corinthians 2:3-4 he says, "I was with you in weakness and in fear and in much trembling. And my message and my preaching were not in persuasive words of wisdom, but in demonstration of the Spirit and of power." So, if, as you obey God, you sometimes feel fearful and weak, you are in good company. Gideon felt that way, and Paul felt that way, but faith obeys, even in the midst of fear.

THE RESULTS OF OBEDIENCE

Obedience, even in the darkness of night, produced results visible in daylight, and the next morning, Gideon's work was open and available for all to see. Judges 6 highlights three specific results.

1. *The anger of the townspeople (vv. 28-30).* As Alexander Whyte perceptively comments, "The worshipers of Baal never neglected their morning devotions. 'Early will I seek thee' they could say to their god with truth and a good conscience."[1] But when they got to the altar to worship their false god, they were first shocked, then infuriated by what they saw.

Verse 30 is probably the most graphic picture of the total apostasy of Israel in the book of Judges. The living God had done great things for Israel, but they had seen His name profaned and degraded and had openly given their approval. But in the name of a god to whom they owed only defeat and degradation, they were ready to kill Gideon.

"Bring him out so that we can kill him." How twisted their perspective had become!

2. *The transformation of Joash (v. 31).* The second result of Gideon's act was a thoroughly unexpected one. When Joash realized what Gideon had done, I believe that he was both shamed and challenged. He knew that Gideon's actions were right, and that he should have done the same thing years earlier. So he defended Gideon in a striking way. "Listen, what you are doing is blasphemy. If Baal really is God, he does not need you to defend him. If he cannot defend himself, he is not worthy of worship. If he is really God, Gideon will be struck dead." It was a basic lesson in Baal theology!

Gideon had been so fearful of his father and his family that he had attacked the altar in the darkness of night. Now the man that he most feared had become his greatest defender. How often that is true. Our obedience to the Lord Jesus can do great things in the lives of the most unexpected people. People whose reactions we fear the most are often the first to respond when they see the reality of our commitment to Jesus Christ.

3. *The reputation of Gideon (v. 32).* Joash had set up the test, and the results were obvious, as verse 32 reveals. Gideon had challenged Baal, and lived to tell the story. Baal did not strike him dead. Instead, on that day, Gideon acquired a new name. *Jerubbaal* literally means "Let Baal contend," based on Joash's challenge. It came to mean "Baal-fighter" or "Baal-conqueror." Every time men looked at Gideon, they had visible proof of the weakness of Baal and the power of God. Because God had made him strong, Gideon had won a great victory in his backyard, and that victory established him in the eyes of the people as God's appointed deliverer.

There was a strikingly similar event in the life of John Knox, the great Scottish Reformer. In 1548, he was a prisoner on a French slave ship, chained to a rowing bench and lashed constantly by the guards. He was there because of his preaching of the Word of God and his refusal to submit to Catholicism. One day the lieutenant brought aboard a wooden image of the virgin Mary and demanded that the slaves kiss it. Knox refused, and they pushed it violently against his face. He grabbed it and threw it overboard, shouting, "Let our Lady now save herself: she is light enough; let her learn to swim."

When no divine judgment fell on Knox, two things happened. Never again were believers required to engage in Catholic exercises against their wishes, and men began to look to Knox as their leader. Eventually, the Scottish Reformation was the result.

Our courage to commit ourselves decisively and finally to the lordship of Jesus Christ can be used by God in the lives of others. Tearing down Baal's altar was Gideon's first assignment, but it was only the first. The next stage in Gideon's spiritual preparation was God's response to his obedience. In verse 34, we learn of Gideon's divine empowerment.

GIDEON'S DIVINE EMPOWERMENT—6:34-35

THE HOLY SPIRIT IN GIDEON'S LIFE

The first words of verse 34 introduce us to a concept that explains the change in Gideon's character. Our passage reads literally, "So the Spirit of the LORD clothed Himself with Gideon." The word is used elsewhere to describe a man putting on his clothes (Gen. 28:20), or a warrior putting on a suit of armor (Isa. 59:17). What a delightful picture! The Holy Spirit wore Gideon the way a man puts on a suit of clothes. It is a vivid way of saying that God the Holy Spirit took possession of Gideon, indwelling and controlling him. Two other times we have this phrase in the Old Testament. In 1 Chronicles 12:18 we read of Amasai, one of David's brave soldiers, being so empowered, and in 2 Chronicles 24:20 the phrase is used of Zechariah the priest who, with great boldness, charged a sinful people with apostasy, and as a result lay down his life as a martyr.

THE HOLY SPIRIT IN THE OLD AND NEW COVENANTS

Inevitably, a phrase like this forces us to ask some important questions about the ministry of God the Holy Spirit to men like Gideon in Old Testament times and His ministry to believers now. Gideon's victory was directly due to the Spirit of God. Our effectiveness is directly dependent upon Him as well; so the more we understand about the ministry of the Spirit, the better prepared we are to live for Him in a secular society.

THE HOLY SPIRIT IN THE OLD COVENANT

There are four things true of the work of Gideon and other Old Testament believers.

1. *His ministry was limited in extent.* The Old Testament believers were not all indwelt by the Holy Spirit. For example, verse 34 records that He entered Gideon in this special way at this specific time. One of the great promises of the New Covenant prophecy in Jeremiah and Ezekiel was that, one day, all God's children would be indwelt by the Spirit. But that is a New Covenant, not an Old Covenant, blessing.

2. *His ministry was limited in purpose.* When we read about the Spirit coming into men's lives, it was for a special service or work that God had for that person to do. In the book of Judges, we are specifically told how He came upon the judges—Othniel, Deborah, Gideon, Jephthah, and Samson. But we do not read of Him entering the lives of ordinary men for ordinary life.

3. *His ministry was limited in time.* The Holy Spirit did not always permanently indwell His people. We read of His departing from Samson in Judges 16:20 and from Saul in 1 Samuel 16:14.

4. *His ministry was limited in effect.* When Gideon was clothed with the Holy Spirit, it was the external man, not the inner man who was affected. He was not transformed morally, so much as externally. Thus this "Spirit-

clothed" man would lead the nation into apostasy in Judges 8. Jephthah was "filled with the Spirit," but he made a sinful, superstitious vow, The Holy Spirit came upon Samson and made him physically powerful. But he remained a morally weak man. Strange as it seems, the Holy Spirit did not always produce the fruit of the Spirit in the lives of the people He indwelt in Old Testament times.

THE HOLY SPIRIT IN THE NEW COVENANT

We are not emphasizing the limitations of the Old Covenant ministry of the Spirit to minimize that Covenant, but rather to maximize the blessing, by contrast, of the New Covenant. Our position in Jesus Christ is infinitely richer. Each limitation of the Old Covenant is removed in the New Covenant.

1. *He is unlimited in extent.* Every believer is indwelt by the Spirit. He is not for some believers or for special believers, but for all believers (Rom. 8:9; John 7:39).

2. *He is unlimited in purpose.* He is not given just for Christian service, but for life and living. It is by the Spirit that we are made adequate as servants of the New Covenant (2 Cor. 3:5-6).

3. *He is unlimited in duration.* The Lord Jesus promised the Holy Spirit will be with us forever (John 14:16-17). By God's Holy Spirit, we have been sealed and given God's pledge of eternal life (2 Cor. 1:20-22, Eph. 1:13-14).

4. *He is spiritual in effect.* His ministry in our lives is evidenced, above all else, by a transformation in our character (Gal. 5:22-23). He does not simply strengthen our external man. Rather, we are "strengthened with power through His Spirit in the inner man" (Eph. 3:16). Life's greatest needs are inner resources and godly character, and that is exactly the Holy Spirit's ministry.

THE HOLY SPIRIT IN OUR LIVES

The teaching of Scripture is clear. The same Holy Spirit who clothed Himself with Gideon has come to indwell you as a child of God. You are His temple, His dwelling place, and His ministry in your life is even richer than His ministry in Gideon's life.

We can learn two significant lessons from the way God worked in Gideon's life. First, the Holy Spirit does not destroy our individuality. When Gideon was indwelt by the Spirit, he remained Gideon. He did not become Othniel or Samson or Jephthah. The Holy Spirit does not bring a dull conformity into our lives, but the power to be what God calls us uniquely to be.

We see an obvious illustration of this every day. In my kitchen, I have all kinds of electrical appliances. I can take an electric light, or a radio, or an electric can opener, or an electric dishwasher, or a toaster and plug them one by one into exactly the same outlet. But they do not all do the same thing. They use the same power, but they do not have the same function. In fact, that power enables them to function individualistically. Until they are plugged in, they are all the same, none of this is doing anything.

The application is obvious. God made me an individual, and when the Holy Spirit is empowering me, I will function as God intends me to function.

The second lesson is that the ministry of God the Holy Spirit is directly related to obedience. A comparison of Ephesians 5:18 and Colossians 3:16 makes that point very apparent. So does the picture of the Holy Spirit clothing Himself with Gideon. Clothing does not fight its wearer. It submits to the human body and moves with it. But human beings are not passive garments. We can quench the Spirit and resist His work in our lives.

One of my seminary professors, Howard Hendricks, was fond of telling us, "Men, every morning I pray, 'Lord, here I am. I want to be Your suit of clothes today. I want You to take me and use me. Lord, just walk around in me today.'" I have never forgotten that. I do not know whether or not he took his idea from Judges 6:34, but I do know that his prayer expresses the truth of this verse.

God's empowering had an immediate effect in Gideon's life. Once again the Midianites invaded the land. For seven years, they had simply walked in and met virtually no opposition from the Israelites. Not this year. God had prepared His man. Empowered by the Spirit and encouraged by his obedience, Gideon blew the war trumpet, and men rallied around him. Look where they came from! First came his own family, the Abiezrites. Obedience at home had produced response at home. Then his tribe came— Manasseh, and others from Asher, Zebulun, and Naphtali.

Gideon had come a long way from the weak, defeated man we met in verse 11. As we have seen, there were three things that produced such changes in his life:

1. He had had firsthand contact with the Lord Jesus Christ.
2. He had decisively and publicly committed himself to the Lord by an act of obedience. There was no turning back from that act. He had dealt with Baal, and now God could use him to deal with Midian.
3. He had come under the control of God the Holy Spirit. It was not by might, nor by power, but by God's Spirit that Gideon has been equipped to scrve God.

Those three things are not simply facts in Gideon's life. They are eternal requirements if we want to be effective for Jesus Christ.

NINE

How Not to Know the Will of God

When John Wesley was thirty-two years old, he was a bachelor missionary in the colony of Georgia. While he was serving a church in Savannah, he met a young woman named Sophia Christina Hopkey. She was pretty and intelligent, and Wesley fell head over heels in love with her. But Wesley belonged to a group called the Holy Club, and one of their ideals was that members should remain single. So Wesley was caught in a dilemma. Was it the will of God for him to marry Sophie or not? To find out, he and a friend named Charles Delamotte decided to draw lots. On three pieces of paper they wrote: "Marry"; "Think not of it this year"; and "Think of it no more." Then they put the pieces in a container. Delamotte closed his eyes and drew out the third one, "Think of it no more." Wesley was heartbroken, but he took the result to be the will of God. He ended the courtship, and, not long after, he sailed back to England. In his journal, he wrote over the record of his romance, "Snatched as a brand out of the fire!"

Shortly after his return to England, Wesley came to saving faith in the Lord Jesus, and he began the evangelistic ministry which God used so greatly. During his travels, he fell in love with another woman, a widow and a Bible class teacher named Grace Murray. This time he tried a different approach to finding the will of God about marriage. He listed seven factors he desired in a wife—her roles as "Housekeeper, Nurse, Companion, Friend, and a Fellow Labourer in the Gospel of Christ . . . , Her Gifts, and the Fruits of her Labours." He set out the pros and cons, and then he stated his conclusion:

> Therefore all my seven arguments against marriage are to-
> tally set aside. Nay, some of them seem to prove that I ought
> to marry and that G. M. is the person.

Unfortunately, John's brother Charles did not agree. He
believed that marriage would hamper John's evangelistic
work. When he heard the news, he galloped over to Grace's
home, jumped off his horse, ran in, and said to her, "Grace
Murray, you have broken my heart!" Then he fainted at her
feet. That shook Grace so badly that she hastily married
another man. Strike two for Wesley!

Finally, a year and a half later, at the age of forty-seven,
John did marry, a wealthy widow named Mary Vazeille. I do
not know how Wesley chose her or what Charles had to say,
but John made a mistake. He had a very unhappy marriage,
and, twenty years later, she left him. When she did, Wesley
wrote in his journal, "I have not left her; I would not send
her away; I will not recall her."

Now that story raises some very interesting questions,
not only about Wesley and marriage, but also about how we
find the will of God. Was Wesley right the first time when
he used lots? How about the second time, when he used
common sense? To put it more personally, how do I know
the will of God in my life? Do I look for some kind of
supernatural sign? Do I put God to certain tests?

We want to look at a passage that can teach us a great
deal about knowing the will of God, but its lessons are
basically negative ones. It is a passage that has caught the
imagination of many Christians, and often we hear about
"putting out the fleece." Is that really what we ought to do?
Is that God's way of giving us guidance? Let us turn to
Judges 6:36-40 and see.

> Then Gideon said to God, "If Thou wilt deliver Israel through
> me, as Thou has spoken, behold, I will put a fleece of wool on
> the threshing floor. If there is dew on the fleece only, and it is
> dry on all the ground, then I will know that Thou wilt deliver
> Israel through me, as Thou hast spoken." And it was so.
> When he arose early the next morning and squeezed the

fleece, he drained the dew from the fleece, a bowl full of water. Then Gideon said to God, "Do not let Thine anger burn against me that I may speak once more; please let me make a test once more with the fleece, let it now be dry only on the fleece, and let there be dew on all the ground." And God did so that night; for it was dry only on the fleece, and dew was on all the ground.

THE WILL OF GOD AND FLEECE-SETTING

If you have been a Christian for any length of time, you have probably heard someone refer to these five verses. Perhaps you are wondering whether or not you should follow a particular course of action, and a Christian friend says, "Well, put out a fleece, brother. The Lord will show you." In fact, the practice of fleece setting has become the way many Christians try to discover the will of God. The idea is very simple. You say to the Lord, "Father, I have two options. If You want me to follow Plan A, then please do this by Tuesday. Then I will know that is what You want me to do. If You do not, I will follow Plan B."

Behind the practice of fleece setting stands a very important fact. For a Christian, nothing is more important than to know and do the will of God.

An old Model T Ford was pulled off to the side of the road with its hood up, and a young man was trying desperately to get it running. He had been working at it for a long time without any success when a beautiful, chauffeur-driven limousine stopped behind him, and a well-dressed man got out. He watched the fellow working for awhile and finally suggested that he make a minor adjustment in one part. The young man was skeptical, but nothing else had worked, so he did what he was told. "Now," said the man, "your car will run. Crank it up." So the young man cranked it once, and, sure enough, the engine started running as if it were brand-new.

The young man was amazed that this kind of man knew so much about cars; so he asked him, "How did you know exactly what to do?" "Well," the other man said, "I'm

Henry Ford. I made the car, so I know all about how it works."

It is for precisely that reason that the will of God is so important to me as a believer. God made me. He knows all about me, and what is more, He loves me so much that He sent His Son to die for me. Therefore, if He has a will for my life, nothing should be more important to me than that I know and do it. That applies to every area of life, at every stage of life. In every decision I make, as a Christian, I want to know and do the will of God.

But that brings us back, face to face with the question of fleece setting. Ephesians 5:17 says, "So then do not be foolish, but understand what the will of the Lord is." But how? Is Judges 6:36-40 a pattern that I should follow in my life as I seek to know His will?

The answer is "no." Fleece setting is not God's way of directing His children. God's greatest desire for His children is that we know and do His will. In fact, He is much more concerned about it than we are. But we make a great mistake if we take Judges 6 as a pattern for our lives. We need to look carefully at this passage to discover why that is so. Yet we do not simply want to show how not to know the will of God; we also want to discover some positive principles about knowing and doing God's will.

GIDEON'S FLEECE—6:36-40

THE PROBLEMS OF FLEECE SETTING

As we look at Gideon's actions in "putting out the fleece," four things stand out:

1. *Gideon was not ignorant of God's will.* It is important that we read verses 36-37 very carefully. Notice what Gideon says to the Lord. "If Thou wilt deliver Israel through me, *as Thou hast spoken,* behold, I will put a fleece of wool on the threshing floor. If there is dew on the fleece only, and it is dry on all the ground, then I will know that Thou wilt deliver Israel through me, *as Thou hast spoken*" (itals. added). Twice, in that statement, Gideon repeats the key

phrase—"As You have spoken." You see, Gideon knew very well what God had said. He knew clearly what God wanted him to do. Gideon's problem was not one of knowledge, it was one of faith and obedience. Let us review God's dealings with Gideon to see how clear that is.

In verse 11, we met Gideon beating out wheat with a stick in a hidden winepress. He was the picture of defeat, doubt, and discouragement. But then the Lord Jesus Himself, the Angel of the Lord, appeared to him, and Gideon knew God's transforming presence in his life. There are three things that the Lord did for Gideon:

- He gave him a clear statement of His will, an unmistakable commission. So that Gideon did not have any uncertainty, it was repeated three times—in verses 12, 14, and 16. Nothing could be clearer. Gideon knew God's will.
- The Lord gave Gideon a clear revelation of His person. Through the miracle of verse 21, Gideon was left in no doubt that his commission had come from God Himself.
- Then, the Lord gave Gideon an experience of His power at work in his life. As the Holy Spirit clothed Himself with Gideon, Gideon was able, not only to deal with the Baal in his father's backyard, but also to rally around him 32,000 men.

When we come to verse 36, we need to remember all of these things that God had done for Gideon. As we read verses 36-37, we realize that Gideon knew exactly what God's will was. He knew God's Word.

2. *Fleece setting is an evidence of doubt, not faith.* "If you will do this, then I will know." But God had already promised Gideon He would deliver and work through him. The Lord had already done a miracle to prove to Gideon that He meant what He said. So, by using the fleece, Gideon was saying, "I know what You have said. I know Your command and Your promise. But I am not sure that I really believe You." In other words, he was still fighting the battle of doubt.

When we come to the question of God's will, we have

clear biblical promises that the Lord will never fail to direct and guide us, as we follow Him. Great promises like these are only a small sample:

Psalm 32:8—I will instruct you and teach you in the way which you should go; I will counsel you with My eye upon you.

Psalm 37:23-24—The steps of a good man are established by the LORD; and He delights in his way. When he falls, he shall not be hurled headlong; because the LORD is the One who holds his hand.

Psalm 48:14—For such is God, our God forever and ever; He will guide us until death.

Isaiah 58:11—And the LORD will continually guide you, and satisfy your desire in scorched places, and give strength to your bones; and you will be like a watered garden, And like a spring of water whose waters do not fail.

When I start fleece setting, I do what Gideon did. I doubt the promises of God. I am refusing to rest in His Word, and, what is more serious, I am demanding that the Lord lead me on my terms, not His. That is why fleece setting nearly always is motivated by doubt, not faith.

3. *Fleece setting is dictating to God.* Gideon did not just come to the Lord and say, "Lord, I am still afraid. I have lots of doubts. Please reveal Yourself again to me." That kind of request is always appropriate. No, he came and said, "God, here is my program. You do this and this, and I want it looked after by tomorrow morning. Wet the fleece and keep the ground dry. Please alter the whole course of nature because I tell You to." The sovereign God must do what Gideon said, or else!

When you think about it, Gideon's request was both absurd and presumptuous. Why should God suspend the laws of nature because a man told Him to? Besides, Gideon's job was to obey God, not to dictate to Him. I do not think we should be too hard on Gideon. After all, he was almost the only man in his generation committed to doing God's will. From what we know about the period of the judges, he probably had virtually no exposure to the written Word of God. He had grown up in a thoroughly pagan environment, with an idolatrous father. I can understand Gideon's confusion about dictating to God. But his confusion should not become my example. What was excusable in his life is not excusable in mine.

4. *Fleece setting does not really solve the problem.* The next morning Gideon got up and went to the winepress, and, sure enough, the fleece was wet and the ground was dry. But then he began to think. "How do I really know this was of God? Obviously, the wool would retain moisture, and the rock would dry up quickly. Maybe it was just a coincidence." Doubt plagued him; so he went into the presence of God again. You will notice that he was aware that he was treading on very thin ice. "Please Lord, don't be angry, but we are going to have to run through all this again. I am afraid my test wasn't good enough. This time we will reverse it. Let us wet the ground and keep the wool dry."

You see, the problem with fleece setting is that it does not produce certainty, and it puts God in our little box. Not long ago, a Bible school announced that it was planning to buy a building. The announcement went, "If we have $100,000 by this date, we will know it is God's will. God can do it." Of course He could. But that was not the question. On the appointed day, they only had about $90,000. Now they had a problem. Should they buy the building or not? If it was not God's will, where had the $90,000 come from? Was that Satan's money? Of course not. But the fallacy was that they had expected God to do His work in their way.

Let us take it one step further. Suppose I ask God to do something for me by 10:00 P.M. The phone rings at 10:05. Is that God or Satan? Or, if it rings at 9:59, was that Satan trying to trick me? On this kind of basis, how can I ever be sure? The Word of God can produce certainty, but this kind of subjectivism never can.

No, fleece setting is not the way we are to find the will of God. But before we look at some positive principles, notice one beautiful lesson from this story.

The lesson is found in the first six words of Judges 6:40: "And God did so that night." The amazing thing about this passage is not what it shows about Gideon's fleece, but what it teaches about God's patience. Gideon was a special student in God's slow-learner class. You or I would have forgotten Gideon and found someone else. The Lord had done all those things in Gideon's life, yet he was still saying, "if," and putting out tests. But God kept on loving and working with him.

I thank God for that because I am afraid that I am one of God's slow learners, too. It takes me so long to learn such simple lessons. Over and over I have learned to be thankful that my God is a God "slow to anger, and abounding in loyal love and truth; who keeps loyal love for thousands, who forgives iniquity, transgression, and sin." That is how He describes Himself in Exodus 34:6-7, and that is exactly what He has proved to be in the life of Gary Inrig. What a wonderful God we slow learners have!

Let me share with you a personal illustration about this business of fleece setting. When we were teaching in Winnipeg, the Lord made it very clear that He wanted us to leave teaching to be involved in a local church ministry. At the same time, He made it abundantly clear that we were meant to come to Bethany Chapel in Calgary. It was undeniable guidance both for us and for the elders of the assembly in Calgary. Humanly speaking, the call was unexpected, but it came from God. But we had a house to sell in Winnipeg; so we put out a fleece. It was February, and we began to pray, "Lord, if you want us to go to Calgary, sell our house by April at such and such a price." You know what? He did not! But we felt sure about His guidance, so we changed the fleece. "By June, Lord." Well, to make the story short, the house did not sell. In fact, it did not sell until the very Sunday in August when I first preached in Bethany Chapel, and at a price which meant we lost the equity we had in the house. What happened? Wasn't it God's will for us to come to Calgary? Yes, it was. We have never had clearer guidance in our lives about anything, and over and over God has confirmed that to us.

How did we know it was His will? After all, the fleece did not work. I believe God was teaching us not to trust in fleeces. But we knew His will, and that knowledge came by applying some basic principles.

KNOWING GOD'S WILL

Let me suggest five clear biblical principles about God's guidance in our lives.

BIBLICAL PRINCIPLES OF GUIDANCE

The first principle is the most important.

1. *God does not give us guidance, as much as He gives us a Guide.* Imagine you are driving in a strange city. Which would you rather have with you—a road map and a list of addresses, or someone who knows the city intimately, knows where you want to go and how to get there? The answer is obvious. Given a choice, we will choose a guide over guidance any time.

As I read the Bible, I discover that is exactly the way God works in my life. In fact, the word *guidance* does not occur in the Bible, but over and over I read of the Guide, the Lord Jesus, who personally leads and directs me. That is how Gideon knew God's will—by personal contact with the Lord Jesus.

Therefore, the first thing I need to realize about the will of God is that it is never mechanical. It is not a matter of plugging the right questions into a heavenly computer but of walking with the Lord Jesus Christ. Guidance comes from the Guide, and, if we are out of fellowship with the Lord Jesus, we can be walking encyclopedias about the will of

God, but we will not know His will personally. Nothing can take the place of this, and the interesting thing I discover is that, as I concentrate on following the Shepherd, the issue of the will of God looks after itself. If I would know His guidance, I must enjoy His fellowship.

A second principle is almost as important as that first one.

2. *Guidance is based on the principles and precepts of the Word of God.* Gideon did not know God's will by putting out the fleece but by obeying the revealed Word of God. Underline this in your mind. God's Word is God's will for your life. God inspired it so that you might be thoroughly equipped for every good work. In the Bible, I have two kinds of guidance: *specific direct commands,* the basic requirements of God for my life as His child, and *general principles,* which apply to many areas of my life. When I take these precepts and principles of Scripture and apply them to my life, I get a clear picture of God's will. In the process, I discover a very important fact. God is much more concerned about what I am, than about where I am, or what I am doing. If I am not the right person because my life is ordered by Scripture, then it will do me little good to be in the right location or vocation. So God's will majors on my character.

3. *Guidance is confirmed through the indwelling peace of God.* In Colossians 3:15 we read, "Let the peace of Christ rule in your hearts." That verse has several applications, but one of the things it tells me is that the Holy Spirit will give me a deep inner peace and contentment about the Father's will for my life. Often it is peace in the middle of turmoil, but it is a real inward peace that comes through my fellowship with the Prince of peace in prayer and the Word.

Philippians 4:6-7 is also relevant. "Be anxious for nothing, but in everything by prayer and supplication with thanksgiving let your requests be made known to God. And the peace of God which surpasses all comprehension, shall guard your hearts and your minds in Christ Jesus." Nothing causes Christians more anxiety than the question of whether or not a particular action is God's will. Anxiety solves nothing, but prayer does! When we commit those anxieties to Him, He places His peace as a fortress around our desires and our understanding.

4. *Guidance is communicated through the desires God gives us.* As we live in fellowship with the Lord through His Word, He plants compulsions and desires in our heart. One of the most beautiful sections on guidance in the Bible is found in Psalm 37:3-4: "Trust in the LORD, and do good; dwell in the land and feed on His faithfulness. Delight yourself in the LORD; and He will give you the desires of your heart." As David says elsewhere, "He will fulfill the desires of those who fear Him" (Psalm 145:19).

Sometimes we hear people talk about "surrendering to the will of God" or "giving in to God," and we get the sense that God's will is something destructive and life negating. I do not want to minimize the reality of our sinful natures or the temptation to rationalize God's will, so that we end up doing what we want, quite independently of God. But the wonderful truth is that, when we submit unreservedly to our Guide, we are never so happy and fulfilled as when we are doing His will. He plants hungers and desires in our hearts, and His will is acceptable and pleasant, for "God is at work within us to produce both the willing and the doing of His good pleasure" (Phil. 2:13).

5. *Guidance comes through the counsel of other believers.* This has been called the "fourth and one" principle. If you are a football fan, you have often seen a quarterback call a time out at a critical point in the game and walk over to the sidelines to get advice from the coach. After all, the coach is a man with more experience and resources, and he has the advantage of being an observer, not a participant whose perspective is limited.

At the fourth and one situations in our lives, when we must make decisions, we need to thank God for the spiritual gifts, experiences, and spiritual discernment He has given other believers and draw upon those resources. But be sure that the counsel comes from mature, spiritual believers. After all, when Roger Staubach calls time out, he does not go to the sidelines and place a long-distance call to Gary Inrig watching the game on television. He goes to Tom Landry to draw upon his experience. Advice is only as good as its source, so seek out godly counselors.

We can know the will of God. It is not a mystical or magical or mysterious process that leaves us perpetually in doubt. It is simply a matter of walking with the Shepherd. We do not *need* fleece setting to know His will. Gideon's problem was not that he did not know God's will, but that he hesitated in doing it.

What is the will of God? It is the voice of the Shepherd. The Lord Jesus said, "My sheep hear My voice and I know them and they follow Me." If you want to know His will, listen to His voice, then follow Him. As His child, you can rest in the fact that His will perfectly reflects His character. His will is good, gracious, holy, wise, and perfect, because He is all of those things. You can also rest in the fact that His guidance is certain. He leads us "for His name's sake" (Psalm 23:3). If He fails to guide, He will lose His reputation as the Good Shepherd.

Trust Him. Keep your eyes fixed on Him and follow where He leads, and you will be able to rejoice with Asaph:

> Nevertheless I am continually with Thee;
> Thou hast taken hold of my right hand.
> With Thy counsel Thou will guide me,
> And afterward receive me to glory (Psalm 73:23-24).

TEN

Prepared for Victory

A Frenchman named Emile Coue flourished in the early part of this century. He claimed to have discovered and developed an almost infallible method of healing. Basically it was this: When you were sick, if you kept insisting to yourself that you were really getting better, you could quite literally talk yourself out of your illness. You were to repeat a little phrase twenty times in a row on two occasions daily.

> Every day, in every way, I am getting better and better.
> Every day, in every way, I am getting better and better.

Coue claimed that he had seen people cured of heart trouble, ulcers, bronchitis, clubfeet, bad nerves, and a multitude of other problems, by following his method. Believe you're getting better, and you will. And often you do.

Coue is only one of hundreds of people in various walks of life who hold the belief that a positive outlook on life and a strong sense of self-confidence will take care of their problems. "If we believe we can, we can." Convinced of that, an athlete "psyches himself up" before a big game, a coach inspires his athletes with a pep talk, a sales manager conducts a motivation seminar, and a general tries to convince his men that they cannot possibly lose. "Men, we can do it. We've got what it takes. Let's go get 'em!"

That reminds me of the little ditty that goes like this:

> He tackled the thing that couldn't be done
> With a will he went right to it.
> He tackled the thing that couldn't be done
> And he found he couldn't do it.

It is interesting to see the way God prepares His men for the battles they will face. The Coues, the Churchills, and the Vince Lombardis of the world seek to prepare us by building our self-confidence and stiffening our backbone. God does something entirely different. He does not build our self-confidence, but our dependence upon Him. It is a process that is repeated many times in the Word of God. When God wants a man or a woman to do great things for Him, He builds into that man or woman not self-confidence but God-confidence.

There are few places where that principle is more obvious than in Judges 7, when God prepared Gideon for battle against Midian. As we see the way God prepared Gideon, we also must realize that God's method of preparing us for spiritual warfare is exactly the same in principle, if not in procedure. The process is described in Judges 7:1-15.

> Then Jerubbaal (that is, Gideon) and all the people who were with him, rose early and camped beside the spring of Harod; and the camp of Midian was on the north side of them by the hill of Moreh in the valley. And the LORD said to Gideon, "The people who are with you are too many for Me to give Midian into their hands, lest Israel become boastful, saying, 'My own power has delivered me.' Now therefore come, proclaim in the hearing of the people, saying, 'Whoever is afraid and trembling, let him return and depart from Mount Gilead.' " So 22,000 people returned, but 10,000 remained. Then the LORD said to Gideon, "The people are still too many; bring them down to the water and I will test them for you there. Therefore it shall be that he of whom I say to you, 'This one shall go with you,' he shall go with you; but everyone of whom I say to you, 'This one shall not go with you,' he shall not go." So he brought the people down to the water. And the LORD said to Gideon, "You shall separate everyone who laps the water with his tongue, as a dog laps, as well as everyone who kneels to drink." Now the number of those who lapped, puttting their hand to their mouth, was 300 men; but all the rest of the people kneeled to drink water. And the LORD said to Gideon, "I will deliver you with the 300

men who lapped and will give the Midianites into your hands; so let all the other people go, each man to his home." So the 300 men took the people's provisions and their trumpets into their hands. And Gideon sent all the other men of Israel, each to his tent, but retained the 300 men; and the camp of Midian was below him in the valley. Now the same night it came about that the LORD said to him, "Arise, go down against the camp, for I have given it into your hands. But if you are afraid to go down, go with Purah your servant down to the camp, and you will hear what they say; and afterward your hands will be strengthened that you may go down against the camp." So he went with Purah his servant down to the outposts of the army that was in the camp. Now the Midianites and the Amalikites and all the sons of the east were lying in the valley as numerous as locusts; and their camels were without number, as numerous as the sand on the seashore. When Gideon came, behold, a man was relating a dream to his friend. And he said, "Behold, I had a dream; a loaf of barley bread was tumbling into the camp of Midian, and it came to the tent and struck it so that it fell, and turned it upside down so that the tent lay flat." And his friend answered and said, "This is nothing less than the sword of Gideon the son of Joash, a man of Israel; God has given Midian and all the camp into his hand." And it came about when Gideon heard the account of the dream and its interpretation, that he bowed in worship. He returned to the camp of Israel and said, "Arise, for the LORD has given the camp of Midian into your hands."

Of all the upsets celebrated by military historians or sports fans, none is more astonishing than the one God accomplished through Gideon. Outnumbered about 450 to 1, Gideon's army won a crushing victory over the powerful hosts of Midian. If a football team composed of junior high school girls were to challenge the Super Bowl champions and defeat them 49-0, you would have an approximation of Gideon's victory.

But before God used Gideon in this way, He had a work of preparation to do. First, God had to teach Gideon's army radical dependence upon Him. Then He brought Gideon to the place of wholehearted confidence in God. Finally, He conditioned Midian for defeat by breathing a mysterious sense of fear into their midst. Let us follow the process.

THE PREPARATIONS OF THE ARMY—7:1-8

For the eighth year in a row the desert-dwelling Midianites had invaded the land at harvest time. This year an enemy force of 135,000 Midianites (8:10) had camped in the Valley of Jezreel, the strategic north central highlands of Israel. They came fully expecting to carry out their usual policy of an uncontested stripping of the land and a triumphant return to their desert home.

But this time there was a difference. God had raised up a man who was prepared to lead Israel against Midian. Gideon, empowered by the Spirit, had raised an army of 32,000 men, and now he marched them to the hills of Mt. Gilboa (called Mt. Gilead in verse 3). Midian was camped to the north, on the plain by the hills of Moreh, and between the two armies was a valley, containing the spring of Harod. That was the only water available for Gideon's men, and it made getting a drink a rather interesting adventure. To drink, a man had to go down in full view of the enemy, and the lush growth of reeds and shrubs around the spring made an ambush a constant possibility.

From his vantage point, Gideon could probably see a great part of the Midianite army. It would be a terrifying sight. The army is described in verse 12: "Now the Midianites and the Amalekites and all the sons of the east were lying in the valley as numerous as locusts; and their camels were without number, as numerous as the sand on the seashore." An army of 135,000 men armed to the teeth. Then, as Gideon looked at his men, he would see 32,000 men with virtually no weapons. I can imagine his feelings: "Lord, how can we do it? We don't have a chance. There's not enough of us!"

As those thoughts were running through Gideon's

mind, God came to him with one of the most amazing sentences I think any man has ever heard. "Gideon, you have too many people. You are too big. We have got to cut down your numbers." Judges 7:2 is one of the most important verses in the Bible for understanding God's principles of spiritual warfare. God is not interested in simply giving His people victory. He is concerned with teaching us trust. In fact, if our victories make us self-reliant, they are ultimately more disastrous than defeat. It happens over and over again. We trust God, and He does good things for us. We begin to see growth and progress; other people begin to applaud us, and pretty soon we begin to take the credit for what God has done. We take the glory due God alone for ourselves. That is what verse 2 is all about. God demanded a troop reduction "lest Israel become boastful, saying, 'My own power has delivered me.' "

Some travelers happened upon a remote island where they found the people there worshiping the moon. The visitors talked with them about it and then said, "It is really very strange that you worship the moon. If you really want to worship something in the skies, why do you not worship the sun?" And the people replied, "It is very simple; the sun only shines by day when it is light, and we do not need it; but the moon shines in the night when it is dark and we cannot see!"

Of course, what they did not understand is that the light of the moon depends entirely on the sun. But every time we take the credit and the glory for what God has done through us, we do exactly the same thing.

Do you see the significance of that? You cannot be too small for God to use, but you can be too big. If you want the credit for what God is doing, God will not use you. "I am the LORD, that is My name," He says. "I will not give My glory to another." This is why, as you look around, you will see God working in a powerful way in the lives of some very weak people. They are people who are careful to give God the glory.

Let me underline that. Does it bother you that you are not very significant? Does it discourage you that you have no prominent gifts? Praise God. You are just the kind of person God delights to use. But if you sit there thinking, "God is sure lucky He has me. I am a natural leader. I can do this or that," then you are in for a bitter disappointment.

However, God's way of reducing the army was not arbitrary or insignificant. He applied two tests, and both tests reveal the kind of things God looks for in the people He uses.

THE TEST OF FEARLESSNESS

In Deuteronomy 20:1-4, 8, God gave a standing order about how Israel was to enter battle. It is an order based on a great promise.

> When you go out to battle against your enemies and see horses [read camels against Midian!] and chariots and people more numerous than you [135,000 to 32,000!], do not be afraid of them; for the LORD your God, who brought you up from the land of Egypt, is with you. Now it shall come about, that when you are approaching the battle, the priest shall come near and speak to the people. And he shall say to them, "Hear, O Israel, you are approaching the battle against your enemies today. Do not be fainthearted. Do not be afraid, or panic, or tremble before them, for the LORD your God is the one who goes with you, to fight for you against your enemies, to save you."
>
> Then the officers shall speak further to the people, and they shall say, "Who is the man that is afraid and fainthearted? Let him depart and return to his house, so that he might not make his brothers' hearts melt like his heart."

When we meet an obstacle of any kind in our lives, God comes with the promise of His presence and power. "I am with you, I am fighting for you. Do not be afraid." But if our fear persists, God will not force us into the fight. In fact, He removes us, because fear is contagious. It focuses upon the problem, not upon the God who is far greater than those problems.

Can you imagine how Gideon felt when He announced, in the words of verse 3, "Whoever is afraid and trembling, let him return and depart from Mt. Gilead" (which is probably another name for Mt. Gilboa), and 22,000 people left? He probably expected a few people to go, but two-thirds of his army? If I know anything about Gideon, by this time his heart was in his boots.

But God was not finished with Gideon yet. In verse 4, He came to Gideon again and said, "Gideon, you still have too many men," and then He announced a second test by which He intended to purify and refine His people.

THE TEST OF FERVENCY

There are three characteristics of this second test.

1. *It was a simple test.* This time God commanded Gideon to send his 10,000 men down to the spring for a drink of water. The spring was in plain view of the Midianites, and there was always the possibility of an ambush. Gideon was to watch how the men drank. Some of the people would scoop up water in one hand, holding their spear in the other, and then lap it like a dog. Others would fall flat on their faces, forgetting about everything else and drink to their heart's content.

2. *It was a secret test.* All the people knew was that Gideon told them to get a drink of water. They had no idea that what they were doing was significant. Even Gideon did not know whether God would choose the lappers or the kneelers.

But it is extremely important for us to realize that God's test usually comes when we are totally unaware of it. What we are then reveals what we really are.

3. *It was a significant test.* Thirst quenching is a necessity of life. But in this case, it had added significance. What the manner of drinking revealed was an attitude to the enemy. Most of the soldiers had their mind only on drinking. They forgot all about Midian. But there were 300 men, 3 percent of the 10,000, who had a different perspective.

They would not take their eyes off the enemy, even to satisfy their thirst. In a time of warfare, they would not forget their central purpose, and they would not take unnecessary time even with life's necessities.

There were 32,000 faithful men who were willing to fight. There were 10,000 men who were fearless because they had a God who was greater than their enemy. But these 300 men were fervent, committed wholeheartedly to engaging the enemy in battle. God chose less than 1 percent of the group that Gideon began with, to do battle with Midian. Imagine, 300 men going out to do battle with 135,000, outnumbered 450 to 1! But here was a group of men who were prepared for battle because God had stripped away everything that would keep them from trusting in Him.

As you apply this to your life, do you know what it is to be fervent in your commitment to Jesus Christ? Is it the burning desire of your heart, the thing that matters to you more than anything else, that Jesus Christ uses you to do battle for Him? Gideon's 300 remind you that God is not looking for great Christians but for believing Christians, people who can be showcases for His glory. He is looking for fervent, wholehearted believers who want their lives to count for Him.

That is the first part of God's preparation. Gideon's army had been reduced to such proportions that they had no alternative. They could either depend totally upon God, or they could perish. Their only hope lay in God. Now comes the second stage of preparation. With their self-confidence destroyed, they were now prepared to learn the lesson of confidence in God.

THE PREPARATION OF GIDEON—7:9-15

I don't imagine that Gideon was sleeping very well that night. I certainly wouldn't be! Only 300 men left! Then, in the middle of the night, God came again to Gideon. Gideon's first thought was probably, "Oh no! Not again!" But this time, the Lord's message was very different. He came with a command and a promise. Basically, it was a command to attack: "Arise, go down against the camp, for I have given it into your hand."

Gideon was hardly in an attacking mood, and the Lord was sensitive to Gideon's feelings. He knew that Gideon needed to have his courage built up. Therefore, having commanded an attack, God said, "But if you are afraid, take Purah, your right hand man, and go down and do some eavesdropping. I am going to use what you hear to strengthen you for the attack."

That was good news for Gideon who immediately called Purah, and they set out for the enemy camp. Carefully, they made their way across the valley into the outskirts of the Midianite camp. Just as they came up to one of the tents, they heard two men talking. Apparently one of the men had just awakened and shaken his friend awake. Just at the right time for Gideon to hear, the Midianite soldier said, "Hey, I just had the craziest dream! I saw a little barley bun come rolling down into our camp and it hit our tent, flipped it over, and flattened it! What do you make of that?"

Surprisingly, the other man instantly understood the dream. Barley was a food very poor people ate. It was a fitting picture of Israel. Midian had seized their wheat and turned Israel into eaters of barley, animal food. The tent was an obvious symbol of the nomadic Midianites. So the Midianite said, "That barley bun is nothing less than the sword of Gideon, the son of Joash. God has given Midian and all the camp into his hand."

This is a beautiful example of the sovereignty of God, who is in control of the world of men. He directed the steps of Gideon and Purah, so they came to exactly the right tent at exactly the right time. He protected Gideon so that he was not observed, and He planted that dream in that Midianite's head—a dream that was totally appropriate. Imagine a little bun destroying a tent! Imagine 300 men defeating 135,000 Midianites! And God led the other Midianite to interpret it precisely, even using Gideon's name.

As Gideon listened to those words, he realized as he never had before, that it was not a battle between 300 Israelites and 135,000 Midianites. It was God who was fighting Midian, and the 300 men were just His channels. Right there, beside a Midianite camp, Gideon learned the greatest lesson of his life, and he bowed in worship before God. For the first time, Gideon had come to realize the greatness of God.

In a very real sense we are never prepared for battle until we know what it is to bow in worship before God. That is why we read in Daniel 11:32, "The people who know their God will display strength and take action." Notice what Gideon said, as he went back to his little band of men, "Arise, for the LORD has given the camp of Midian into your hands" (v. 15). Gideon had become strong because God had taught him that victory is not gained by self-confidence but by God-confidence.

THE PREPARATION OF MIDIAN—7:13-14

There is a third kind of preparation in Judges 7. Not only had God prepared Gideon and his army, He also had been setting up Midian, by planting fear in their hearts. How, on human terms, can you possibly explain Judges 7:13-14? Midian knew very well what was going on in the camp of Israel. They had seen an army of 32,000 turn into a band of 300. They may not have known why, but they would have seen 31,700 men pack their belongings and head home. Why would an army of 135,000 men be afraid of an army of 300 soldiers, with no proper weapons, led by a man with no military experience? I do not think the President of the United States lies awake at night worrying about an invasion by Lichtenstein. Why this strange anxiety in Midian?

The only answer is that God had planted fear in their hearts. God had already prepared Midian for Gideon. And when God calls us to do battle for Him, He always goes before us. That is why we read in 2 Corinthians 2:14, "Thanks be to God, who always leads us in His triumph in

Christ." Note the wording of that verse. He does not lead us into our triumph. It is His triumph, it is His victory, and we enter into it in union with Christ.

In God's grace, we are destined for victory in the Lord Jesus. On a practical level, we enter into that victory when we learn the lessons of preparation for victory. God does not call us to believe in ourselves and in our own adequacy. Rather, He strips us bare, taking us down to the place where we must depend on Him. Then, in grace, He takes us by the hand and teaches us that we can trust completely in Him. We need to learn the lesson of dependence, so we may move on to learn the lesson of confidence. We learn that we can do nothing without Him. Then we delight to discover that we can rely completely upon Him. Having learned those great lessons, we are prepared for victory.

ELEVEN

Satan's Game Plan

When a football team is about to play an important game, the coaches spend hours studying the game films of their opponents. They are looking for the habits and patterns of the other team, the kinds of things they are likely to do in certain circumstances. What kind of play does the quarterback prefer on third and long? Will the linebackers blitz, and is there any way to detect when they are coming? The more they know about their opponents, the better they are able to prepare for them.

The Apostle Paul had something like that in mind when he wrote, "[I am doing this] in order that no advantage be taken of us by Satan; for we are not ignorant of his schemes" (2 Cor. 2:11). Satan has schemes and devices in dealing with the children of God that he has used over and over again. Through the centuries, he has developed some techniques and strategies which have proved extremely successful, and he loves to fall back upon those classic methods, as he seeks to blunt the effectiveness of God's children.

We become aware of Satan's devices by studying the Word of God and carefully analyzing what he has done in the past. It would be foolish for a team to face its opponents in the Super Bowl with no knowledge of its past performances. In the same way, it is both foolish and dangerous for Christians to live in ignorance of Satan's game plan. That is one of the values of studying the way Satan attacked Gideon in the middle of history's most glorious military victory. It is not an archaic strategy. In fact, church history contains countless illustrations of Satan adopting exactly the same method in the course of apparent victory for God's people and turning that victory into a bitter defeat. But we do not learn about Satan's strategy from the perspective of Gideon's failure. Gideon met Satan's tactic successfully, and as we learn from him, so can we.

There are three parts to the battle. There was Gideon's initial victory followed by two counterattacks of Satan, which Gideon met successfully.

GIDEON'S GREAT VICTORY—7:15-25

And it came about when Gideon heard the account of the dream and its interpretation, that he bowed in worship. He returned to the camp of Israel and said, "Arise for the LORD has given the camp of Midian into your hands." And he divided the 300 men into three companies, and he put trumpets and empty pitchers into the hands of all of them, with torches inside the pitchers. And he said to them, "Look at me, and do likewise. And behold, when I come to the outskirts of the camp, do as I do. When I and all who are with me blow the trumpet, then you also blow the trumpets all around the camp, and say, 'For the LORD and for Gideon.'" So Gideon and the hundred men who were with him came to the outskirts of the camp at the beginning of the middle watch, when they had just posted the watch; and they blew the trumpets and smashed the pitchers that were in their hands. When the three companies blew the trumpets and broke the pitchers, they held the torches in their left hands and the trumpets in their right hands for blowing, and cried, "A sword for the LORD and for Gideon!" And each stood in his place around the camp; and all the army ran, crying out as they fled. And when they blew 300 trumpets, the LORD set the sword of one against another even throughout the whole army; and the army fled as far as Beth-shittah toward Zererah, as far as the edge of Abel-meholah, by Tabbath. And the men of Israel were summoned from Naphtali and Asher and all Manasseh, and they pursued Midian. And Gideon sent messengers throughout all the hill country of Ephraim, saying, "Come down against Midian and take the waters before them, as far as Beth-barah and the Jordan." So all the men of Ephraim were summoned, and they took the waters as far as Beth-barah and the Jordan. And they captured the two leaders of Midian, Oreb and Zeeb, and they killed Oreb at the rock of Oreb, and they killed Zeeb at the winepress of Zeeb, while they pursued Midian; and they brought the heads of Oreb and Zeeb to Gideon from across the Jordan.

At the final dress rehearsal for Queen Elizabeth's coronation in 1953, everyone was very tense. For many of the people involved, the next day would be the most important day in their lives. They worked through the ceremony in Westminster Abbey, up to the place where the queen would enter. The orchestra had just finished, the archbishop dressed in all his robes stood at the altar, all the officers of state were at attention. There was a spine-tingling fanfare of trumpets to signal the queen's imminent entrance. Just at that moment, four charwomen pushing carpet sweepers walked in and proceeded to sweep up any feathers or dust which had collected around the throne or on the gold carpet.

The whole abbey rocked with laughter at the timing. Obviously, those servant girls had a job to do, and it had its importance. But they hardly deserved a fanfare of trumpets with everyone standing at attention. That honor belonged to the queen.

That is exactly what God was trying to teach His people in Judges 7. He had taken an army of 32,000 men and reduced it to a little group of 300, and He was calling those 300 men to do battle with 135,000 Midianites. He had taken Gideon and changed him into a leader who could lead those men into victory. But none could really believe that it was Gideon or Gideon's 300 who were responsible for the victory. They were God's carpet sweepers, but the glory belonged to God and to God alone.

THE PLAN OF ATTACK (VV. 15-18)

Earlier in the evening, God had told Gideon to take his

servant and go down into the camp of the Midianites. There Gideon heard information that built his confidence in God. So, as verse 15 tells us, he worshiped God; then he went back to his men, woke them up, and said, "Arise, for the LORD has given the camp of Midian into your hands."

Now Gideon prepared for the attack. He divided them into three groups of 100 men each, then passed out their equipment. Imagine for a minute that you were one of those 300 men. You were a faithful, fearless, fervent person, otherwise you would not be there. But no matter how fearless you were, you would be wondering just how Gideon was planning to pull this off. After all, you were outnumbered 450 to 1! Now you get your weapons, and what are they? A horn, a torch, and a jar! No shields, no arrows, no swords. I can imagine Gideon's 300 looking at those things and wondering how they could ever win a victory with such unmilitary objects.

Then Gideon explained how the things were to be used, and I am not sure they felt any better as a result. They were to keep their eyes on Gideon and do exactly what he did. They had

> —a horn to blow
> —a jar to shatter
> —a torch to shine
> —a voice to shout.

That was it! Before, Gideon had said, "Whoever is afraid and trembling, let him depart." If I had managed to make it into the 300, at this point, I think I would have traded in my horn, jar, and torch and headed home. However, those men knew what it was to trust God. Even though they could not have understood all that God was going to do, they did trust Him, and they knew that He was the One behind Gideon's plans. There is a great lesson here. It is not our responsibility to understand how God is going to keep His Word and accomplish His work. It is our responsibility to obey Him and to do what He commands.

THE PLAN IN OPERATION (VV. 19-22)

Now Gideon put God's plan into action. He waited until the middle watch had just been posted. That was about 10:30 P.M., when some of the men had been asleep for three or four hours and were now in the deepest part of their sleep. The men who had just been relieved from guard duty would still be moving through the camp, and the men who had just gone on duty would still be rubbing sleep out of their eyes.

Suddenly, there was a huge noise all around them. The rams' horns were signaling an enemy attack. Then the clay pitchers smashed on the ground, sounding like armies clashing into one another. The Midianites looked up, and they were surrounded on three sides by lights and torches. Finally, a great shout shattered the silence, "A sword for the LORD and for Gideon." To the half-asleep men, everything that moved became an enemy. Every shadow was an Israelite. In all the confusion, the camels stampeded, and, in the chaos and tumult that resulted, the panicked Midianites began to slaughter one another. All this time, Gideon's men did not move. They stood in their place, blowing their trumpets, waving their torches, and shouting their slogan.

THE ROUT OF MIDIAN (VV. 23-25)

Finally, the Midianites gained enough sense to flee, and they headed for home as fast as they could. They streamed east down the valley toward the Jordan River, so they could cross, and head into the desert. As they fled, Gideon recruited two kinds of help. He called the 32,000 men who had come in the first place, and they joined in the chase. Then, because the Midianites were headed straight for the territory of Ephraim, he sent messengers to Ephraim to recruit a force to stop the enemy when they tried to cross the little rivers before the Jordan. Ephraim did that, and more. They captured two of the major leaders of Midian, men named "Raven" (Oreb) and "Wolf" (Zeeb).

THE PRINCIPLES OF VICTORY

I do not think there is a better commentary on the victory of

Gideon and his men than Paul's words in 2 Corinthians 10:3-4: "Though we walk in the flesh, we do not war according to the flesh, for the weapons of our warfare are not of the flesh, but divinely powerful for the destruction of fortresses." It is utterly absurd to believe that 300 men equipped with jars, torches, and horns could do anything at all against 135,000 men. But they did, because God was with them.

Years later, in Judah's history, King Asa was confronted with an army of over a million Ethiopians, led by 300 chariots. He could fight them with 580,000 footsoldiers, but the odds were obviously overwhelming. In response to that problem, Asa prayed one of the great prayers of Scripture, "LORD, there is no one besides You to help in the battle between the powerful and those who have no strength; so help us, O LORD our God, for we support ourselves on You, and in Your name we have come against this multitude. O LORD, You are our God: let not man prevail against You" (2 Chron. 14:11). God answered that prayer with a resounding victory over the Ethiopians. It also provides us with a great pattern for our prayer life. In times of need, we support ourselves by leaning upon the Lord. When we go in His name, we can rely upon His promise that we can depend upon His power.

Or choose another example. Here are eleven men and a few women. A few days before, they had been so terrified that their leader has turned into a blaspheming coward in front of a servant girl. Not one of them is educated, wealthy, or famous. But God the Holy Spirit took those weak, unequipped people and used them to bring into being the church of Jesus Christ and to turn first Jerusalem and then the world upside down. One of the most intriguing interviews of history took place when John and Peter were brought before the Jewish council and asked, "By what name or by what power have you done this?" And we read that, "Peter, filled with the Holy Spirit" preached the gospel. Then, having heard God's Word through Peter, the whole council was left absolutely befuddled.

"Now as they observed the confidence of Peter and John, and understood that they were uneducated and untrained men, they were marveling, and began to recognize them as having been with Jesus" (Acts 4:13). When they sent the disciples out of the room, they began to confer with one another, "What shall we do with these men? For the fact that a noteworthy miracle has taken place through them is apparent to all who live in Jerusalem, and we cannot deny it!" (4:16).

Do you see their problem? You can deal with men who are your equals. But how do you fight against weak, ignorant men who are filled with confidence because they have been with Jesus and are filled with His Spirit? You can fight an army that comes at you with swords and shields, but how do you handle 300 men, outnumbered 450 to 1, who attack you with pots, torches, and horns, who have God's power working through them? Goliath can handle Saul, but how can he handle a teenager who comes at him with five stones and the promise of God? Oh, that we would trust God, in all of our weakness, to work through us for His glory!

Perhaps it was this very passage that Paul had in mind when he wrote in 2 Corinthians 4:6-7:

> For God, who said "Light shall shine out of darkness," is the One who has shone in our hearts to give the light of the knowledge of the glory of God in the face of Christ. *But we have this treasure in clay pots, that the surpassing greatness of the power may be of God and not from ourselves* (itals. added).

There is a striking parallel between the book of Acts and Judges 8. As God is blessing the church and thousands of people are coming to know the Savior, and the Jewish leaders are in total confusion, Satan counterattacks. He attacks from exactly the same direction as he does here against Gideon, and he continues to use the same tactics against believers today.

The Attack of Disunity—8:1-3

Then the men of Ephraim said to him, "What is this thing you have done to us, not calling us when you went to fight against Midian?" And they contended with him vigorously. But he said to them, "What have I done now in comparison with you? Is not the gleaning of the grapes of Ephraim better than the vintage of Abiezer? God has given the leaders of Midian, Oreb and Zeeb into your hands; and what was I able to do in comparison with you?" Then the anger toward him subsided when he said that.

At this time in history, Ephraim was the largest and most important of the tribes. They would be the first to tell you how important they were. After all, the tabernacle was located in their territory at Shiloh, and they could claim the great Joshua as an Ephraimite. But they came to Gideon with a festering complaint. "Why did you not call us to fight Midian? Why were we not included?" On the surface, that was a valid question. Gideon had not called them, although judging from their attitude, there was probably a good reason for that. However, as we examine the question a little more closely, we recognize that something was seriously wrong. Ephraim had made no effort to attack Midian on its own, and although they had probably heard of Gideon's effort to raise an army, none of them had volunteered to go.

Their complaint was almost entirely motivated by personal jealousy and injured pride. Gideon had won an astonishing victory, one from which Ephraim would greatly profit. But there was no joy at what God had done through Gideon, no enthusiasm for the wonderful victory God had given His people, no gladness and thanksgiving before God. There was only bitterness of heart. To put it bluntly, Ephraim was totally selfish. They put a priority on their own problems, and they wanted Gideon to stop the battle until their little need was met.

It is sadly true that in a time of victory the greatest danger often comes from within, from fellow believers. It would have been very easy for Gideon to be absolutely furious with those people. After all, it is easy to sit back and criticize after the battle has been fought, to be brave when the victory is won, to be a spectator who points out all the mistakes of others. There is nothing that Satan loves more than to see Christians fighting with one another. In the book of Acts, when Satan had tried all kinds of attacks on the church from outside and totally failed, what did he do? He tried to destroy the unity of believers over the actions of Ananias and Sapphira. When that did not work, he stirred up a fuss over the language tensions between Greek-speaking and Hebrew-speaking Christians, and the way widows were being looked after. If we are fighting ourselves, we are not pursuing the enemy. Satan can get us so confused that we believe fellow believers are our enemies.

This is not a tired tactic from the past. Satan uses it time and again. When people are trusting Christ, young Christians are being discipled, and established believers are growing and maturing, Satan will bend every effort to sow disunity. He does not care why we are divided, he just cares that we are. It may be division because of pride or hurt feelings, or over our differences economically, socially, or educationally. It could be over personalities or differences in minor doctrines. But Satan loves to see us divided.

THE RESPONSE OF GIDEON

That is why it is so important for us to see what Gideon did. He could have put those Ephraimites in their place with a few choice words or defended himself and shredded them for their attitudes. But he utterly refused to do that. Listen to what he says: "What have I done now in comparison with you? Isn't the gleaning of Ephraim better than the vintage of Abiezer? God has given the leaders of Midian, Oreb and Zeeb, into your hand; what was I able to do in comparison with you?"

Do you think that really makes sense? Was it really

greater for Ephraim to kill two kings than for Gideon to attack 135,000 men with 300, and to conquer them? Of course not. But we learn two great lessons from Gideon.

1. *The unity of God's people is more important than personal pride.* So what if he was wronged, mistreated, criticized? It was more important for God's people to be one than for Gideon to be vindicated. What a great lesson for us to learn. None of us likes to be wronged, or to be misrepresented the way Gideon was. But how much better to take that hurt to the Lord and let Him deal with it, than to be on the outs with my brother.

2. *We must not take our eyes off the enemy.* Quite frankly, Gideon did not have time to fight with Ephraim. He had his eyes on the Midianites. Gideon refused to be deflected from God's call for his life. That really was Ephraim's problem. They had lots of time to discuss their feelings because they had no burden to do God's work. They had no sense of God's purpose for them; so naturally they were out of step with Gideon. Often people who find lots to criticize in the lives of other people are people who have no sense of urgency about God's call for their lives.

Someone once told of a conversation he had with Dr. Charles Fuller, a man greatly used by God in radio evangelism. During the conversation, a man's name came up who had been publicly attacking Dr. Fuller. Fuller said, "Yes, God bless him." Another man said, "You don't seem too upset, Dr. Fuller." And Fuller replied, "Why should I let someone else decide how I'm going to act?" What a great attitude for every believer to cultivate!

With that attack met, Gideon crossed the Jordan and continued his pursuit of Midian. Satan had not given up yet. He often tries to draw us into division where there ought to be unity; he also loves to draw us into unity where there ought to be division. It was so in the early church. Over the widows' issue, there could be no division, but with the hypocrisy of Ananias and Sapphira, there could be no unity.

THE ATTACK OF FALSE UNITY—8:4-21

Then Gideon and the 300 men who were with him came to the Jordan and crossed over, weary yet pursuing. And he said to the men of Succoth, "Please give loaves of bread to the people who are following me, for they are weary, and I am pursuing Zebah and Zalmunna, the kings of Midian." And the leaders of Succoth said, "Are the hands of Zebah and Zalmunna already in your hands, that we should give bread to your army?" And Gideon said, "All right, when the LORD has given Zebah and Zalmunna into my hand, then I will thrash your bodies with the thorns of the wilderness, and with briers." And he went up from there to Penuel, and spoke similarly to them; and the men of Penuel answered him just as the men of Succoth had answered. So he spoke also to the men of Penuel, saying, "When I return safely, I will tear down this tower." Now Zebah and Zalmunna were in Karkor, and their armies with them, about 15,000 men, all who were left of the entire army of the sons of the east; for the fallen were 120,000 swordsmen. And Gideon went up by the way of those who lived in tents on the east of Nobah and Jogbehah, and attacked the camp, when the camp was unsuspecting. When Zebah and Zalmunna fled, he pursued them and captured the two kings of Midian, Zebah and Zalmunna, and routed the whole army. Then Gideon the son of Joash returned from the battle by the ascent of Heres. And he captured a youth from Succoth and questioned him. Then the youth wrote down for him the princes of Succoth and its elders, seventy-seven men. And he came to the men of Succoth and said, "Behold Zebah and Zalmunna, concerning whom you taunted me, saying, 'Are the hands of Zebah and Zalmunna already in your hand, that we should give bread to your men who are weary?' " And he took the elders of the city, and thorns of the wilderness, and briers, and he disciplined the men of Succoth with them. And he tore down the tower of Penuel and killed the men of the city. Then he said to Zebah and Zalmunna, "What kind of men were they whom you killed at Tabor?" And they said, "They were like you, each one resembling the son of a king." And he said, "They were my brothers, the sons of my mother. As the LORD lives, if only you had let them live, I would not kill you." So he said to Jether his first-born, "Rise, kill them." But the youth did not draw his sword, for he was afraid, because he was still a youth. Then Zebah and Zalmunna said, "Rise up yourself, and fall on us; for as the man, so is his strength." So Gideon arose and killed Zebah and Zalmunna, and took the crescent ornaments which were on their camels' necks.

Gideon left behind the trouble with Ephraim and pressed on after Midian. By now, his men had traveled many miles and many days, and they were obviously exhausted. But Gideon had a commission from God, and he was committed to carrying it out.

In the course of his travels, he came to Succoth, one of the Israelite towns on the other side of the Jordan, and he begged them for food. They should have been excited about what God had done through Gideon. He had liberated them from Midian. Instead, he ran into a group of people who professed to be the people of God, but who had no knowledge of God at all. There was no thankfulness to God, no trust in God, no mention of God. Even the lowest level of human kindness required that they help Gideon, their fellow Israelite. Not only did they not help him, but they mocked him. "Are the hands of Zebah and Zalmunna already in your hands, that we should give bread to your army?" (v 6)

Here were 300 tired, exhausted men, and even though Midian had been badly defeated, they still represented a formidable foe. They were 15,000 strong, led by two fierce kings, and they were reduced to desperation, fighting for their lives. What is more, they were in the refuge town of Karkor. The attitude of Succoth and Penuel could well have convinced Gideon to turn back. "You are right. We have already won a great victory. Why press our luck any further? There is not much chance we can do anything. Let's turn back."

Gideon was not made of that kind of stuff. See how he reacts. This time there is no soft answer turning away wrath from Succoth and Penuel. There can be no unity where there is only an empty religious shell with no reality. At least Ephraim was part of the battle, but Succoth and Penuel were in total unbelief. Scripture teaches that there must be unity among true children of God, but there cannot be unity apart from truth and faith.

That is why there are times when we must say to people, who claim the name of Jesus Christ but who reject the truths of Scripture, that we cannot have unity with them. Such unity is false, and it will destroy the work of God. Our unity must be unity in the Lord Jesus.

But even here we see the character of Gideon. He is going to bring judgment on Succoth and Penuel, but before he does that, he is going to pursue Midian and defeat them. Nothing can stop Gideon from doing what God has called him to do.

There is a great lesson for us in Gideon's persistence. D. L. Moody once said, "Give me a man who says 'This one thing I do' and not 'These fifty things I dabble with.'" Benjamin Disraeli declared, "The secret of success is constancy of purpose." Gideon knew that kind of constancy. "Then Gideon . . . crossed over, weary yet pursuing" (v. 4). I wonder if we know that singleness of purpose in carrying out the will of God. It was that more than anything else that protected Gideon from this attack of Satan.

Gideon carried out his divine calling completely. He finished the job of defeating Midian, and he carried out his threats against Succoth and Penuel. Finally, he slayed the remaining Midianite kings, and the yoke of Midian was removed from Israel once and for all.

God had given Gideon a great victory because he dared to trust Him. Yet, in the middle of that victory, Satan counterattacked in a potentially devastating way. Other men have fallen before such an attack, but because Gideon had an unswerving commitment to God's purpose for his life, God gave him not only a great victory but a complete victory. As we fix our hearts and minds completely on doing the will of God, we will be able to stand against the schemes of the devil. Do we have that kind of commitment to His will in our lives?

TWELVE

Gideon's Sad Ending

On September 29, 1938, Great Britain, France, Germany, and Italy signed the Munich Pact, which granted Adolf Hilter the Sudetenland, the northern part of Czechoslovakia. It was the culmination of a sad series of events based on the premise that Hitler was a reasonable and trustworthy man.

England and France had committed themselves to protect the interests of Czechoslovakia, but Hitler announced that Germany's rights had been abrogated, and he would invade Czechoslovakia unless certain conditions were met. His case was paper thin, but suddenly all Europe seemed about to explode into war.

Neville Chamberlain, the British prime minister, flew to Berlin to meet with Hitler. Under the pressure of Hitler's personality and the threat of war, he caved in. In the middle of the night of the twenty-first of September, the British and French ambassadors wakened the Czech premier to announce that their countries were not going to keep their treaty obligations. Eight days later the Munich Pact was signed, which conceded virtually everything to Hitler, and Chamberlain flew home to England, waving the Pact and proclaiming that this meant "peace in our time, peace with honor." A sense of relief swept through Britain. Chamberlain was acclaimed as a great hero.

One man was not fooled. Winston Churchill arose in the House of Commons to speak some profound and prophetic words:

> Britain and France had to choose between war and dishonor.
> They chose dishonor. They will have war ... (the people)

should know that we have sustained a defeat without war . . . they should know that we have passed an awful milestone in our history...and that terrible words have for the time being been pronounced against the Western democracies: "Thou art weighed in the balance and found wanting." And do not suppose that this is the end. This is only the beginning of the reckoning. This is only the first sip, the first foretaste of a bitter cup which will be proferred to us year by year unless, by a supreme recovery of moral health and martial vigor, we arise again and take our stand for freedom as in the olden times.

Churchill recognized two important things: You cannot compromise with evil. Compromise *is* defeat. The course which follows compromise goes steadily downwards, and, unless that compromise is dealt with, decline and decay are inevitable.

Unfortunately, as we come to Judges 8, we are faced with a story of compromise, defeat, and backsliding—the last chapter in the life of a man who knew the greatest victory of faith set down in the Word of God. I suspect most of us are totally ignorant of this part of Gideon's life, yet the Holy Spirit has recorded it in His Word with some important insights for us.

In Jeremiah 17:5, there is a powerful message of the Holy Spirit to which we need to listen carefully:

> Thus says the LORD,
> "Cursed is the man who trusts in mankind
> And makes flesh his strength,
> And whose heart turns away from the LORD."

That is exactly what we see happening among God's people at the very time God had revealed His supernatural power in an unexpected way. Because God had worked through Gideon and his little band of 300 men, 135,000 Midianites lay dead. It was not their victory, it was God's victory. But how quickly human nature forgets that and tries to take the credit for itself.

There is a sense in which Gideon's greatest victory was won in Judges 8:22-23, and, if we could end his life story with verse 23, it would be one of the happiest biographies in all of Scripture. Sadly, Gideon's greatest triumph was followed by his greatest mistake. Before we dwell on that, let us look at the climax of his career.

GIDEON'S GREATEST VICTORY—8:22-23

> Then the men of Israel said to Gideon, "Rule over us, both you and your son, also your son's son, for you have delivered us from the hand of Midian." But Gideon said to them, "I will not rule over you, nor shall my son rule over you; the LORD shall rule over you."

Before the battle God had refused to allow Gideon to attack Midian with 32,000 men, "Lest Israel become boastful saying, 'My own power has delivered me'" (7:2). God had prevented them from doing that, but they had not learned God's lesson. True, they did not take the credit for themselves, but neither did they give it to God. As 8:22 tells us, they tried to give it to Gideon. "Rule over us ... for *you* have delivered us from the hand of Midian" (itals. added).

Sometimes we can learn more from what is not recorded in Scripture than from what we actually read. That is certainly true in Judges 8. As you read this chapter, you will not find one word of spontaneous praise, gratitude, or thanksgiving to God. Nothing is more indicative of the spiritual condition of Israel than this. Before ever they approached Gideon, they should have been pouring out their hearts in praise to the God who gave them victory, but, that never occurred to them. They did not have the singing faith of Moses or Joshua or Deborah. Their hearts did not ring with praise to their God.

I wonder how often we are guilty of spiritual ingratitude. We do not spontaneously praise God and acknowledge what He has done in our lives. We do not thank Him for the victories that He has wrought for us. If God is not the center of our lives, then everything else is out of balance. A praiseless and thankless heart is the evidence of deep carnality.

THE PEOPLE'S REQUEST OF GIDEON

Out of Israel's unthankful hearts arose an ungodly idea. "Gideon, 'Rule over us, both you and your son, also your son's son, for you have delivered us from the hand of Midian.'"

Notice two things about that request. First, they gave Gideon credit he did not deserve. Apart from what God had done in his life, Gideon was a weak, defeated, discouraged man. Although Gideon was the instrument, he was only the instrument. The credit belonged to God alone.

Second, they made a request that was outside the will of God. God had raised up Gideon to be a judge, but they wanted to make him into a king, to establish a royal dynasty, so that Gideon's son and his grandson would succeed him. That was not God's revealed will or God's plan, but an idea they had borrowed from their pagan neighbors. Israel was the only nation in the Near East at that time that did not have a human king, because God Himself was the King in Israel, as Moses said in Deuteronomy 33:5. God meant Israel to be a theocracy, a nation led and ruled by God Himself rather than by any earthly king. Later it was God's revealed will for the nation of Israel to have a visible king, but at this point Israel was to be a theocracy. Certainly, He had given no indication that He desired Gideon's house to be the royal family in Israel.

It is important for us to recognize this fact, because when we read the New Testament, we discover that it is God's will, not only for Israel, but for the church to be a theocracy. The church has one Head and only one, and that is the Lord Jesus Christ. Whether we are speaking about the universal church or the local church, there is only one

Head, the Savior. You cannot find a single passage in the New Testament which teaches that one man is to act as the visible leader of God's people. That position belongs to Jesus Christ, and only to Him, for the church is His alone. In the New Testament church, there were elders and deacons who served as shepherds and leaders. There were others with gifts of pastoring and teaching who ministered to God's people, but there is *only* one Head, there is only one Chief Shepherd, and this is the Lord Jesus.[1]

One of the oldest tendencies of our sinful hearts is to exalt men to the place that belongs only to God. In the history of the church, there has been a pernicious tendency to elevate men into the position that belongs only to the Lord Jesus. Men are given special titles, special powers, and special clothing and are set apart from ordinary Christians. One of the most evident patterns in the evangelical church today is for men who are pastors to take more and more power. A recent book on church growth has as its first principle: "The pastor has the power in a growing church." There is a danger here that must not be ignored.

In Mark 10:42-45, the Lord Jesus spelled out His principles of leadership. It is a passage to which all Christians need to pay careful attention.

> You know that those who are recognized as rulers of the Gentiles lord it over them; and their great men exercise authority over them. *But it is not so among you, but whoever wishes to become great among you shall be your servant;* and whoever wishes to be first among you shall be slave of all. For even the Son of Man did not come to be served, but to serve, and to give His life as ransom for many (itals. added).

Commenting on this passage and the church's tendency to borrow the authority patterns of the world, Ray Stedman, in his provocative article, "Should a Pastor Play Pope?" writes these words, which deserve serious consideration:

> All too long churches have behaved as if Jesus were far away in heaven, leaving church leaders to make their own deci-

sions and run their own affairs. But Jesus said in the Great Commission, 'Lo, I am with you always, even unto the end of the age.' He is present not only in the church as a whole but in every local church as well. Jesus Himself is the ultimate authority within every body of Christians, and He is quite prepared to exercise His authority through the elderhood.

The task of elders is not to run the church themselves, but to determine how the Lord wishes to run the church. Much of this He has already made known through the Scriptures ... In the day-to-day church decisions, elders are to find the mind of the Lord through an uncoerced unanimity, reached after thorough biblical discussion. Thus, ultimate authority, even in practical matters, is vested in the Lord and no one else.

The point is, no one man is the sole expression of the mind of the Spirit; no one individual has authority from God to direct the church.[2]

Stedman is right, and his reminder is extremely important. The tendency to exalt man and to give the authority of the Lord Jesus to some human leader is just as present today as in Gideon's day, and it is just as dangerous. Nearly every deviation from God's truth occurs when men take the place that belongs to the Lord. Nowhere in Scripture will you find that the Lord Jesus, the Head of the church, has surrendered His position to any man. Men have seized it, but He has never given it. We must be very careful, in our desire for truly biblical authority in our churches and for dynamic growth, that we do not implicitly reject the teaching of the Word of God about church life.

GIDEON'S GREAT REFUSAL

The request to make him king must have been enormously flattering to Gideon. Men love power and prestige, and they were being offered to Gideon on a silver platter. But he knew it was not God's will for him to take that position, and so he gave his answer to the people clearly and unequivocally: "I will not rule over you, nor shall my son rule over you; the

LORD shall rule over you." Israel did not need a king, they had a King. All that a king could be to a nation, the Lord was to Israel, and Gideon was willing to allow God to be the Leader in Israel. The Israelites may have forgotten who deserved credit for the victory. Gideon could not and did not.

That was the high point of Gideon's life. He had not only resisted a very strong temptation, but he had stood for a great biblical truth, the truth of the kingship of God in Israel. If only the story ended there! But it does not, and the irony is that Gideon's decline began in the very moment of his affirmation of God's absolute kingship. Unfortunately, his actions were not consistent with his words.

GIDEON'S GREAT MISTAKE—8:24-28

Yet Gideon said to them, "I would request of you, that each of you give me an earring from his spoil." (For they had gold earrings, because they were Ishmaelites.) And they said, "We will surely give them." So they spread out a garment, and every one of them threw an earring there from his spoil. And the weight of the gold earrings that he requested was 1,700 shekels of gold, besides the crescent ornaments and the pendants and the purple robes which were on the kings of Midian, and besides the neck bands that were on their camels' necks. And Gideon made it into an ephod, and placed it in his city, Ophrah, and all Israel played the harlot with it there, so that it became a snare to Gideon and His household. So Midian was subdued before the sons of Israel, and they did not lift up their heads any more. And the land was undisturbed for forty years in the days of Gideon.

Although Gideon had clearly refused the people's request that he be king, they were deeply grateful to him. So, when he made a request of them, they were quick to respond. "I would request of you, that each of you give me an earring from his spoil." It was the custom for Midianite men to wear an earring, and since that meant the Israelites had collected 135,000 earrings and a great deal of other war booty,

Gideon's request was relatively modest. The people responded gladly. Probably a blanket was spread on the ground, the men filed by, and when the collection was finished, there were about sixty pounds of solid gold earrings (1,700 shekels) on the blanket, worth in modern terms about $150,000.

THE EPHOD

To this point, we have not been told why Gideon wanted the gold. The answer is given in verse 27. He took the gold and made it into an ephod. An ephod was simply a garment that resembled a fancy apron, but it had a very special significance. The ephod was part of the clothing of the high priest. On the front was the linen breastplate which had the two stones the high priest used to discover the will of God, the Urim and the Thummin, and in the course of time, the ephod had become the symbol of the office of the high priest. When the high priest put on the ephod, it was because he wanted to know the will of God.

We will give Gideon the benefit of any doubt. The gold was not for himself. He had no intention of producing something that would become an idol. He was thoroughly committed to carrying out the principle of verse 23, "The LORD shall rule over you." But there was one major problem with the theocracy. The priesthood had become corrupt, and the high priest was totally ineffectual. Not once in the book of Judges do we read of the high priest functioning according to the Word of God and providing spiritual leadership to the people. As Gideon thought about the needs of the people, he knew this spiritual vacuum had to be filled. There could be no theocracy unless there was a way to discover the will of God. Gideon decided that he was the one to fill that vacuum. After all, God had spoken to him in the past, and He could do it again. Therefore, he decided to put on his beautiful ephod, far more impressive than anything Shiloh could offer, and to use that ephod to keep the theocracy functioning. His plan was to supersede the depraved Aaronic priesthood with his own, so that God could speak.

Gideon probably acted from the very best of motives. But it requires more than good intentions to make a good act. Gideon may have meant well, but his act was spiritually disastrous. Verse 27 tells us why: "All Israel played the harlot with it there, so that it became a snare to Gideon and his household." The term "playing the harlot" always refers to spiritual unfaithfulness to God. Verse 33 adds, "It came about, as soon as Gideon was dead, that the sons of Israel again played the harlot with the Baals, and made Baal-berith their god." Despite all the achievements of Gideon, he made no permanent spiritual difference in the life of the nation. The worship of the ephod in his own lifetime was judged by God to be spiritual adultery, and, because it was, it led to total apostasy after Gideon's death. Gideon's ephod became his great mistake.

What was so wrong about the worship of the ephod at Ophrah? No matter how sincere Gideon was, he was totally wrong, because God had commanded worship through the Levitical priesthood at the tabernacle, and God had located the tabernacle at Shiloh, not at Ophrah. Gideon was in direct violation of the Word of God. He had no right to try to solve a genuine problem in his own way. If he wanted to do anything, he should have devoted all his energies to reforming and reestablishing the tabernacle.

It is extremely important that we recognize this. The essence of all compromise, and ultimately of all heresy, is that we believe that we have the right to alter or improve the revealed will of God. Donald Grey Barnhouse illustrates this by imagining a sheepdog which had been stationed by a flock and ordered to stay there, no matter what. The dog stays, but watching sheep is not a very exciting activity. After awhile, a deer bounds by. That dog loved to chase deer, and he was very bored with guarding those stupid woolies. Besides, there was no apparent danger. Now if that dog was like many Christians, it would begin to rationalize like this: "My master didn't foresee this possibility. He's a kind master. He wouldn't deny me a little pleasure. Besides, I've done pretty well so far. One little chase won't hurt anyone." So off he goes.[3]

However, sheepdogs are wiser than Christians who think like that. They learn to be consistently obedient to their masters and to order their lives around the master's will. They do not lean upon their own understanding, and so they stay with the sheep. Gideon did not, and, from his defection, we need to learn that anything less than complete and consistent obedience leads to spiritual disaster. We cannot improve on the precepts of an omniscient, loving Father. Good intentions are not more important than complete obedience. What is right in our own eyes may be terribly wrong in God's eyes. Our need is not clever innovations, but consistent obedience to the Word of God.

This is the first clear illustration of a problem that is a constant problem for believers in a secular and amoral society. People around us live as an authority unto themselves, and we can adopt the same standard. We do what is right in our eyes rather than ordering our lives around the written Word of God. It is a disease which will become a virtual epidemic before we leave the book of Judges, and it is a crucial issue for twentieth-century Christians. We must not put anything in the place of God's Word. It is ironic that Gideon's action involved undermining the authority of God. We fight that battle today, not only as men attack the integrity of the Bible, but as others undermine its sufficiency, by claiming visions and revelations, which supplement or supersede it. The Word of God is complete and absolutely authoritative, and nothing and no one must be allowed to take its place among God's people.

When we reject the authority of God's Word in any way, decline is inevitable. Unfortunately, the ephod episode was not an isolated one in Gideon's life, but only the beginning of his decline. There follows a chapter of his life that is not well known, but we must not miss it. The great Gideon became a backslider, and his life-style became more and more carnal. Even more evident is the effect on the next generation. By denying the complete authority of God's Word in his life, Gideon led his family down a path which led directly to apostasy. That is a pattern which has been reproduced countless times whenever God's Word loses its absolute authority.

GIDEON'S BACKSLIDING—8:29-35

Then Jerubbaal the son of Joash went and lived in his own house. Now Gideon had seventy sons who were his direct descendants, for he had many wives. And his concubine who was in Shechem also bore him a son, and he named him Abimelech. And Gideon the son of Joash died at a ripe old age and was buried in the tomb of his father Joash, in Ophrah of the Abiezrites. Then it came about, as soon as Gideon was dead, that the sons of Israel again played the harlot with the Baals, and made Baal-berith their god. Thus the sons of Israel did not remember the LORD their God, who had delivered them from the hands of all their enemies on every side; nor did they show kindness to the household of Jerubbaal (that is, Gideon), in accord with all the good that he had done to Israel.

In grace, the Holy Spirit does not dwell upon this part of Gideon's biography. However, enough is said for us to realize what happened. The man who refused the throne adopted a very kingly life-style.

1. *His royal harem.* Occasionally, an ordinary Israelite might have more than one wife, but large-scale polygamy was practiced only by rulers because they were the only ones who could afford it. Gideon adopted not only the Canaanite's idea of having a harem but apparently their moral standards as well, because he had a concubine in Shechem.

2. *His royal luxury.* Gideon lived in royal prosperity. He began his career by describing himself as "least in Ma-

nasseh" (6:15), but he ended his life enjoying great luxury. This is exactly what God warned against allowing to happen, in Deuteronomy 17:17: "Neither shall [a king] multiply wives for himself, lest his heart turn away; nor shall he greatly increase silver and gold for himself."

3. *His royal title.* The final evidence of Gideon's backsliding is found in the name he gave his son. Gideon chose his name very deliberately. *Abimelech*—"My father is king." Everytime that boy gave his name, he claimed for his father what Gideon had apparently renounced in verse 23. More than that, chapter 9 reveals that his family received the impression that the next king would come from among Gideon's sons. How far away his great victory was now!

THE LESSONS OF GIDEON'S FAILURE

The ending of Gideon's story is a sad one, but it has some important lessons that we must not overlook.

1. *We cannot compromise our obedience to the Word of God.* The path of partial obedience is the pathway of spiritual defeat, and the path of compromise means that the Lord will not be able to use our lives to make a permanent impact for Jesus Christ. We cannot alter God's Word, and we cannot choose to obey what we deem appropriate. His Word must be supreme.

2. *The most glorious profession of the lordship of Jesus Christ must be followed by the consistent practice of that lordship.* Over the story of Gideon we can write the words of 1 Corinthians 10:12, "Let him who thinks he stands take heed lest he fall." I am always delighted when people share how they have come to a new understanding of the lordship of Jesus Christ in their lives. Often, following a camp or a conference or a stirring message, people will announce that they have dedicated their life in a new and deeper way to the Savior. The testimony is tremendous, but the evidence must be worked out in life over a course of time. Gideon professed the kingship of God in Israel in clear, unequivocal

terms, but then he felt free to alter the King's clear commands. How has your dedication to the Lord altered your life? Is it only a glorious profession, or is it a habit of life? There is no substitute for hard-nosed, consistent obedience.

3. *The only safe place to keep our spiritual eyes is on the Lord Jesus.* Even Gideons may backslide. The most spiritual Christian may fail. Gideon's defection must have had a traumatic effect on sincere believers who were patterning their lives on his. So God the Holy Spirit calls us to run the race before us, looking away from all else unto Jesus, the Source and Perfector of faith (Heb. 12:1-2). He is the unfailing Example.

THIRTEEN

The Christian's Civil War

Five days after Charles Spurgeon trusted the Lord Jesus and knew the assurance of salvation, he came crashing back to earth. Since the Sunday of his conversion, he had been so filled with the joy of his new life that he seemed to be walking in midair. Then, on Friday, an awful realization exploded in his consciousness. He still had some very sinful thoughts and desires which he did not understand. After all, he was now a Christian. He had no doubt that he was trusting entirely in the Lord Jesus Christ, but those sinful desires distressed him.

On Sunday, he went back to the same little chapel where he had trusted Christ, anxious to find an answer. When the preacher turned to Romans 7 and read Paul's description of his inner conflict and struggle with sin, Spurgeon was sure that the Lord Jesus meant this message just for him. Then the preacher began to expound the passage. He said, "Paul was not a believer when he wrote Romans 7," and he went on to say that no child of God ever felt any inner conflict. Spurgeon was so sure that the man was wrong that he picked up his hat and left the chapel in the middle of the message, never to return. Later on, he wrote of churches which teach that doctrine of the Christian life: "They are very good for people who are unconverted to go to, but of very little use for the children of God. . . . They are like the parish pound, it is a good place to put the sheep in when they've strayed, but there is no food inside; they had better be let out as soon as possible to find grass."[1]

Years later, Spurgeon was a speaker at a conference,

along with another man, who publicly proclaimed that Christians could reach a place of sinless perfection where they no longer struggled with sin or had any desire to sin because they were perfected in the love of God. The speaker went on to suggest modestly that he had realized this in his own life. Spurgeon said nothing, but the next morning, at breakfast time, he crept up behind the man and poured a jug of milk on his head. He quickly discovered that the man still had his sinful nature![2]

Spurgeon's method of testing a man's doctrine may be rather unorthodox, but it does face us with a very important fact of Christian experience. A Christian is a person who knows an inner conflict, a struggle with sin, and often finds himself engaged in a civil war within his own being. That does not mean that a Christian does not experience victory. By God's grace, he does. But it is a victory in the midst of conflict, not a victory over conflict, and it is both naive and dangerous to ignore or minimize the nature of the inner battle which we all face until the Lord calls us home.

Judges 9 provides us with an opportunity to examine that civil war. There are significant parallels between God's principles of physical warfare and His principles of spiritual warfare. Most of the enemies during this time are external, invading foreigners, such as Moab, Ammon, or the Philistines. However, in the story of Abimelech, Gideon's son, we have an account of internal division and civil war which provides helpful parallels to a Christian's inner conflict.

THE CONFLICT FOR CONTROL—8:33—9:6

Then it came about, as soon as Gideon was dead, that the sons of Israel again played the harlot with the Baals, and made Baal-berith their god. Thus the sons of Israel did not remember the LORD their God, who had delivered them from the hands of all their enemies on every side; nor did they show kindness to the household of Jerubbaal (that is, Gideon), in accord with all the good that he had done to Israel. And Abimelech the son of Jerubbaal went to Shechem to his mother's relatives, and spoke to them and to the whole clan of the household of his mother's father, saying, "Speak, now, in the hearing of all the leaders of Shechem, 'Which is better for you, that seventy men, all the sons of Jerubbaal, rule over you, or that one man rule over you?' Also, remember that I am your bone and your flesh." And his mother's relatives spoke all these words on his behalf in the hearing of all the leaders of Shechem; and they were inclined to follow Abimelech, for they said, "He is our relative." And they gave him seventy pieces of silver from the house of Baal-berith with which Abimelech hired worthless and reckless fellows, and they followed him. Then he went to his father's house at Ophrah, and killed his brothers the sons of Jerubbaal, seventy men, on one stone. But Jotham the youngest son of Jerubbaal was left, for he hid himself. And all the men of Shechem and all Beth-millo assembled together, and they went and made Abimelech king, by the oak of the pillar which was in Shechem.

The principle which confronts us in this incident is that if we reject the true King, we will be ruled by a usurper. If the throne is not filled by God the King, it will be filled by an Abimelech, a bramble king. That is the experience of Israel in Judges 9, but it is also the experience of a Christian who does not submit to the lordship of Jesus Christ. Paul states the principle in Romans 6:16: "Do you not know that when you present yourselves to someone as slaves for obedience, you are slaves of the one whom you obey, either of sin resulting in death, or of obedience resulting in righteousness?" If I do not walk in the Spirit, I will walk in the flesh. If Jesus Christ does not rule my life, my sinful nature will.

ISRAEL'S SPIRITUAL VACUUM

Nature abhors a vacuum, and something will immediately rush in to fill it. The same principle operated spiritually in the nation of Israel. Sadly, although Gideon was used by God to deliver his people from the Midianites, he left his nation in a spiritual vacuum. It is ironic that Gideon's original victory was due to the fact that he was obedient to

God's Word, but the greatest failure of his life was that he did not consistently practice the Word of God. In fact, as we read the account of Gideon's judgeship, there is no suggestion that the Word of God had a very important place in his life. If he had Scripture at all, he simply ignored it, and that led him to the sin of the ephod and to his backsliding into a royal life-style. Despite the great affirmation of 8:23, "I will not rule over you, nor shall my son rule over you; the LORD shall rule over you," Gideon did not establish God in His rightful place in Israel.

As a result, when Gideon died, his life left no permanent difference on the spiritual life of the people of Israel. For the fifth time in Judges, the cycle of sin began as the people turned away from the living and true God to the depraved pagan worship of Baal. In this case, he was called *Baal-berith*, meaning "Baal of the covenant." This time, however, there was a difference. The oppression did not come from a foreign power, but from within Israel's own ranks.

ABIMELECH'S COUP D'ETAT

Two factors influence a man supremely—his parents and his home environment. Unfortunately, both of these left deep scars on Abimelech. They do not excuse his actions or remove his guilt, but they are important considerations in understanding the man.

The greatest influence on our lives comes from our parents. That may seem to be something in Abimelech's favor. After all, he was a son of Gideon, the hero of faith. But in his case that was not an unmixed blessing, for Abimelech was the product of Gideon's years of backsliding. His mother was a part of Gideon's harem, but Gideon did not even give her the dignity of being his wife. She was a convenience, not a life partner. The son of a concubine was in a very divided situation. Legally, he had no rights from his father, and he belonged to his mother's family. So Abimelech had his father's genes but not his father's name.

He could hardly respect his father for his life-style or his morality, or love him because of his fatherly care.

Gideon not only failed to express love to Abimelech, he failed to communicate spiritual truth to him. We are told that Gideon's ephod was a snare not only to Gideon but to all his family. It engaged his entire family in spiritual adultery and kept them from the truths of God's Word. There was no one snared more severely than Abimelech. His very name "My father is king" bore witness to his father's sad decline. No wonder Abimelech found Baal worship easy to adopt.

The second major influence in Abimelech's life was his city, Shechem, which vividly symbolized the spiritual confusion of the nation. Near the city, Joshua had led the people to commit themselves to God's covenant, as they recited the blessings and cursings from Mt. Ebal and Mt. Gerizim. But when the people refused to obey God and drive out the Canaanites, Shechem became a mixed city. Canaanites and Israelites lived side by side, and together they worshiped Baal-berith, in the house of Baal (9:4). The city was saturated with Baalism, and because Abimelech saw no evidence of a vital faith in the Lord in his father's life, he fell easy prey to the seductive, sensual worship of Baal.

One thing Abimelech had gained from his family tie was the feeling that Gideon's descendants had a right to rule. This again contradicted Gideon's bold affirmation in 8:23, but apparently it was generally expected that one of Gideon's seventy sons, or the entire group, would rule. That expectation was certainly behind his appeal. "'Which is better for you, that seventy men, all the sons of Jerubbaal, rule over you, or that one man rule over you?' Also, remember that I am your bone and your flesh" (9:2). If there was a vacuum of leadership, Abimelech was going to fill it, at whatever cost. He began by establishing his base of power at Shechem and by working through his relatives to rally the Shechemites to his support.

Abimelech was not content to stop with intrigue. He became the official worker of Baal by taking money from the Baal temple in Shechem and using it to hire a group of worthless, wicked men. Then, as their leader, he marched north to Ophrah, and, in a surprise attack, captured Gideon's entire family. In a ruthless and despicable act, he cold-bloodedly executed sixty-nine of his half brothers on a rock near their home, while one escaped. This godless act should have aroused the entire nation against Abimelech. Whatever Gideon's failings, they owed him a great deal. The demands of God's law and simple humanity called for Abimelech to be put to death for his crime, but nobody raised a hand against him. Thus, in this one act, both Israel and Abimelech revealed themselves for what they were. Israel was an immoral, pagan society prepared to tolerate the most atrocious acts, while Abimelech was an utterly ruthless man, prepared to use any means to gain his desired ends.

The people and the man deserved one another. When Abimelech returned to Shechem, he was not exposed as a butcherer, but crowned as king. Abimelech had tasted power and he was committed to extend it throughout the entire nation.

We need to remind ourselves at this point of the basic lesson of Judges 9. If God is not King, a usurper will arise in His place. If God had been kept in His place as King, Abimelech would never have been successful. But when there is a spiritual vacuum, Satan will rush in to fill it.

THE CHRISTIAN'S CIVIL WAR

That same principle operates within Christians. If we are not practicing the lordship of Jesus Christ, there is a power vacuum in our lives which will be filled by a king, every bit as ruthless as Abimelech in his thirst for power. It is important that we understand the nature of this conflict. Paul describes it clearly in Galatians 5:16-18:

> But I say, walk by the Spirit, and you will not carry out the
> desire of the flesh. For the flesh sets its desire against the
> Spirit, and the Spirit against the flesh; for these are in opposi-
> tion to one another, so that you may not do the things that
> you please. But if you are led by the Spirit, you are not under
> the law.

The Apostle Paul is always utterly realistic about the Christian life. He is not interested in covering it over with layers
of sentiment or disguising the real issues. Here he tells us
that *the believer is involved in a constant inner conflict.* He
is not describing an occasional experience or an experience
we outgrow. Literally, he says, "For the flesh *keeps on
setting* its desire against the Spirit, and the Spirit against the
flesh."

When we, as sinners, come to the Lord Jesus in faith, we
are instantly born again and become new creatures in Christ
Jesus. God the Holy Spirit comes to live within us, and our
basic nature is changed. We are new people in Christ.

At the same time, there remains within us our old
Adamic nature—a sinful drive which opposes God. It is not
God's purpose to remove that from us until death or the
rapture. That old nature goes by many names in the Bible,
and here, in Galatians 5, it is called the flesh. It is not the
physical body although it does work through it. Suddenly,
we find ourselves thrown into the middle of an inner conflict. Before we were Christians, there were things we
would do without a second thought, but now, as we begin
to do them, the Holy Spirit says, "No, you should not do
that as a child of God." The flesh responds back, "Oh, come
on. Don't be fanatical about this!" and the conflict goes on.
Or the Holy Spirit moves us to do the will of God, and the
flesh shouts "No" in our ears. The result is a constant inner
conflict in Christians.

It is extremely important that you understand yourself
as a Christian. You are not schizophrenic or a split personality, but you do have two drives within you. Do not under-
estimate the ugliness and sinfulness of the flesh. It is capable

of incredible evil, and Abimelech is a fitting symbol of it.

God's Word does not have us locked in hopeless conflict, however. Paul tells us in these same verses that *the only resolution of the conflict is to walk in the Spirit*. If that language is too nebulous, to walk in the Spirit is to live in conscious submission, obedience, and dependence upon the Lord Jesus (note the comparison between Eph. 5:18 and Col. 3:16). Remember, if you are rightly related to one member of the Trinity, you cannot be wrongly related to another. To be in fellowship with the Lord Jesus is to be walking in the Spirit.

That is the promise of Galatians 5:16. "Walk by the Spirit, and you *will not* carry out the desire of the flesh" (itals. added). Please understand this. The flesh flourishes only in a power vacuum, and that vacuum exists whenever the Lord Jesus is not controlling your life. Those are the only two alternatives, the flesh or the Spirit. The new nature has no power in and of itself, and, if I do not consciously allow God the Spirit to rule in my life on a day to day basis, the flesh will imitate Abimelech.

Remember the principle of Judges 9. If God had been truly King, Abimelech could not have been king. So it is in my life. The flesh cannot rule where the Spirit is King. That means that the Christian life is not lived by beating down the flesh and trying as hard as I can to keep my old nature in its place. The crucial issue is whether I am keeping the Lord Jesus in His place.

David Watson tells of a time when Corrie ten Boom had a week's meeting in the Anglican church in which he was ministering. At the end of the week, the three very proper clergymen of the church, all dressed in their clerical collars and dark grey suits and looking very official, took her to the train. Corrie got on, and they stood on the platform to watch her go. Just as the train began to pull out, Corrie leaned out the window and shouted a last message for them—and she shouted loudly so everyone could hear—"Don't wrestle, just nestle!" Watson said they all went pink, but he has never forgotten that message. "Don't wrestle, just nestle!"[3] The way we have victory in the conflict with the flesh is not to wrestle with the flesh, but to nestle close to the King. There is conflict, but there is victory in that conflict as the Lord Jesus is honored as King and Lord in our lives. Discipline is necessary, but we will never overcome the flesh by self-discipline. Victory comes when we look away from the flesh to the Lord Jesus, and fill the throne of our lives with Him.

THE PRINCIPLE OF CONTROL—9:7-21

Now when they told Jotham, he went and stood on the top of Mount Gerizim, and lifted his voice and called out. Thus he said to them, "Listen to me, O men of Shechem, that God may listen to you. Once the trees went forth to anoint a king over them, and they said to the olive tree, 'Reign over us!' But the olive tree said to them, 'Shall I leave my fatness with which God and men are honored, and go to wave over the trees?' Then the trees said to the fig tree, 'You come, reign over us!' But the fig tree said to them, 'Shall I leave my sweetness and my good fruit, and go to wave over the trees?' Then the trees said to the vine, 'You come, reign over us!' But the vine said to them, 'Shall I leave my new wine, which cheers God and men, and go to wave over the trees?' Finally all the trees said to the bramble, 'You come, reign over us!' And the bramble said to the trees, 'If in truth you are anointing me as king over you, come and take refuge in my shade; but if not, may fire come out from the bramble and consume the cedars of Lebanon.' Now therefore, if you have dealt in truth and integrity in making Abimelech king, and if you have dealt well with Jerubbaal and his house, and have dealt with him as he deserved—for my father fought for you and risked his life and delivered you from the hand of Midian; but you have risen against my father's house today and have killed his sons, seventy men, on one stone, and have made Abimelech, the son of his maidservant, king over the men of Shechem, because he is your relative—if then you have dealt in truth and integrity with Jerubbaal and his house this day, rejoice in Abimelech, and let him also rejoice in you. But if

not, let fire come out from Abimelech and consume the men
of Shechem and Beth-millo; and let fire come out from the
men of Shechem and from Beth-millo, and consume
Abimelech." Then Jotham escaped and fled, and went to
Beer and remained there because of Abimelech his brother.

If Abimelech's coup d'etat introduced us to the conflict for
control, Jotham's parable reminded us of the nature of the
struggle. Suddenly, in the middle of Abimelech's coronation ceremony, there was an interruption. The people
turned their eyes to follow the sound which rang through
the natural amphitheater and there, in the distance, they
saw Abimelech's only remaining half brother. Jotham alone
had survived Abimelech's butchery, and now he used the
first recorded biblical parable to teach a great lesson.

THE FIRST PARABLE

It is a parable of the trees which, for some reason, decided to
appoint a king. So they approached the olive tree, a valuable and prized tree, and got a flat "No." "Why should I
leave my fatness with which God and men are honored, and
go to sway over the trees?" So the nominating committee
went to the fig tree and got a very similar reply. "Why
should I leave my sweetness and good fruit for such a silly
function?" Then they turned to the grape, and there was the
same response. "Shall I leave my wine which cheers God
and man?"

There are several things we should notice about these
trees. They recognized that they already had a king—God.
What good was a king of the trees? They did not want to rule,
they simply wanted to function as God intended them to
function. Next, they were all fruit-bearing trees. As long as
they were being what God made them to be, they brought
blessing to God and man.

Finally, they came to the bramble bush, the buck thorn.
It was not a tree at all, but a bush that was useless because it
bore no fruit. It was dangerous as well, because in the heat
of summer it could catch on fire and set the countryside

ablaze. The bramble was a product of God's curse on the earth in Genesis 3, a nuisance, which could provide absolutely no shade.

Verse 15 is filled with sarcasm. Imagine a bramble king! It was the most worthless tree imaginable, but it had delusions of grandeur. It willingly accepted the offer and loudly called the other trees to take refuge in its shade. What shade can a bramble bush offer a cedar of Lebanon?

Jotham's point is obvious. When they crowned Abimelech, they were choosing an absolutely worthless man. He could not give them the protection they wanted. Besides, he was dangerous, and he would destroy them. Jotham finished his message with a very pointed prediction in 9:19-20:

> If then you have dealt in truth and integrity with Jerubbaal and his house this day, rejoice in Abimelech, and let him also rejoice in you. But if not, let fire come out from Abimelech and consume the men of Shechem and Beth-millo; and let fire come out from the men of Shechem and from Beth-millo, and consume Abimelech.

It was a prediction fulfilled in precise detail as the conclusion of the chapter reveals.

THE PRINCIPLE OF THE PARABLE

The parable of Jotham contained the lesson God the Holy Spirit intended His people to see in this episode. The spiritual vacuum in Israel was not filled by fruit-bearing, useful, godly men. They refused to usurp God's place, to take what He had not given them. The vacuum was filled by a useless, worthless, dangerous bramble named Abimelech.

The flesh is a bramble. If it takes control of my life, it will not produce fruit, but rather the ugly, destructive works of the flesh. Paul catalogues them in Galatians 5:19-21, and I need to reflect soberly on that list. In radical contrast stands the fruit of the Spirit, the product of His growth in my life. The principle of control is clear. My life will show the results of who controls it. The flesh will produce destructive bramble-works. The Holy Spirit will produce within me a Christlike character.

James Montgomery Boice has an excellent illustration of this which does not deal with all the details but does help us think more clearly about this situation in our lives.[4] He suggests that we compare a man to an airplane cruising at 35,000 feet. The body of the man is the fuselage, the pilot is the soul, and the spirit is the motor. When the motor is running, the body of that plane is an asset, because the wings keep the plane up and the rest of the body assists in flying. But when the motor stops, the fuselage is a distinct liability, because it is too heavy and the plane will crash.

Now when I do allow the Holy Spirit to fuel my human spirit and keep it moving ahead, there are growth and progress. My body moved by the Holy Spirit becomes an instrument for God's glory. But when I cut off the fuel supply, my spiritual motor stops running and, suddenly, I am dominated by my body and its desires, not by my fellowship with God. When that happens, I am headed for a crash. My body, when it is not under the control of God the Spirit, can become an instrument through which my evil flesh works. But under His control, it becomes "a vessel for honor...useful to the Master, prepared for every good work" (2 Tim. 2:21).

THE OUTCOME OF THE CONFLICT—9:22-57

Now Abimelech ruled over Israel three years. Then God sent an evil spirit between Abimelech and the men of Shechem; and the men of Shechem dealt treacherously with Abimelech, in order that the violence done to the seventy sons of Jerubbaal might come, and their blood might be laid on Abimelech their brother, who killed them, and on the men of Shechem, who strengthened his hands to kill his brothers. And the men of Shechem set men in ambush against him on the tops of the mountains, and they robbed all who might pass by them along the road; and it was told to Abimelech. Now Gaal the son of Ebed came with his relatives, and crossed over into Shechem; and the men of

Shechem put their trust in him. And they went out into the field and gathered the grapes of their vineyards and trod them, and held a festival; and they went into the house of their god, and ate and drank and cursed Abimelech. Then Gaal the son of Ebed said, "Who is Abimelech and who is Shechem, that we should serve him? Is he not the son of Jerubbaal, and is Zebul not his lieutenant? Serve the men of Hamor the father of Shechem; but why should we serve him? Would, therefore, that this people were under my authority! Then I would remove Abimelech." And he said to Abimelech, "Increase your army, and come out." And when Zebul the ruler of the city heard the words of Gaal the son of Ebed, his anger burned. And he sent messengers to Abimelech deceitfully, saying, "Behold, Gaal the son of Ebed and his relatives have come to Shechem; and behold, they are stirring up the city against you. Now therefore, arise by night, you and the people who are with you, and lie in wait in the field. And it shall come about in the morning, as soon as the sun is up, that you shall rise early and rush upon the city; and behold, when he and the people who are with him come out against you, you shall do to them whatever you can." So Abimelech and all the people who were with him arose by night and lay in wait against Shechem in four companies. Now Gaal the son of Ebed went out and stood in the entrance of the city gate; and Abimelech and the people who were with him arose from the ambush. And when Gaal saw the people, he said to Zebul, "Look, people are coming down from the tops of the mountains." But Zebul said to him, "You are seeing the shadow of the mountains as if they were men." And Gaal spoke again and said, "Behold, people are coming down from the highest part of the land, and one company comes by the way of the diviners' oak." Then Zebul said to him. "Where is your boasting now with which you said, 'Who is Abimelech that we should serve him?' Is this not the people whom you despised? Go out now and fight with them?" So Gaal went out before the leaders of Shechem and fought with Abimelech. And Abimelech chased him, and he fled before him; and many fell wounded up to the entrance of the gate. Then Abimelech remained at Arumah, but Zebul drove out Gaal and his relatives so that they could not remain in Shechem. Now it came about the next day, that the people went out to the field, and it was told to Abimelech. So he took his people and divided them into three companies, and lay in wait in the field; when he looked and saw the people coming out from the city, he arose against them and slew them. Then Abimelech and the company who was with him dashed forward and stood in the entrance of the city gate; the other two companies then dashed against all who were in the field and slew them. And Abimelech fought against the city all that day, and he captured the city and killed the people who were in it; then he razed the city and sowed it with salt. When all the leaders of the tower of Shechem heard of it, they entered the inner chamber of the temple of El-berith. And it was told Abimelech that all the leaders of the tower of Shechem were gathered together. So Abimelech went up to Mount Zalmon, he and all the people who were with him; and Abimelech took an axe in his hand and cut down a branch from the trees, and lifted it and laid it on his shoulder. Then he said to the people who were with him, "What you have seen me do, hurry and do likewise." And all the people also cut down each one his branch and followed Abimelech, and put them on the inner chamber and set the inner chamber on fire over those inside, so that all the men of the tower of Shechem also died, about a thousand men and women. Then Abimelech went to Thebez, and he camped against Thebez and captured it. But there was a strong tower in the center of the city, and all the men and women with all the leaders of the city fled there and shut themselves in; and they went up on the roof of the tower. So Abimelech came to the tower and fought against it, and approached the entrance of the tower to burn it with fire. But a certain woman threw an upper millstone on Abimelech's head, crushing his skull. Then he called quickly to the young man, his armor bearer, and said to him, "Draw your sword and kill me, lest it be said of me, 'A woman slew him.' " So the young man pierced him through, and he died. And when the men of Israel saw that Abimelech was dead, each departed to his home. Thus God repaid the wickedness of Abimelech, which he had done to his father, in killing his seventy brothers. Also God returned all the wickedness of the men of Shechem on their heads, and the curse of Jotham the son of Jerubbaal came upon them.

Abimelech had come with great promises. "Remember, I am your flesh and blood. I will be the king who really gives you freedom." It is the kind of promise that a false king loves to give, and no one loves that kind of promise more than the flesh. "Indulge me, and you will find life!" I am reminded of the false teachers Peter describes in 2 Peter 2:19, "Who promise them freedom while they themselves are slaves of corruption."

But false promises are followed by disillusionment, and that is exactly what happened to the people of Shechem. They quickly realized that Abimelech was not a liberator; he was a tyrant, and they tried to break away from him.

All too often I have seen Christians turn away from the lordship of Jesus Christ and embrace a false promise of freedom. For awhile, it seems to be very good. There is the enjoyment of the pleasure of sin, for a short time. After all, Abimelech reigned for three years before his rule turned to ashes in their mouths. Then, in despair, they recognize their mistake and try to deal with it. All too often, in the midst of this kind of disillusionment, Christians do exactly what these Shechemites did. What they should have done was turn to God in radical repentance and submit to Him as King. Instead, they tried to deal with Abimelech on their own, still leaving God out.

The result was self-destruction. As the rest of chapter 9 relates, when they turned away from Abimelech, Abimelech turned on them in total fury, and utterly destroyed them. And, as we leave Judges 9, both Shechem and Abimelech are destroyed.

The apostle puts it this way in Galatians 6:7-9: "Do not be deceived, God is not mocked [and by the way, he is talking about God as the Lord of our pocketbooks]; for whatever a man sows, this he will also reap. For the one who sows to his own flesh shall from the flesh reap corruption, but the one who sows to the Spirit shall from the Spirit reap eternal life. And let us not lose heart in doing good, for in due time we shall reap if we do not grow weary."

Judges 9 poses the great question: Is there a power vacuum in your life? If Jesus Christ is not King and Lord, in word and deed, then the bramble king of the flesh will seize control. If you are not walking in the Spirit, you are walking in the flesh. Those are the inevitable realities of your spiritual experience. There are no other alternatives. Which is true of you?

FOURTEEN

Rejected by Men, Accepted by God

One day when I went for lunch, I found myself waiting in line behind a huge man who was talking a great deal about football. If he had been wearing his uniform, I would have immediately recognized him as an all-pro defensive lineman, considered to be the strongest man in the Canadian Football League. When I realized who he was, I was suddenly glad that my childhood dreams of athletic stardom had been only dreams. They had not included any realities as big as this!

It reminded me of the time in the Chicago airport when I found myself standing next to the tallest man I had ever seen. It did not take much intelligence to realize he was a basketball player (he was carrying some equipment), but it took a lot of self-control not to stare. In my mind, I imagined myself trying to get a jump shot over his head, and I realized that I would get a very sore nose from all the shots he would catapult back at me. A few minutes later, when I discovered that he was a well-known 7′ 3″ center in the National Basketball Association, I gained a new respect for the "little men" in the N.B.A.

When I was in junior high school, I wanted very badly to be a basketball player. Everyone knows that midgets do not make very effective basketball players, and I certainly was not endowed with an abundance of height. If wishing could make you grow, I would have stood well over six feet. Day after day, I would come home from school and measure myself, but the result was always depressingly the same. If my basketball career was dependent on my size, I was going to pick up a lot of splinters from sitting on the bench. I just did not measure up.

Sometimes in the spiritual realm, we get the impression that before God can use us in His service, we must have certain characteristics. If we do not have the right family background, social standing, or educational training, we are destined to be water boys watching the spiritual first-string accomplish God's real work. At the best, we can cheer them on in their efforts for the Lord, but without the proper credentials, we are not the kind of people the Lord can or will use.

As we have already seen, that is not the pattern we find in God's Word. God is not a God of stereotypes, and, if we need any confirmation of that, we have it in abundance in the study of another judge, a unique man named Jephthah. He was a man in whom we find great conflicts and contrasts. There are some ugly blotches in his life, but there are also some glorious victories.

To understand Jephthah, it is essential for us to understand the times in which he lived and served God. That background is given in Judges 10:6-18.

THE TIMES OF JEPHTHAH—10:6-18

Then the sons of Israel again did evil in the sight of the LORD, served the Baals and the Ashtaroth, the gods of Syria, the gods of Sidon, the gods of Moab, the gods of the sons of Ammon, and the gods of the Philistines; thus they forsook the LORD and did not serve Him. And the anger of the LORD burned against Israel, and He sold them into the hands of the Philistines, and into the hands of the sons of Ammon. And they afflicted and crushed the sons of Israel that year; for eighteen years they afflicted all the sons of Israel who were beyond the Jordan in Gilead in the land of the Amorites. And the sons of Ammon crossed the Jordan to fight also against Judah, Benjamin, and the house of Ephraim, so that Israel was greatly distressed. Then the sons of Israel cried out to the LORD, saying, "We have sinned against Thee, for indeed, we have forsaken our God and served the Baals." And the LORD said to the sons of Israel, "Did I not deliver you from the Egyptians, the Amorites, the sons of Ammon, and the Philistines? Also when the Sidonians, the Amalekites and the Maonites oppressed you, you cried out to Me, and I delivered you from their hands. Yet you have forsaken Me and served other gods; therefore I will deliver you no more. Go and cry out to the gods which you have chosen; let them deliver you in the time of your distress." And the sons of Israel said to the LORD, "We have sinned, do to us whatever seems good to Thee; only please deliver us this day." So they put away the foreign gods from among them, and served the LORD; and He could bear the misery of Israel no longer. Then the sons of Ammon were summoned, and they camped in Gilead. And the sons of Israel gathered together, and camped in Mizpah. And the people, the leaders of Gilead, said to one another, "Who is the man who will begin to fight against the sons of Ammon? He shall become head over all the inhabitants of Gilead."

A preacher was visiting a man who professed to be a Christian, but who had drifted a long way from the Lord Jesus. They talked for a while, and then the preacher said, "I want you to go outside and look up to heaven. You will receive a revelation."

"But it is pouring rain. I will get soaked," the man protested.

"Just do what I say. It is important."

So the man went outside, and, ten minutes later, he came in soaking wet. He was absolutely drenched, and he said to the preacher, rather angrily, "Well, I kept looking up to heaven, but I sure did not get any revelation. I am just drenched, and I feel like an idiot."

"Not bad," said the preacher. "That is quite a revelation for a first try!"

Unfortunately, not many of us realize the stupidity of sin. We may think of it as unfortunate or as enjoyable, but we rarely recognize it for what it is—spiritual insanity. There is a very striking phrase in the story of the prodigal son. He had left his father until, one day, watching pigs fill their bellies with corn husks, he *came to himself*. In other words, he came to his senses. He came back to reality. It does not matter how intelligent a man is or how well educated he is, when he is separated from God by sin, he is in a state of spiritual insanity, because he is out of touch with reality.

Only when we see sin like that can we properly appreciate the seriousness of Israel's apostasy. Judges 10:6 records the sixth time that we see the Israelites turning their backs on the living and true God to throw themselves into the worship of pagan gods. They had seen God's hand miraculously revealed through Gideon. They had seen the disaster of apostasy in the life of Abimelech. They had known the leadership of two minor judges named Tola and Jair, but still they turned away from God.

It is important to recognize that although Israel kept doing the same thing, they were not going around and around in the same circle. Each time they did *the evil* in the sight of God and chose paganism over God's truth, they sank lower and lower until, finally, here in Judges 10, they reached one of the bleakest times spiritually in the nation's history. In fact, as we read verse 6, we realize they would have worshiped almost anything or anyone, rather than the Lord God. There are seven false religions mentioned here, and they include some of the most perverted and depraved practices ever known to man. Every part of the country is involved. But the really important fact is found in the last clause, "They forsook the LORD and did not serve Him."

Once again exactly the same thing happened. God delivered them over to two nations—one on the east and the other on the west. The western enemy was the Philistines, and we will learn more about them in the story of Samson. On the east, the enemy was Ammon. They were a desert people who lived on the eastern side of the Dead Sea. They first overpowered the two and one-half tribes which had chosen to stay in the area east of the Jordan River, a region called Gilead, and occupied by Reuben, Gad, and half the tribe of Manasseh. Then Ammon gained sufficient power to cross the Jordan and to attack the central tribes in Israel— Judah, Benjamin, and Ephraim.

Finally, when God had put their backs right against the wall, Israel gained enough sense to cry out to Him. "LORD, we have sinned." But the striking thing is God's reply. In effect He says, "Listen, I am not going to help you. You turned away from Me to other gods, and if you want help, you go to them."

We need to recognize there is a great difference between regret and repentance. A Christian who was visiting a man in jail said to him, "I hope you have repented of what you have done, so you will not make the same mistakes when you are released." And he said, "No ma'am, I sure won't. Next time I pull a job, I'll be sure to wear gloves." That is regret, not repentance. Paul puts the distinction like this, in 2 Corinthians 7:9-10:

> I now rejoice, not that you were made sorrowful [regret], but that you were made sorrowful to the point of repentance; for you were made sorrowful according to the will of God, in order that you might not suffer loss in anything through us. For the sorrow that is according to the will of God produces a repentance without regret, leading to salvation; but the sorrow [regret] of the world produces death.

Regret touches the emotions, but it may go no deeper than that. We read that Judas regretted what he had done (Matt. 27:3). But repentance involves a change of mind, a change of will. You can have repentance without sorrow, and you can have sorrow without repentance. Regret is remorse over the consequences of an act, but repentance involves a reordering of our lives around God.

That is why many of us, even as Christians, have never known God at work in our lives. Until we deal on a radical level with our sin in the presence of God and fill our minds with God's truth so that we act upon it, we will not know His power.

The Lord's refusal to respond to superficial regret drove the Israelites to examine their hearts more deeply. The result was genuine repentance, to which the Lord responded in His loving grace. "So they put away the foreign gods from among them, and served the LORD; and He could bear the misery of Israel no longer." In the Hebrew text, that last phrase is a beautiful insight into the heart of God. "His soul reached the limit of its endurance with the trouble of Israel." Do you see what that says? Here were God's people undergoing the discipline which they richly deserved. God could have written them off, and the angels would not have missed one note of their eternal praise. But God's heart was in turmoil over what Israel was suffering, and finally He said, "That is enough. I cannot take any more."

I hope that after our studies in the book of Judges you will never again believe Satan's lie that the God of the Old Testament is a stern, unforgiving God, who delights in judgment. He is a God of incessant love and infinite mercy. Over and over He displays these characteristics, not only in the way He dealt with Israel back then, but in the way He works in our lives now. He is the God of all grace.

God's grace manifested itself in giving Israel the initiative and courage to draw up their forces at Mizpah, to do battle against the Ammonites. But there was one urgent need. "Who is the man who will begin to fight against the sons of Ammon?" That is a constant cry of God's people, and it is worth noticing that it does not do a great deal of good to say to one another, as the Israelites did, "Where is the leader?" That is a question we need to bring to the Lord, for we do not need leaders chosen and approved by men. We need God's leaders, and often He will surprise us with His choices. The men He chooses often would not be our choice, but they are always the right choices.

God had a man for these times, a unique man named Jephthah. He was one of the most unusual men in the Old Testament; a man with a tragic past, checkered career, and a strong character, grained with great flaws. Nothing about

Jephthah was painted in pale colors. His gifts and weaknesses were painted in bold colors, and his inner conflicts ran deep. But he was the man God used to accomplish His will among His people.

JEPHTHAH, GOD'S MAN FOR THE TIME—11:1-3

Now Jephthah the Gileadite was a valiant warrior, but he was the son of a harlot. And Gilead was the father of Jephthah. And Gilead's wife bore him sons; and when his wife's sons grew up, they drove Jephthah out and said to him, "You shall not have an inheritance in our father's house, for you are the son of another woman." So Jephthah fled from his brothers and lived in the land of Tob; and worthless fellows gathered themselves about Jephthah, and they went out with him.

The Lord does not produce Christians the way General Motors produces cars, rolling them off an assembly line, differing only in a few options. We search Scripture in vain for the stereotype into which we must fit before He can use us. Yet many Christians suffer from a severe inferiority complex because they do not "fit the mold." Sometimes the fault is their's; often the complex comes from listening to other Christians. Thank God, there is no such mold. Recently, I read a letter from a friend who was commenting on his experiences as a missionary in Ethiopia. Among other things, he wrote:

The key to the exciting growth of the church in Ethiopia is the Holy Spirit. His human agents in all of this are the Ethiopian evangelists. Nine of them share the work here. . . . Each man is supported by his home church which provides him with about $20 a month. All of them have families, and, as you can well imagine, find it very difficult to make ends meet on such meagre allowances.

As for the men themselves, there is little, humanly speaking, to commend them as missionaries. Without exception, they would be rejected by North American mission societies. Their average education is grade four. Some of them have no formal Bible training.

Take Indreas, for example. With his wife—a former barmaid—and four children—one of whom is a hunch back—he preaches and teaches at a remote point two full days journey from Bonga. Last time I went to his church, I attended the baptism of 88 believers!

Or take Arshe, a young man of about 25. He has six fingers on his hand. He is well educated by local standards, having completed grade six as well as some Bible training. His wife has T.B. His church, too, is growing, with 24 baptized one month, while many more believed.

Jephthah was an Old Testament man like that—a leader of the society of the unacceptable. Yet God, in His sovereign wisdom, chose to use and work through him.

THE MAN NOBODY WANTED (11:1-3)

The first obvious fact of Jephthah's life was his family background. His mother was a common prostitute, and Jephthah was the unwanted, illegitimate son of his parents. Apparently his father had enough concern for him to take him into his own house, and to give him some kind of legal status, but Jephthah grew up with the scars of his parents' sins. Then, when his younger half brothers became old enough, they drove Jephthah away from his family and his home, and he became a social outcast. In the society of that day, this was a terrible situation in which to be. Jephthah was a man alone in the world.

Alone except for God. The grace of God was at work in this man's life, rescuing him from an apparently hopeless future. God does not submit to human prejudices, and He is not limited by the social, parental, and environmental factors that men consider determinative. A Christian knows that God is the great Determiner, and in that knowledge there is freedom. I am not a prisoner of my past, no matter how desperate that past was. God delights in using the unusable and in making the ugly beautiful.

An often unrealized example of this truth in Scripture occurred in a man whose life bore many resemblances to

Jephthah's. That man was David. As we study his life, we do not learn a great deal about his parents, but the evidence suggests that his home was very confused. By the time David was born, his father was an old man who had had several families by different wives. David's brothers had sons as old as David was himself, and his sisters were much older. From all indications, his family did not have much time for David. In fact, when Samuel told Jesse to call all his sons, they did not even bother with David. They just left him out looking after the sheep. Apparently, he had a lonely, unhappy childhood.

But David learned a great truth, which is found in Psalm 27:10, "For my father and my mother have forsaken me, but the LORD will take me up." I thank God for my parents, and they certainly have not forsaken me. Their love and encouragement are constant, but all are not so fortunate. So I thank God that, no matter what our family background, God is able to use us for His glory. We are not prisoners of our past.

THE BANDIT CHIEF (11:3)

The second stage of Jephthah's life followed his rejection by his family; it is briefly recorded in verse 3. Jephthah left home, and in his desperation, headed north to the frontier area of Tob. It was the kind of place where the Israelites and their enemies lived in constant conflict, and, apparently, Jephthah became a kind of Hebrew Robin Hood, a leader of a military band who functioned as an unofficial police force. He skillfully brought together this refugee band, and, for a price, they protected the Hebrews and attacked the enemy. This provides another interesting parallel to the life of David because he did exactly the same thing in the period while he was hiding from King Saul.

But this period was enormously important for Jephthah in three ways:

1. *Jephthah learned military warfare and strategy, and God later used that for His glory.* God does not ignore a

man's gifts and talents, and God was, in that period of Jephthah's life, overseeing his gifts, long before they were to be used in God's service.

God never wastes anything in one of His children's lives. The gifts and talents that you have can be used in some way for His glory and service. I think that one of the best illustrations of this is in the life of a man to whom I owe a great deal in my knowledge of the Word, Dr. S. Lewis Johnson. When Dr. Johnson was a university student, he was an ardent golfer, and he found that if he wanted to play on the golf team, the only course that would fit his schedule was classical Greek. He had no interest in Greek, and he was not a Christian, but he loved golf, so he took Greek. He came to love Greek so much that the next year he dropped his golf to pursue Greek.

Dr. Johnson graduated and went into business. Classical Greek was not very helpful in selling insurance. Then God, in His sovereign love, reached into his life, and Dr. Johnson was brought to a saving faith in the Lord Jesus. As he grew in the Lord, he felt called to prepare himself to minister God's Word. That in turn led to a rich and God-blessed ministry of teaching the Greek New Testament at Dallas Theological Seminary. That schedule conflict which seemed so accidental years before was part of God's eternal purpose.

Sometimes Christians fall into the trap of viewing their preconversion experience as a vast wasteland from which nothing can be redeemed. That is never so. The same Lord, who was sovereign in your salvation, was sovereign before your salvation; nothing brought to Him is wasted. In His hands, even broken fragments have purpose and meaning.

2. *Jephthah learned leadership.* It was no small job to take a group of "worthless men," as they are called, and turn them into an effective force. But Jephthah succeeded, and the lessons he learned in practical leadership were things I am sure he fell back on over and over again in later life.

3. *Jephthah learned to know God.* Jephthah was full of contradictions. While he knew God, he had some glaring misconceptions in his knowledge, a fact that is hardly surprising when you realize Jephthah's family background and the total neglect of God's Word in his time. But for all of that, Jephthah used the personal name of God more than any other person in the book of Judges. He knew Jehovah, the covenant-keeping God of Israel, and despite his spiritual immaturity, he was committed to God. His knowledge of God was not deep, but it was real.

A group of broadcasters was holding a conference with some Soviet Christians, and one of the men asked a Russian, "Brother, how did you manage to survive thirty-two years of Soviet labor-camp?" The writer says that he expected some tale of terror or an outburst of anger. Instead, the man quietly and gently answered, "Brethren, even a desert looks like a flower garden when you are in communion with the Lord."

Perhaps Jephthah knew something of that kind of experience. He did not have a father or mother to accept him, but he did have the Lord. He knew what it was to be taken up by the Lord when even those closest to him had rejected him, and because that rejection drew him to the Lord, it made Jephthah the man he was for God.

FROM OUTLAW TO LEADER (11:4-11)

And it came about after a while that the sons of Ammon fought against Israel. And it happened when the sons of Ammon fought against Israel that the elders of Gilead went to get Jephthah from the land of Tob; and they said to Jephthah, "Come and be our chief that we may fight against the sons of Ammon." Then Jephthah said to the elders of Gilead, "Did you not hate me and drive me from my father's house? So why have you come to me now when you are in trouble?" And the elders of Gilead said to Jephthah, "For this reason we have now returned to you, that you may go with us and fight with the sons of Ammon and become head over all the inhabitants of Gilead." So Jephthah said to the elders of Gilead, "If you take me back to fight against the sons of Ammon and the LORD gives them up to me, will I become your head?" And the elders of Gilead said to Jephthah, "The LORD is witness between us; surely we will do as you have said." Then Jephthah went with the elders of Gilead, and the people made him head and chief over them; and Jephthah spoke all his words before the LORD at Mizpah.

The third stage in Jephthah's experience was the call to leadership in verses 4-11. It must have been a great moment for Jephthah when those elders came and asked him to come back to be their leader. It was not a position he had applied, worked, or negotiated for, but in God's own time the door opened, and Jephthah was elevated to the position of chief and leader in Gilead.

My responsibility in my Christian life is to be involved where I am, in doing the will of God where He has put me, to learn the lessons that He is teaching me. It is God's job to open doors of opportunity. An available heart will always find lots to do for the Lord. Jephthah had learned that lesson. Verse 11 makes it clear that he was living his life in the conscious presence of his God: "Jephthah spoke all his words before the LORD at Mizpah."

As a young man, Charles Spurgeon was pondering his future, especially in relation to his education. He says that, as he was walking one night, running the alternatives through his mind, he heard God say to him, "Seekest thou great things for thyself? Seek them not!" "At that moment," he said, "I realized I would never go to Cambridge, and I would never amount to anything more than preaching to a congregation of two hundred people." He committed himself to doing God's will, whatever the cost. Six months later, as a young man only nineteen years old, he was preaching to 2,500 people a Sunday in London. That happened because he was willing to allow God to open the doors in his life and to be faithful where he was then. Live enthusiastically for Him in the present, and He will concern Himself with your future.

JEPHTHAH THE DIPLOMAT (11:12-28)

Now Jephthah sent messengers to the king of the sons of Ammon, saying, "What is between you and me, that you have come to me to fight against my land?" And the king of the sons of Ammon said to the messengers of Jephthah, "Because Israel took away my land when they came up from Egypt, from the Arnon as far as the Jabbok and the Jordan; therefore, return them peacably now." But Jephthah sent messengers again to the king of the sons of Ammon, and they said to him, "Thus says Jephthah, 'Israel did not take away the land of Moab, nor the land of the sons of Ammon. For when they came up from Egypt, and Israel went through the wilderness to the Red Sea and came to Kadesh, then Israel sent messengers to the king of Edom, saying, "Please let us pass through your land," but the king of Edom would not listen. And they also sent to the king of Moab, but he would not consent. So Israel remained at Kadesh. Then they went through the wilderness and around the land of Edom and the land of Moab, and came to the east side of the land of Moab, and they camped beyond the Arnon; but they did not enter the territory of Moab, for the Arnon was the border of Moab. And Israel sent messengers to Sihon king of the Amorites, the king of Heshbon, and Israel said to him, "Please let us pass through your land to our place." But Sihon did not trust Israel to pass through his territory; so Sihon gathered all his people and camped in Jahaz, and fought with Israel. And the LORD, the God of Israel, gave Sihon and all his people into the hand of Israel, and they defeated them; so Israel possessed all the land of the Amorites, the inhabitants of that country. So they possessed all the territory of the Amorites, from the Arnon as far as the Jabbok, and from the wilderness as far as the Jordan. Since now the LORD, the God of Israel, drove out the Amorites from before His people Israel, are you then to possess it? Do you not possess what Chemosh your god gives you to possess? So whatever the LORD our God has driven out before us, we will possess it. And now are you any better than Balak the son of Zippor, king of Moab? Did he ever strive with Israel, or did he ever fight against them? While Israel lived in Heshbon and its villages, and in Aroer and its villages, and in all the cities that are on the banks of the

Arnon, three hundred years, why did you not recover them within that time? I therefore have not sinned against you, but you are doing me wrong by making war against me; may the LORD, the Judge, judge today between the sons of Israel and the sons of Ammon.'" But the king of the sons of Ammon disregarded the message which Jephthah sent him.

The fourth stage of Jephthah's career puts him in a very different role. It was the period of negotiation, and it brought Jephthah into an encounter with the king of Ammon. From his background, we might expect him to strike first and to ask questions later. That is not God's way. Before Jephthah entered into battle with Ammon, he was concerned to confront them with the truth, and Jephthah was a man with a firm grasp of the truth. Where Jephthah gained his thorough knowledge of Israel's history, we cannot tell, but he knew it in detail, and he recognized that Israel's history was really God's history, the record of what the Lord had done for His people.

Before he drew up battle lines, Jephthah sent messengers to Ammon, asking the obvious question, "What is the problem? Why are you invading us and fighting against our land?" The reply came back, "Because Israel took away my land, at the time of Joshua, so return it peacefully now." Jephthah's reply was simple but powerful. He told the king, check your history. We captured the land from Sihon, the king of the Amorites, not the Ammonites (vv. 15-22). Next, check your theology. The Lord God of Israel gave us this land, and we cannot surrender His gift. Live in the land your false god Chemosh has given you (vv. 23-25). Finally, check your logic. For 300 years, we have held the land and you have done nothing to recapture it. It is too late for native land claims now (vv. 26-27).

The significant thing is that Jephthah's answer was grounded in the truths of history. He did not argue probability or dispute possibility. He stood firmly on fact. That is where a Christian always stands. The early Christians did not set their world aflame by expressing opinions or exchanging experiences, but by insisting upon the truth of who the Lord Jesus is and what He did. Our calling is the same. We do not go into the world telling men of our experience, but proclaiming Jesus Christ, telling men who He is and what He did, and the great evidences for the gospel. We may add our testimony to that, but we attack Satan on the ground of truth, not on the ground of experience or feelings.

THE CONQUERING HERO (11:29-33)

Now the Spirit of the LORD came upon Jephthah, so that he passed through Gilead and Manasseh, then he passed through Mizpah of Gilead, and from Mizpah of Gilead he went on to the sons of Ammon. And Jephthah made a vow to the LORD and said, "If Thou wilt indeed give the sons of Ammon into my hand, then it shall be that whatever comes out of the doors of my house to meet me when I return in peace from the sons of Ammon, it shall be the LORD'S, or I will offer it up as a burnt offering." So Jephthah crossed over to the sons of Ammon to fight against them; and the LORD gave them into his hand. And he struck them with a very great slaughter from Aroer to the entrance of Minnith, twenty cities, and as far as Abel-keramin. So the sons of Ammon were subdued before the sons of Israel.

The final stage of Jephthah's development from outcast to hero of faith was found in the victory which God gave him over Ammon. The king was not prepared to listen to truth, so the time had come to stop talking and act. Jephthah attacked in the power of God the Holy Spirit. For all of his experience in war, it was not Jephthah's skill which brought victory, it was God. "Now the Spirit of the LORD came upon Jephthah" (v. 29). "And the LORD gave them into his hand" (v. 32). Jephthah was led and controlled by the Spirit.

But that leading was not a quiet inactivity. Jephthah did not sit down and passively observe while God accomplished His will. He traveled through the region to gather troops; he organized them; he developed strategy; he led the attack. To be led by the Spirit is always to be led into activity and into the battle for God.

Gideon was a weak man who was transformed by God into a fearless warrior. Jephthah was a valiant warrior. Because of his tragic family life, he had had to become strong to survive. The story of his life is of God taking a strong man, and, by His Spirit, turning him into a usable man. Whatever our strengths and weaknesses, the secret of our usefulness is our availability to our God.

God's grace had taken Jephthah from the scrap heap of Israel and transformed him into the liberator of his people. We would have seen nothing that God could use in Jephthah, an illegitimate outcast with a graduate degree in violence and survival. But the Lord took him and transformed him into His man. The Lord delights to do that. No one is beyond His capacity to use for His glory. Your past may not be as sordid as Jephthah's nor your gifts so unusual, but the God who used him will use you as you trust Him.

FIFTEEN

The Danger of Spiritual Ignorance

Canada and the United States have long been the best of friends, justly proud of the undefended border between them. It has not always been so. During the War of 1812, between the United States and Britain, the Americans crossed the border and destroyed York, modern day Toronto. The British retaliated by burning Washington, D.C. Finally, on December 24, 1814, representatives of the two countries, who had been meeting in Belgium signed the Treaty of Ghent, which agreed on the details of an armistice.

Unfortunately, the news of the peace was delayed, and, on January 8, 1815, unaware of the armistice, the two armies met in the Battle of New Orleans. More than 2,000 men lost their lives in a totally unnecessary battle, because they were ignorant of the peace treaty.

There is an old cliché that says, "Ignorance is bliss." In fact, ignorance can be extremely dangerous and have tragic consequences, and, if that is generally true, it is particularly true of spiritual ignorance. Enormous evils have resulted because men and women have not understood the character of God, as He has revealed Himself in Scripture. Personal problems are often the direct result of ignorance of God's truth and God's will as it is found in God's Word. Sometimes Christians can fall into the trap of believing that an understanding of God and His Word is a nice thing to have, but it is really a spiritual luxury that does not have much to do with everyday life. In fact, to be ignorant of spiritual truth is profoundly dangerous. It not only robs us of many of God's blessings, it can result in serious damage both to us and through us to others.

James Packer, in his excellent book, *Knowing God*, writes:

> Knowing about God is crucially important for the living of our lives. As it would be cruel to an Amazonian tribesman to fly him to London, put him down without explanation in Trafalgar Square and leave him, as one who knew nothing of English or England, to fend for himself, so we are cruel to ourselves if we try to live in this world without knowing about the God whose world it is and who runs it. The world becomes a strange, mad, painful place, and life with it a disappointing and unpleasant business, for those who do not know God. Disregard the study of God and you sentence yourself to stumble and blunder through life blindfolded, as it were, with no sense of direction and no understanding of what surrounds you. This way you can waste your life and lose your soul.[1]

In Judges 11 and 12, we have a case history of the consequences of spiritual ignorance. What makes the study even more startling is that this ignorance is found in a man who had a great zeal for God. In fact, he took his own life in his hands for God. But zeal without biblical understanding becomes a fanaticism which destroys everything it touches. Jephthah was not alone in his ignorance, but the effects in his life were so tragic that they brand the lesson on our minds. Daniel said, "The people who know their God will display strength and take action" (Dan 11:32). In Jephthah's hand the verse becomes, "The people who are ignorant of God will display stupidity and wreak havoc."

Several years ago, a book was written, entitled *Terror in the Name of God*. The title is entirely appropriate to describe Jephthah's career. The first description of the man reads, "Now Jephthah was a valiant warrior"; he was also a man with a zeal for God. When his fighting skills and commitment to the Lord were harnessed by the will of God, Jephthah was God's man to break the bondage of the Ammonites. But when Jephthah's zeal outran his understanding, those same abilities became weapons of terror and destruction, aimed, not at the enemy, but at his own daughter and his own countrymen. This is not a pretty picture, but it is important that our revulsion against Jephthah's excesses does not blind us to the very important lessons we need to learn from Jephthah's failures.

IGNORANCE OF GOD'S PERSON—11:29-40

Now the Spirit of the LORD came upon Jephthah, so that he passed through Gilead and Manasseh, then he passed through Mizpah of Gilead, and from Mizpah of Gilead he went on to the sons of Ammon. And Jephthah made a vow to the LORD and said, "If Thou wilt indeed give the sons of Ammon into my hand, then it shall be that whatever comes out of the doors of my house to meet me when I return in peace from the sons of Ammon, it shall be the LORD'S, or I will offer it up as a burnt offering." So Jephthah crossed over to the sons of Ammon to fight against them; and the LORD gave them into his hand. And he struck them with a very great slaughter from Aroer to the entrance of Minnith, twenty cities, and as far as Abel-keramin. So the sons of Ammon were subdued before the sons of Israel. When Jephthah came to his house at Mizpah, behold, his daughter was coming out to meet him with tambourines and with dancing. Now she was his one and only child; besides her he had neither son nor daughter. And it came about when he saw her, that he tore his clothes and said, "Alas, my daugher! You have brought me very low, and you are among those who trouble me; for I have given my word to the LORD, and I cannot take it back." So she said to him, "My father, you have given your word to the LORD; do to me as you have said, since the LORD has avenged you of your enemies, the sons of Ammon." And she said to her father, "Let this thing be done for me; let me alone two months, that I may go to the mountains and weep because of my virginity, I and my companions." Then he said, "Go." So he sent her away for two months; and she left with her companions, and wept on the mountains because of her virginity. And it came about at the end of two months that she returned to her father, who did to her according to the vow which he had made; and she had no relations with a man. Thus it became a custom in Israel, that the daughters of

Israel went yearly to commemorate the daughter of Jephthah
the Gileadite four days in the year.

The earlier part of Judges 11 has told us how God led the
people of Israel to turn to Jephthah to be their military
leader against the Ammonites. Even though he was the
illegitimate son of a prostitute, a refugee from his own
family, he was the man God had prepared to deliver His
people after eighteen years of oppression. The first thing he
did was to enter into negotiations with the king of Ammon,
to try to solve the problem peacefully. That failed; so,
Jephthah prepared for war (v. 29). He gathered an army from
the people of Gilead, and, empowered by the Holy Spirit, he
marched out to war.

But before he went out to confront the Ammonites,
Jephthah tried to strike a bargain with God by putting
himself under a vow. "If Thou wilt indeed give the sons of
Ammon into my hand, then it shall be that whatever comes
out of the doors of my house to meet me when I return in
peace from the sons of Ammon, it shall be the LORD'S and
I will offer it up as a burnt offering."[2]

We need to understand exactly what Jephthah was
vowing to do. "God, if we do not win, we are going to be
enslaved forever. So, let us make a deal. If You help me win,
I am going to offer You, as a burnt offering, the first person
who comes out of my house to greet me when I return." We
may not appreciate his vow, but there can be no doubt that
Jephthah was vowing to make a human sacrifice. Three
observations clinch this. First, animals were not kept in-
doors. Second, it would be a mockery to vow to God whatever animal happened out the door. It was customary to
express praise and gratitude by offering a lamb or a bull,
and Jephthah was making an extraordinary vow. If he intended an animal sacrifice, he would have vowed his very
best animals, not just whatever wandered out the door.
Third, he intended a sacrifice, as the word translated "burnt
offering" indicates. Every time the word is used in the Old

Testament, it refers to a blood sacrifice, and that must be its meaning in Judges 13:16.

This was a hideous vow, which contradicted the clear teaching of God's Word. But before we consider why Jephthah made this vow, we need to understand the Old Testament teaching on vows. Basically, a vow was a promise to God to acknowledge publicly an answer to prayer, and Moses gave this instruction about vows, in Deuteronomy 23:21-23:

> When you make a vow to the LORD your God, you shall not delay to pay it, for it would be sin in you, and the LORD your God will surely require it of you. However, if you refrain from vowing, it would not be sin in you. You shall be careful to perform what goes out from your lips, just as you have voluntarily vowed to the LORD, your God, what you have promised.

A vow was a purely voluntary act, but once a vow was made, a man was committed before God. For that reason, God warned against making rash or thoughtless vows. If you are going to make a commitment to God, do it carefully and thoughtfully. As we read in Proverbs 20:25, "It is a snare for a man to say rashly, 'It is holy!' and after the vows to make inquiry," and, in Ecclesiastes 5:4-5, "When you make a vow to God, do not be late in paying it, for He takes no delight in fools. Pay what you vow! It is better that you should not vow than that you should vow and not pay."

That still leaves us with the question of why Jephthah would vow to offer a human sacrifice to God, when the Bible so clearly forbids such a thing (Lev. 18:21; 20:2-5; Deut. 12:31; 18:10). Many Bible scholars are convinced that Jephthah could never have done such a thing. But remember the times in which he lived. There was apostasy; there was ignorance of the Word of God; and there was the horrible example of other religions. Years later, even after the godly ministry of Samuel, Saul was ready to kill his son Jonathan, because of a foolish vow Saul had made.

The real lack in Jephthah's life was not a lack of sincerity. Jephthah's vow was the prayer of a sincere heart, zealous before God. Jephthah was totally sincere, but he was totally wrong. We do not need simply a sincere faith; we need a sincere and understanding faith. Jephthah's sincerity was destructive because he had a false view of God.

He had a false view of God because he believed that God had to be bargained with and bribed. He thought he could buy God's help, at the cost of a human life. He could have claimed God's promises to Israel, but instead he tried to bargain. Rather than resting in God's grace, he tried to wrestle the favor of a reluctant God, by paying a terrible price.

He had a false view of God because he believed that God delighted in what hurts. If it was really unpleasant, that was something that would please God. God was a sadistic God to Jephthah, not a God slow to anger and abounding in loyal love. He was not the God who says to His people, "I know the plans that I have for you, . . . plans for welfare and not for calamity to give you a future and a hope" (Jer. 29:11). Instead, Jephthah thought he had an unhappy God who made others unhappy.

He had a false view of God because he believed that God might abandon him halfway through the job. Verse 29 clearly states that the Holy Spirit empowered him to raise his army, but Jephthah did not trust God to complete what He had begun; so he bargained with God. He did not accept the fact that the One who had begun a good work could be trusted to keep on doing it.

Behind it all stands an ignorance of the Word of God. Jephthah had a zeal for God, but zeal without truth is dangerous. Dedication without understanding produces fanaticism. What a person believes about God is the most important fact about that individual, and one can only think properly about God when he thinks biblically about Him.

I have met many Christians who think their God is like Jephthah's false view of God. He is a stern and sadistic God, a legalistic God, who squeezes the joy out of life and delights in the unpleasant. He is a God who must be bargained with, and whose favor must be earned, whose presence cannot be counted on. But that is not the God of the Bible. Unless we know God in truth, we cannot live in truth.

THE FULFILLMENT OF THE VOW

God, in His grace and love for His people in their need, gave them victory. Jephthah's vow had nothing to do with God's blessing. God worked despite, not because of, Jephthah's vow.

But then, in the moment of victory, tragedy hit Jephthah. Dancing out to meet him, full of life and joy, came his daughter. She was his only child, and, at a time when a man's family was extremely important to him, that made her doubly precious to Jephthah. She was not only his daughter, she was his hope for the future. When he saw her dancing with joy, Jephthah was crushed.

Jephthah's daughter was a girl of extraordinary character. Her father may have been ignorant of God. She was not. When she heard for the first time of the vow her father had made, she immediately submitted to it. It was a vow made to God, and that vow was binding. But she requested two months postponement, and during that time she wept, not just that she was going to die, but that she was going to die childless—the supreme tragedy for a Hebrew woman. Her death would mark the end of Jephthah's line, a tragedy even greater than the loss of her life.

Then, in verse 39, we read simply, "And it came about at the end of two months that she returned to her father, who did to her according to the vow which he had made." There are many commentators who believe that Jephthah did not put his daughter to death, but that he committed her to a life of perpetual virginity and service at the tabernacle. I would like to believe that, but I cannot. The plain sense of the text is that Jephthah's daughter was offered up in sacrifice, and it is interesting to note that this is how the passage was always understood by the earlier Jewish and Christian scholars.

Horrible as Jephthah's action was, there was one positive feature that challenges us. Jephthah had made a vow to God, and he took that commitment seriously, despite an agonizing personal cost. It is not hard to criticize Jephthah. His action was grotesque and intolerable. But how often do we make pledges to God which we do not honor? Perhaps it is as we study Scripture, or as we hear God's Word ministered. We are moved, and we respond by dedicating ourselves again to the Lord. "Lord Jesus, I want to do this or that for You." But it ends there. Because it never becomes part of our lives, it becomes simply a cheap emotional sentiment. Before God, Jephthah is more honorable than that kind of person!

There is an even greater tragedy in Jephthah's story. He could not take back his vow. He was committed before God. But he could have carried it out biblically. You see, God had clearly spelled out the solution of Jephthah's problem in Leviticus 27. It tells how, when a person is committed to the Lord, that person's life is redeemed by the payment of a certain amount of money. If only Jephthah had known God's Word, if only someone had taught him God's Word, his daughter never would have died. In fact, one of the Jewish commentaries on Judges tells us that the reason they held the annual mourning for Jephthah's daughter was "In order that none should make his son or daughter a burnt offering, as Jephthah did, and did not consult Phineas the priest. Had he done so, he would have redeemed her with money."[3]

Do you see how devastating ignorance of the Word of God is? Jephthah's daughter died because he did not know the Word of God. Our ignorance may not have such tragic consequences, but there will be tragic consequences. Ignorance of God is the greatest ignorance of all.

Ignorance breeds ignorance. In the first verse of Judges

12, there is another form of ignorance, this time on the part of Gideon's old friends, the men of Ephraim.

IGNORANCE OF PERSONAL RESPONSIBILITY—12:1-4

Then the men of Ephraim were summoned, and they crossed to Zaphon and said to Jephthah, "Why did you cross over to fight against the sons of Ammon without calling us to go with you? We will burn your house down on you." And Jephthah said to them, "I and my people were at great strife with the sons of Ammon; when I called you, you did not deliver me from their hand. And when I saw that you would not deliver me, I took my life in my hands and crossed over against the sons of Ammon, and the LORD gave them into my hand. Why then have you come up to me this day, to fight against me?" Then Jephthah gathered all the men of Gilead and fought Ephraim; and the men of Gilead defeated Ephraim, because they said, "You are fugitives of Ephraim, O Gileadites, in the midst of Ephraim and in the midst of Manasseh."

If the results were not so serious, the story would be utterly absurd. For eighteen years the Ammonites had overrun the area of Gilead, and Ephraim had totally ignored the needs of their brothers there. They had not raised a spear in anger against Ammon. But now, when the battle was over, they crossed the Jordan, armed to the teeth for war, and challenged Jephthah. "Why did you cross over to fight against the sons of Ammon without calling us to go with you? We will burn your house down on you." They threatened to burn Jephthah alive because they had not been included in the battle.

It is hard to imagine a more obnoxious attitude. They had reacted to Gideon in a similar way in the middle of his battle with Midian. Ephraim was always brave after the battle. Obviously, the Ephraimites were an arrogant, critical, envious group. Although a small tribe, they were very sure of their own rights, but totally unwilling to accept their responsibilities. They were always ready to fight with their brothers, but never against the enemy.

This time they had made a serious mistake. Gideon had been willing, in the middle of a battle, to humor Ephraim to keep Israel united. But this battle was over, and Jephthah was not Gideon. At first he responded gently. He pointed out that he had, in fact, called Ephraim, and they had not come. Then, at the risk of his life, while Ephraim basked in safety, he had rushed into battle against Ammon, and the Lord had given him victory. The Ephraimites had nothing about which to complain.

The Ephraimites were not willing to listen to logic or truth. They began to sneer at Jephthah's men as renegades and refugees. They aggravated them and goaded them on, until, finally, Jephthah and his men could contain their anger no longer. They turned in fury on the men of Ephraim.

It is important that we realize the kind of ignorance the Ephraimites represent. It was an ignorance of their God-given responsibility. They were very happy gathering up the spoil, and they were very quick to defend their rights and their privileges, but they had no taste for battle. God had called them to join in the fight against the people on the land, but Ephraim was only willing to stand back and criticize until the battle was won.

I am afraid that there are far too many Christians who are Ephraimites when it comes to understanding their God-given responsibilities. They are more than willing to let other believers move out into the world, and to let other Christians confront the world with the gospel. Other people should get involved in teaching Sunday school or doing menial work or going to the mission field or engaging in Christian service. But these people reserve the right to criticize from the sidelines or even to condemn what these other Christians do. They are very critical of their brothers, but they are not involved in confronting the enemy.

I am reminded of the story of the man who came up to D. L. Moody and said, "Mr. Moody, I don't like the way you preach the gospel."

"You know," Mr. Moody said, "I'm always willing to learn. Tell me about the method you use."

"I guess I don't really have one," the man said.

"I'll tell you what," Moody said, "I like the way I do it better than the way you don't do it."

The Ephraimite attitude is destructive and divisive. The church of Jesus Christ does not need grandstand quarterbacks or armchair generals. It needs believers who are willing to take their God-given responsibility to serve God and other believers. It is contemptible to have the heart of an Ephraimite. Do not complain and criticize. Instead, lead by example, encouragement, and edification!

The final stage of the story brings us back to Jephthah. Once again we see the destructiveness of zeal without understanding.

IGNORANCE DUE TO LEGALISM—12:5-7

And the Gileadites captured the fords of the Jordan opposite Ephraim. And it happened when any of the fugitives of Ephraim said, "Let me cross over," the men of Gilead would say to him, "Are you an Ephraimite?" If he said, "No," then they would say to him, "Say now 'Shibboleth.'" But he said "Sibboleth," for he could not pronounce it correctly. Then they seized him and slew him at the fords of the Jordan. Thus there fell at that time 42,000 of Ephraim. And Jephthah judged Israel six years. Then Jephthah the Gileadite died and was buried in one of the cities of Gilead.

The battle with Ephraim was not Jephthah's fault. The Ephraimites richly deserved to be taught a lesson. But in the midst of that lesson, Jephthah once again showed his ignorance of God's will and God's way. Ephraim was beaten, and the Ephraimites began to stream back toward the Jordan, fleeing for their lives. But Jephthah and his men seized the crossings of the Jordan. Then they gave each refugee a simple test. You can often tell people by their speech. A Canadian says "eh!" It doesn't take long to recognize a native of Brooklyn or Texas. Apparently, the Ephraimites had a dialect which did not use "sh." So they pronounced the word *Shibboleth* "Sibboleth." Whenever a man came along who could not say Shibboleth, Jephthah's men put him to death, and, by the end of the battle, 42,000 Ephraimites were dead.

Do you see the problem? Jephthah treated fellow Israelites as if they were Ammonites. It is one thing to be provoked to battle, but it is quite another thing to stand at the fords of the Jordan and cold-bloodedly execute Ephraimites. Jephthah was a hardheaded legalist. He had experienced God's grace in his own life, but he did not practice it in his relations with others. He knew nothing of the tenderness and love and grace of God.

Jephthah is not alone, unfortunately. Many times Christians have treated their brothers as if they were enemies. Martin Luther led God's people into the truth of justification by faith, and the authority of God's Word, but he also turned in fury on some Anabaptists who wanted to practice God's Word. The Puritans fled England to find religious liberty in New England, and then they denied that same liberty to Roger Williams and others. Many other Christians have seized on their differences with other believers and treated them as if they were enemies of the gospel.

Legalism is a deadly thing, and, more than that, it is a disaster. Jephthah's view of God was that He was stern and joyless, an unhappy Judge who robbed life of joy. How sad it is to see Christians bound up in the ignorance of legalism. There is a great old hymn that is based on the 100th psalm which originally went like this:

All people that on earth do dwell,
Sing to the Lord with cheerful voice,
Him serve with mirth, His praise foretell,
Come ye before Him and rejoice.

Now that is beautifully biblical and faithful to what the psalmist wrote. But someone viewed it as flippant, and as a result changed it to "Him serve with fear." Of course, reverence has its place in worship; but so does mirth, and how sad it is that someone with a long-faced God found it necessary to change the hymn.

If there is one great message from this sad story of Jephthah, it is the danger of spiritual ignorance. To be ignorant of God and of God's Word is the pathway to spiritual disaster.

The last time Harry Ironside lectured at Dallas Theological Seminary, he was almost blind. His wife would read the text of Isaiah, and he would expound it. Now Dr. Ironside had been a lifelong student of God's Word and one of the great Bible teachers of his day. He was a great reader of all kinds of books, but, during that series of lectures, he held up his Bible and said, "Men, I wish I had read other books less and this Book more!"

There is no substitute for the knowledge of God that comes through the knowledge of His Word. It is God's cure for spiritual ignorance.

SIXTEEN

Separation: What's It All About?

At first, I did not know what to make of the experience. We were driving along a busy highway when, suddenly, we had to pull out to pass a black, horse-drawn buggy, driven by a man dressed entirely in black. My host told me that the man was not protesting against the high cost of gasoline, but he was a member of a group who had separated themselves from a twentieth-century life-style. In the name of religion, they had turned their backs on automobiles, electricity, and bright colors. The first sign of creeping worldliness was noted if a person put rubber wheels on his buggy. That might entice him on to a steel-wheeled tractor, which might be followed by one with the comforts of rubber wheels. A sign of deep-seated worldliness would be to own a car, a black one with all the chrome painted black.

Here was a group of people who lived in the twentieth century but were certainly not a part of it. Unfortunately, such groups demonstrate great sincerity in following their beliefs, but all too often they know nothing of a deep personal faith in Jesus Christ. Their Christianity has become a cultural way of life. However, although I may consider some of their practices bizarre, I could not help but ask myself as I looked at that man in his buggy: What does it mean to be separated from the world? In what way is a Christian to be in the world but not of it?

No one who reads God's Word can fail to notice that it speaks in direct and strong language about Christians' relationships to the world. For example, in 1 John 2:15, we read, "Do not love the world, nor the things in the world. If anyone loves the world, the love of the Father is not in him." James goes one step further. "Don't you know that friendship with the world is hostility toward God? Therefore whoever wishes to be a friend of the world constitutes himself an enemy of God" (James 4:4). Clearly the world can be very dangerous to the believer and his relationship to God.

But that is not all the Bible says. The Lord Jesus calls us to live in the world to His glory. We are, He says, the salt of the earth and the light of the world. Salt is only valuable when it leaves the shaker and permeates. Light is only helpful when it shines in the darkness. We have been sent into all the world to make disciples of all nations, and Paul clearly says, in 1 Corinthians 5:10, that this means associating with immoral, sinful people.

How do we put those facts together—in the world but separated from it; involved in the world but not loving it or being conformed to it; using the world but not making friends of it?

It has been hard for Christians to resolve those commands. Many have emphasized the side of separation, and usually their logic has taken three steps. They begin by calling us to be *separated from sin*. That much is obvious. The next step is to call Christians to *abstain from specific practices*, practices the Bible does not specifically condemn, but which some Christians have found dangerous. Then they take the final step of calling Christians to be *separated from sinners*. A wise Christian, they say, will have as little as possible to do with non-Christians; so a "separated" Christian often ends up being an isolated Christian, living in a gospel ghetto, carefully walled off from the world.

Other Christians have wanted nothing to do with that life-style. They realize *isolationism* is a distortion of biblical truth. They want to take seriously our mandate to go into the world for the Lord Jesus. Unfortunately, many younger Christians have overreacted to a position of *assimilation*.

They have been so concerned about associating with non-Christians that many have ended up assimilating the values and life-styles of unbelievers. Too often, associating with sinners has meant associating with sin; so they have lost their Christian distinctiveness.

The question remains. What is biblical separation? The answer is not to be found in either of the extremes. Isolation, external separation, is no more biblical than assimilation. We are not to be chameleons, conforming to our environment, but neither are we to be hermits, sealed off from the world of men. We can only resolve the question by setting aside our preconceived ideas and listening carefully to the Word of God.

We can learn a great deal about biblical separation by carefully investigating the life of Samson. Unfortunately, not all the lessons of his life are positive ones. Samson was largely a failure; yet the failures of his life are very instructional. He was not an especially attractive figure, but he was a significant one, and more scriptural space is given to his life than that of any other judge. Almost everything about the man was unique; that was especially true of his birth and calling by God.

THE TIMES FOR THE MAN—13:1

Now the sons of Israel again did evil in the sight of the LORD, so that the LORD gave them into the hands of the Philistines forty years.

Once again we find the same dreary pattern repeated. There are times in Judges where we get the feeling that the needle is stuck. Only the names are changed to reveal the guilty. So, in Judges 13, we have the seventh cycle of Israel's downward spiral into anarchy and apostasy. However, verse 1 is not a simple repetition. It announces two facts that are essential to a proper understanding of the life and ministry of Samson.

THE PHILISTINES

During Samson's life, the Philistines appeared as Israel's major enemy. They had appeared briefly during the ministry of Shamgar (3:31), but it was during Samson's time that they became public enemy number one. The Philistines were a people who had been forced out of their homeland in the area of Greece and the Aegean Sea. They had set out by sea to look for a new home, and, around 1200 B.C., a main force of "Sea People" had attacked Egypt. They were defeated; so they moved up the coast to the southern coastal plain of Palestine where some earlier refugees had settled, and, by Samson's time, they had established themselves in five main cities—Gaza, Ashdod, Ashkelon, Ekron, and Gath.

What makes the Philistines especially important is the method they used. They had a great military strength because they had learned how to smelt iron. With their iron weapons, they could have overrun Israel by direct attack, as the other nations had. They did not. Rather than marching as an obvious enemy, the two main weapons they used were trade and intermarriage. If the Israelites wanted a plow or an axe, they had to go to the Philistines to get one (see 1 Sam. 13:19-21). If they wanted to marry their sons or daughters, the Philistines had no objection. In both those ways, the Philistines were gaining a stranglehold on the Israelites, slowly choking them to death by compromise and assimilation. Israel was not being enslaved by military dominance but by spiritual and cultural seduction.

THE APATHY OF ISRAEL

That leads us to the second thing we need to see in verse 1. Actually, it is hard to see because it is something which is not there. Sometimes silence is eloquent, and that is true here. At every point in the book of Judges, when the people turned from God and experienced God's judgment of political bondage, they reached a point where, as a nation, they repented and cried out to God for a deliverer, a judge to liberate them.

That never happened against the Philistines. Not once did the people realize their danger and cry out to God to deliver them. Things were going too well for that. It was a time of affluence. Because there was no national repentance, there was no national deliverer. The people were slowly but surely losing their identity, but they were so ignorant of what was going on that when God did send Samson, they were ready to hand him over to death rather than to upset the Philistines.

Those two facts—Philistine assimilation and Hebrew apathy—were the keys to God's purposes through Samson. Israel was facing a unique situation. They had not repented, so the Lord did not send a national liberator. Samson was an individualist, fighting personal battles. The other major judges—Othniel, Ehud, Deborah, Gideon, and Jephthah—led a repentant people against the enemy. Samson, by contrast, fought alone, and his battles were very personal affairs. Not once was he joined in battle by so much as one man. Therefore, when we study his life and see his enormous failures, we need to balance our disgust with the recognition that Samson singlehandedly exposed the dangers of the Philistines and held back their control of Israel. He was the one man of his day who realized that a person or nation could not compromise and remain free to serve God.

The pressures which Samson faced make him a contemporary figure. Twentieth-century Christians face the danger of assimilation, of being slowly and imperceptibly squeezed into the mold of the world around us. Therefore, what God did with and through Samson has a special meaning for our times.

GOD'S MAN FOR THE TIMES—
THE UNIQUENESS OF SAMSON—13:2-25

And there was a certain man of Zorah, of the family of the Danites, whose name was Manoah; and his wife was barren and had borne no children. Then the angel of the LORD appeared to the woman, and said to her, "Behold now, you are barren and have borne no children, but you shall conceive and give birth to a son. Now therefore, be careful not to drink wine or strong drink, nor eat any unclean thing. For behold, you shall conceive and give birth to a son, and no razor shall come upon his head, for the boy shall be a Nazirite to God from the womb; and he shall begin to deliver Israel from the hands of the Philistines." Then the woman came and told her husband, saying, "A man of God came to me and his appearance was like the appearance of the angel of God, very awesome. And I did not ask him where he came from, nor did he tell me his name. But he said to me, 'Behold, you shall conceive and give birth to a son, and now you shall not drink wine or strong drink nor eat any unclean thing, for the boy shall be a Nazirite to God from the womb to the day of his death.'" Then Manoah entreated the LORD and said, "O LORD, please let the man of God whom Thou hast sent come to us again that he may teach us what to do for the boy who is to be born." And God listened to the voice of Manoah; and the angel of God came again to the woman as she was sitting in the field, but Manoah her husband was not with her. So the woman ran quickly and told her husband, "Behold, the man who came the other day has appeared to me." Then Manoah arose and followed his wife, and when he came to the man he said to him, "Are you the man who spoke to the woman?" And he said, "I am." And Manoah said, "Now when your words come to pass, what shall be the boy's mode of life and his vocation?" So the angel of the LORD said to Manoah, "Let the woman pay attention to all that I said. She should not eat anything that comes from the vine nor drink wine or strong drink, nor eat any unclean thing; let her observe all that I commanded." Then Manoah said to the angel of the LORD, "Please let us detain you so that we may prepare a kid for you." And the angel of the LORD said to Manoah, "Though you detain me, I will not eat your food, but if you prepare a burnt offering, then offer it to the LORD." For Manoah did not know that he was the angel of the LORD. And Manoah said to the angel of the LORD, "What is your name, so that when your words come to pass, we may honor you?" But the angel of the LORD said to him, "Why do you ask my name, seeing it is wonderful?" So Manoah took the kid with the grain offering and offered it on the rock to the LORD, and He performed wonders while Manoah and his wife looked on. For it came about when the flame went up from the altar toward heaven, that the angel of the LORD ascended in the flame of the altar. When Manoah and his wife saw this, they fell on their faces to the ground. Now the angel of the LORD appeared no more to Manoah or his wife. Then Manoah knew that he was the angel of the LORD. So Manoah said to his wife, "We shall surely die, for we have seen God." But his wife said to him, "If the LORD had desired to kill us, He would not have accepted a burnt offering and a grain offering from our hands, nor would He have showed us all these things, nor would He have let us hear things like this at this time." Then the woman gave birth to a son and named him Samson; and the child grew up and the LORD blessed him. And the Spirit of the LORD began to stir him in Mahaneh-dan, between Zorah and Eshtaol.

As we have already noticed, Samson was a unique man for a unique time, and that uniqueness is clearly indicated in this chapter which introduces him to us. Three particular things stand out.

HIS UNIQUE BIRTH

In verse 2, we meet Samson's parents. The majority of the tribe of Dan had moved north to Laish by this time (cf. Judg. 18), but Manoah was one of the Danites who had remained in their God-given area. He lived in Zorah, a border city wedged between Israel and the Philistines. Samson's parents were a genuinely godly couple, with a heart for God and a hunger to obey His Word. In a time of apostasy, those characteristics must have made them very unusual. But they were also a couple with a heartbreak. They had no children, and they would never have children. Manoah's wife was barren, and, for a Hebrew woman, that was a shattering and shameful condition.

Then God, in His grace, reached into this couple's lives. Suddenly, the angel of the Lord Himself appeared to Manoah's wife and announced to her, "Behold now, you are barren and have borne no children, but you shall conceive and give birth to a son" (v. 3). She drank in every word, and immediately rushed off to tell her husband. Actually, she was not even sure to whom she had been speaking. She called him a man of God, a prophet, and said he looked like an angel, but she did not know His name or His origin. The striking thing is that Manoah did not pass this off as a hysterical emotional experience of his wife. He believed her and prayed for an instant replay.

That was exactly what happened. The angel of the Lord appeared again, but He did not add a single thing to what He had said before. He did not return to give added information about the child, but added information about Himself. Obviously, at this point God wanted both of them to know that something very special was taking place. God was supernaturally going to intervene in the body of a barren woman and bring forth a special child. Furthermore, He sent the news special delivery by an angel. Those two facts alone are enough to cause us to pay special attention to the birth of Samson.

But the angel was not just an angel. He was called "the angel of the LORD," and we need to recall the distinction between *an* angel and "the angel of the LORD." An angel is a created being, a heavenly messenger, sent by God on a particular mission. The Angel of the Lord is none other than God Himself, appearing to men to communicate His will. As Gideon's experience suggested, the Angel of the Lord is the Lord Jesus Christ, taking a temporary human form.

The Angel did three things to indicate to Manoah who He was. First, in verse 18, He declared His name, "Why do you ask my name, seeing it is wonderful?" This goes beyond saying that it is a wonderful name. To the Hebrews, a person's name indicated his character, and the Angel used the same name prophetically given to the Savior in Isaiah

9:6, "Wonderful Counsellor." Not only is His name "Wonderful," but He is wonderful. The Lord Jesus then worked wonders, while Manoah and his wife looked on. He did what His name suggested. Finally, to confirm His identity, the Lord Jesus mysteriously disappeared in the flame of the fire. These things had an immediate effect on the couple. Manoah realized that he had seen the Angel of the Lord and then trembled with fear, "For we have seen God" (v. 22).

All of this was meant to emphasize that Samson was going to be a most unusual child. Not only was he born by God's miraculous intervention, but his birth was announced by the Lord God Himself. In all of Scripture, there is only one other child of whom that is true, and that is Isaac. John the Baptist was born of a barren mother, but his birth was announced by Gabriel, who is only an angel, not the Angel of the Lord. Obviously, Samson occupied a very special place in God's purposes since He sent His own Son to announce his birth.

HIS UNIQUE LIFE-STYLE

Not only was Samson's birth announced in a unique way, but the content of his birth announcement was unusual. In verse 5, we read, "Behold, you shall conceive and give birth to a son, and no razor shall come upon his head, for the boy shall be a Nazirite to God from the womb." To understand the Angel's command, it is necessary to understand what it meant to be a Nazirite. The word *Nazir* in Hebrew means "to set apart" or "to separate," and so a Nazirite was a person who had dedicated or separated himself to God.

Numbers 6 is the basic passage on the Nazirite vow, and it indicates four things about the vow.

1. *It was voluntary.* A Nazirite vow was an act of personal, spontaneous commitment to the Lord, motivated by love and faith.

2. *It was purposeful.* As the last phrase of verse 2 puts it, a Nazirite dedicated himself to the Lord. It is a phrase that is repeated over and over again—verse 5, "He separated

himself to the LORD"; verse 6, "separation to the LORD"; verse 7, "his separation to God"; verse 8, "all the days of his separation he is holy to the LORD." The purpose of the vow was for a man to cut himself off from other things, so that he could devote himself especially to the Lord.

3. *The Nazirite vow was symbolic.* A person was to do three things as part of his vow:

■ He was to abstain from the fruit of the vine. This was not because there was anything sinful about wine or grapes or raisins. But all those things were signs of luxurious living; so, during the time of the vow, he was to live a simple life.

■ He was not to cut his hair. Now that was obviously the public sign of his vow. It was certainly not wrong to get a haircut. In fact, Paul tells us in 1 Corinthians 11 that the opposite is true, but a Nazirite's uncut hair became a public sign of his vow to God.

■ He was to avoid contact with a dead person. This was a sign of the preeminence of God in his life. Contact with death made a man unfit for the tabernacle, and so a man vowed to stay in constant fellowship with God.

4. *It was temporary.* A Nazirite vow was not a lifelong condition, but one which lasted for a set period of time.

For Samson, to be a Nazirite, meant that he was bound by all of these obligations. But he was to be a Nazirite with a difference. All his life, he was to live under the vow. There was nothing temporary about it. In fact, his mother was to live under the vow while he was still in her womb. He was not a Nazirite by a personal commitment, but by a divine command. His separation was not voluntary, but commanded by God.

Obviously, Samson was going to be a striking figure, because nothing represented his position more than the hair on his head. Men could not see whether he drank wine or was around the dead, but they could see his long, braided hair and know that this man was set apart in a special way to God. In his Nazirite life-style, as well as in his birth, Samson was unique.

HIS UNIQUE MINISTRY

The third distinctive of Samson was his God-given role. The Angel announced, "He shall begin to deliver Israel from the hands of the Philistines" (v. 5). The key word in that statement is the word "begin." Samson's lifework was not going to be completed. Because Israel had not repented, the Lord was not yet ready to break the yoke of the Philistines. But neither would He abandon Israel. In grace, He raised up Samson to begin the process of liberation. In that, he was unique. The other judges had known military victory, Samson would not. He would prevent complete defeat, but he would accomplish only partial victory.

Coupled with this unique ministry was a unique endowment of God's Holy Spirit in his life. Verse 25 indicates how "the Spirit of the LORD began to stir him" as a young man. The distinctive effect of the Spirit's work was Samson's legendary physical strength. Once again this was related to God's unique purpose for his life. The other judges were great military leaders, but Samson was called by God to fight alone, unaided by any human companions. Therefore, God the Spirit gave him great personal strength to fight great personal battles.

GOD'S PURPOSE IN SAMSON

We need to remember that none of this happened by accident. God specifically and sovereignly raised up Samson for a definite purpose. Samson was unique because God made him unique. God intended Samson to be a lesson, carved in flesh, to confront His people with some great truths about separation.

1. *Separation is a positive dedication to the Lord Jesus.* The great danger posed by the Philistines was assimilation, and in contrast to that, Samson was a living embodiment of separation, a lifelong Nazirite under the vow of God. True, he was a man separated from certain things, but most of all, he was a man separated unto the Lord.

It is right there that the tragedy of Samson lies, because

Samson's separation turned out to be purely negative. He vowed not to take wine, not to cut his hair, and not to go near the dead. He knew the code, but he did not understand the concept. The point of the Nazirite vow was not separation from, it was *separation unto.* If it was not in the code, Samson went ahead and did it, but he lacked a warm-hearted love for God. By his position, Samson was dedicated to the will of God. But in his heart, he was not dedicated to the God whose will it was. His separation was formal and legalistic.

Some Christians understand separation the way Samson did. They live by a strict code. If you were to ask them, "Are you a separated Christian?" they would say, "Of course I am. I don't do this; I don't do that; I don't go there, and I don't own that; and, besides, I don't hang around with the people who do." But negative separation is not biblical separation. If spirituality is determined by what a person cannot do, then quadriplegia is close to godliness. Paralysis is not spirituality.

God does not call us to isolationism. Nor does He call us to a life-negating, joyless asceticism. Separation is, above all else, a positive, joy-filled relationship with Jesus Christ. A truly separated Christian is a believer whose heart and life are set apart to God, and who lives life for Him.

2. *Strength comes from separation.* All around Samson were hundreds of thousands of Hebrews, but not one of them lifted a finger against the Philistines. They had been assimilated, compromised, and integrated. It was the separated Samson who had strength to fight, and when he lost the last symbol of his separation, he lost his strength.

If God does not call us to isolation from the world, it is equally true that He does not call us to become like the world. It is not an easy thing to live in the world and not to become like it, but that is exactly what God calls us to do. Assimilation may sound easier; it may even seem to be necessary to evangelize. But strength comes from separation.

3. *Separation is always accompanied by enablement.*

God not only called Samson to live a separated life; He also equipped him to live that kind of life. God had given him the Holy Spirit to enable him to live his life for God.

Our relationship to the Holy Spirit is not the same as Samson's. His ministry in our lives is much richer, fuller, and deeper than anything Samson knew. God does not throw us into the middle of the Philistines and say, "Do the best you can, but do not be assimilated." He gives us His Spirit to enable us to live distinctively for Him in the world.

4. *The pattern for Christian separation is the Lord Jesus.* We can learn important lessons about separation from Samson's life: Unfortunately, they are usually insights gleaned from his failures. So then, if separation is not isolation from the world, if it is not assimilation to the world, what is it? The best answer is found in the Lord's words, in John 17: 15-17, as He prays to the Father about us:

> I do not ask Thee to take them out of the world, but to keep them from the evil one. They are not of the world, even as I am not of the world. Sanctify [separate] them in the truth; Thy word is truth.

The basis of the Lord's prayer is a very simple fact. To be separated from the world is to be related to the world as Jesus Christ was. We do not leave the world, we live in the world for Him. The Lord Jesus was not separated from sinners geographically. He spent time with them and ministered to them. What is more, in a way that infuriated the Pharisees, He deliberately sought out sinful people. At the same time, He was, on occasion, separated from the activities of sinners. He did not and could not do all that they did. And He was always separated from the world in His character. He never compromised or sinned or accepted men's values. He was separated because he was *distinct*.

John 17:17 tells the story. God sets us apart in the truth. His means of doing that is the Word of God. A separated Christian is a Bible-centered, Christ-controlled Christian, in whom God is reproducing His character by the Holy Spirit.

SEVENTEEN

Squandered Resources

An old woman, known to all her neighbors as "Garbage Mary," lived in a small town in Florida. Every day she would be seen dressed in her rags, walking the streets, scavenging through garbage cans for food, which she hoarded in her car or in her tiny two-room apartment. She was a recluse with no friends, and, as she scrounged cigarettes and ice cubes from anyone who was available, it was logical to believe that she was an old woman who was rapidly losing her mind and living on the verge of destitution.

Finally, Garbage Mary was picked up by police and confined in a psychiatric institution. But, when some court officials went to her apartment to collect a few of her personal effects, they were amazed to discover that there was money everywhere. Scattered through her apartment and her car were bank books, stock securities, oil-drilling rights, real-estate documents, and cash, which indicated that Garbage Mary was worth more than a million dollars. These documents also indicated that she was not an old woman, but a forty-eight-year-old college graduate, who had inherited a great deal of money when her father died in 1974.

Further investigation revealed that she had experienced two unhappy marriages, and her brother felt the resulting trauma may have caused her mental problems. Her psychiatrist conjectured that, living alone, she had fallen into a mental rut because she had nothing to excite her. Whatever the reason, the tragedy remains. Here was a woman, abounding in the physical resources she needed to meet her physical needs, foraging through garbage and living in rags, while her resources went unused and neglected. While her money collected interest, she collected garbage!

The tragedy of Garbage Mary is neglected resources. There are others who live as derelicts because they have squandered their resources. Money has gone through their hands like water, and, because they could not control their appetites and impulses, they feed their bodies from garbage cans, when once they had lived in mansions.

Samson was a kind of spiritual "Garbage Mary." He did not end his life as a hopeless derelict. He was the leader of his countrymen, a famous hero. But Samson squandered and ignored the resources God had given him. He was a man of great potential and even greater tragedy, because his life was a story of waste. And in that there is a lesson for us. We who are in Christ have enormous resources, far beyond anything that Samson knew. In the Lord Jesus, we have been given all things that relate to life and godliness. But we can dissipate those resources and live far below them, if we do not learn the lesson that Samson never learned—the lesson of self-discipline and wholehearted commitment to the Lord Jesus.

Note the events in Judges 14:1-20:

Then Samson went down to Timnah and saw a woman in Timnah, one of the daughters of the Philistines. So he came back and told his father and mother, "I saw a woman in Timnah, one of the daughters of the Philistines; now therefore, get her for me as a wife." Then his father and his mother said to him, "Is there no woman among the daughters of your relatives, or among all our people, that you go to take a wife from the uncircumcised Philistines?" But Samson said to his father, "Get her for me, for she looks good to me." However, his father and mother did not know that it was of the LORD, for He was seeking an occasion against the Philistines. Now at that time the Philistines were ruling over Israel. Then Samson went down to Timnah with his father and mother,

and came as far as the vineyards of Timnah; and behold, a
young lion came roaring toward him. And the spirit of the
LORD came upon him mightily, so that he tore him as one
tears a kid though he had nothing in his hand; but he did
not tell his father or mother what he had done. So he went
down and talked to the woman; and she looked good to
Samson. When he returned later to take her, he turned
aside to look at the carcass of the lion; and behold, a swarm
of bees and honey were in the body of the lion. So he scraped
the honey into his hands and went on, eating as he went.
When he came to his father and mother, he gave some to
them and they ate it; but he did not tell them that he had
scraped the honey out of the body of the lion. Then his
father went down to the woman; and Samson made a feast
there, for the young men customarily did this. And it came
about when they saw him that they brought thirty companions to be with him. Then Samson said to them, "Let
me now propound a riddle to you; if you will indeed tell it to
me within the seven days of the feast, and find it out, then
I will give you thirty linen wraps and thirty changes of
clothes. But if you are unable to tell me, then you shall
give me thirty linen wraps and thirty changes of clothes."
And they said to him, "Propound your riddle, that we may
hear it." So he said to them, "Out of the eater came something to eat, and out of the strong came something sweet."
But they could not tell the riddle in three days. Then it
came about on the fourth day that they said to Samson's
wife, "Entice your husband, that he may tell us the riddle,
lest we burn you and your father's house with fire. Have you
invited us to impoverish us? Is this not so?" And Samson's
wife wept before him and said, "You only hate me, and you
do not love me; you have propounded a riddle to the sons of
my people, and have not told it to me." And he said to her,
"Behold, I have not told it to my father or mother; so should I
tell you?" However she wept before him seven days while
their feast lasted. And it came about on the seventh day that
he told her because she pressed him so hard. She then told
the riddle to the sons of her people. So the men of the city
said to him on the seventh day before the sun went down,
"What is sweeter than honey? And what is stronger than a

lion?" And he said to them, "If you had not plowed with my heifer, you would not have found out my riddle." Then the Spirit of the LORD came upon him mightily, and he went down to Ashkelon and killed thirty of them and took their spoil, and gave the changes of clothes to those who told the riddle. And his anger burned, and he went up to his father's house. But Samson's wife was given to his companion who had been his friend.

There is no way of proving it, but Samson may well have been the strongest man who ever lived. To say the least, he would have made Charles Atlas feel like a 90-pound weakling. Yet, for all his strength, Samson was a weak man, because he never learned to control himself. Proverbs 16:32 could have been spoken directly to Samson: "He who rules his spirit [is better] than he who captures a city." Although he was fully capable of singlehandedly capturing a city, Samson did not discipline and rule his own desires and lusts. As a result, for all his strength, he was a weak man.

In Judges 13, we had a description of the great events that accompanied the birth of Samson and his early life. Here, in Judges 14, we have the first record of Samson's life as a man, and, in this very first episode, we have the three themes which will run all through his story—his enormous potential under God, his fatal flaw which dissipates that potential, and the providences of God in his life.

SAMSON'S GREAT POTENTIAL

Almost in passing, the Holy Spirit indicates to us the exact situation of Israel at this point of history. "Now at that time the Philistines were ruling over Israel" (v. 4). It was a domination which would continue and increase until the battle of Aphek (1 Sam. 4), when the Ark of the Covenant was captured, and Israelite pride shattered. But not only was Israel controlled, it was compromised. Intermarriage with the Philistines and cultural integration were increasingly evident, and, without a struggle, Israel was being assimilated.

At the same time, the priests were giving no spiritual leadership. The priesthood was under the control of Eli's two sons, Hophni and Phinehas. They were utterly godless and corrupt men, who stole the offerings and apparently practiced a form of prostitution in the tabernacle, a typically Canaanite perversion (1 Sam. 2:12-25). It was a time of great spiritual darkness, and none were in greater darkness than the two leading priests. The verdict of Scripture is, "Word from the LORD was rare in those days" (1 Sam. 3:1).

God's man for the time was Samson, a man who, under God, had a greater potential than almost any other man in the Old Testament. God had built some great resources into his life. There were his godly parents. Manoah and his wife knew God in a personal way, and they were committed to obeying Him at a time when that meant being part of a very small minority. Josephus recounts the Jewish tradition about Samson's parents:

> There was one Manoah, a person of such great virtue that he had few men his equals, and without dispute, the principal person of his country. He had a wife celebrated for her beauty and excelling her contemporaries.

Since those statements are traditional and not biblical, we cannot be certain of each one. But, undeniably, Samson knew a godly home life.

As well, he was a man born miraculously, by the direct intervention of God. That fact would give him great security, as he set out on his God-appointed mission. Furthermore, he was a man with a unique life-style, a lifelong Nazirite, set apart conspicuously to God. Finally, he was a man blessed with a special ministry of the Holy Spirit. God had given His Spirit to Samson in an unparalleled way; so that whenever Samson stood in need of physical strength, it was unreservedly supplied to him.

That unique divine enablement is graphically revealed in two episodes in Judges 14. The first is found in the famous story of Samson and the lion, recorded in verses 5-9.

As Samson made his way to Timnah to see the Philistine girl to whom he had been attracted, he left his parents for a time. Suddenly, while he was alone, he was attacked by a full-grown young lion, in the maturity of its strength. Immediately, Samson knew the power of God in his life, and he tore the lion in pieces with his bare hands, as if it were only a baby goat.

The second incident is recorded in verse 19. Whatever our concerns about the morality of Samson's act, we cannot overlook the display of enormous physical power which enabled him to attack and kill thirty men singlehandedly. It is a vivid illustration of the way in which God had fully equipped him for the task He had assigned him. In terms of available resources, Samson lacked nothing.

It cannot be stressed often enough that the believer in the Lord Jesus is in exactly the same position. God has given us the resources of His own person, for it is God the Holy Spirit who lives within us to meet the deepest needs of our lives. Paul expressed the wealth of a believer's position when he wrote, "By His doing you are in Christ Jesus, who became to us wisdom from God, even righteousness and sanctification, and redemption" (1 Cor. 1:30). "In Him dwells all the fulness of the divine nature in bodily form, and you are filled full in Him" (Col. 2:9-10).

The great blessing of justification is that a believer has been eternally united to the Lord Jesus. He is "in Christ" by the action of God the Father and God the Holy Spirit. Suppose I take a piece of paper and place it in my Bible. To see that paper, I must first look at my Bible. To deal with it, I must first touch my Bible. In scriptural terms, that paper is "in Bible." So it is with my position in the Lord Jesus. The Father never sees me without first seeing the Son He loves. He never deals with me without first dealing with the Lord Jesus. My life has been hidden with Christ in God (Col. 3:3), and God the Father always deals with me on the basis of my relation to the Lord Jesus.

There is one great weakness with the illustration. That

piece of paper can fall out of my Bible. It can be separated from it. I cannot fall out of Christ. I am permanently and organically a part of Christ, so intimately one with Him that He would be incomplete without me. I am in Him forever by His grace.

It is wonderful that I am in Christ, but God's Word goes further to tell me that He is in me, and He is in me to be my Resource for life. The little chorus sings it well, "Jesus Christ is made to me all I need, all I need." That was Paul's emphasis. We are in Christ. He has become wisdom to us from God. Whatever we need, He is. We have been "filled full in Him" (Col. 2:9-10).

Samson had a constant resource of physical strength by God's Holy Spirit. We have something far more than that—we have God's Spirit indwelling us constantly to make available God's resurrection power in every area of our lives. As Peter puts it, "His divine power has granted to us everything pertaining to life and godliness" (2 Pet. 1:3). If only we realized and claimed a small fragment of our riches in Christ!

But with all his resources and potential, Samson had a great weakness which led him to live a Garbage-Mary kind of life. Samson could have accomplished so much for the Lord, but he did not, and the reason for his failure is very obvious in Judges 14.

SAMSON'S FATAL FLAW

One day Samson went down to a Philistine town not far from his home in Zorah. There he saw a beautiful Philistine woman, and it was lust at first sight. Now, in that society, you did not try to get a date or to arrange a meeting or to follow her home. You turned the whole project over to your parents. So Samson headed home and broke the news to his parents. "Well, mom and dad, I have seen the girl of my dreams. She looks terrific. That is the girl I want to marry, so will you get her for me, make all the arrangements?"

"Oh, I am glad you have found the girl the Lord has for you, son. Who is she?"

"She is a Philistine girl from Timnah."

And with that statement, Samson's parents' world fell apart. His parents knew all about his miraculous birth and God's call for his life, and for years they had been praying for him, that God would use their son to deliver Israel. Now their son, whom God had called to live a life of separation, wanted to marry one of the enemy. That was not only a betrayal of his calling, it was direct disobedience to the Word of God, because God had told His people not to intermarry with the pagan people who lived in the land (Deut. 7:3-4).

Immediately, Manoah tried to talk some sense into his son, "Is there not a single Hebrew girl you could marry? Do you really have to marry a Philistine girl? Those people are uncircumcised. They are outside of God's covenant. Does God's program not mean anything to you? Oh, Samson, you cannot marry her."

And Samson replied, in a single sentence that tells an immense amount about the character of the man. "Get her for me, for she looks good to me." As nothing else could, that simple sentence epitomizes the kind of man Samson was.

The first thing it tells us is that he was a man who rejected authority. There were two reasons why Samson ought not to have married that woman. As we have already seen, intermarriage with pagans was directly contrary to God's Word. It was also against the clear wishes of his godly parents. Samson refused to submit to parental authority. The principle of Samson's life was very clear: If I want to do it, I am going to do it. To get the clear implications of what Samson is saying, let me translate the Hebrew very literally: "Take her for me, for she is right, pleasing in my 'eyes.' "

In the book of Judges, God gives us twice over His divine diagnosis for the spiritual decadence and moral pollution in the time of the Judges. In 17:6 and 21:25, we read that diagnosis: "In those days there was no king in Israel; everyone did what was right [or pleasing] in his own eyes." Exactly those same words are used by Samson to describe himself. He was a self-confessed spiritual anarchist, a man who had adopted the social values of his pagan contemporaries.

Somehow that makes Samson a very modern man, because if there is a phrase which describes twentieth-century Western society, it is, "Everyone is doing what is right in his own eyes." "If it feels good, do it." "Let it all hang out." It does not take a genius to recognize that we live in a period of moral, spiritual, and ethical anarchy. But what is especially sad is when believers adopt that world view as their own. There are many excuses or sophisticated arguments that we may try to use, but, ultimately, it all comes down to whether we are going to live by God's authority or by the authority of what is right in our own eyes. The great battleground of our time is the battleground of authority.

Samson's response to his father also tells us that he was a man who not only rebelled against external authority, but he also refused to practice self-discipline. His obedience to God was legalistic and incomplete. "Get her for me, for she looks good to me." He kept his Nazirite vow, at least in part, but he missed the moral and ethical implications of that vow. If the vow did not explicity forbid something, Samson indulged himself freely. It was meaningless to keep his hair cut while he allowed his lust to flow unfettered. It is obvious that Samson focused on the code of separation, not the concept of holiness. As Milton points out in *Samson Agonistes:*

> What boots it at one gate to make defense
> And at another to let in the foe?

Samson was a man controlled by his passions. He had never even met this girl, but she attracted him sexually and he wanted her. The sad part about Samson's life is there were things that he was very careful not to do. He would not think of cutting his hair—that would break his vow. But outside of that restriction, Samson was an undisciplined man. His ritual obedience was careful, but it went no further than that. Strange as it seems, Samson was a legalist at heart, at the same time as he lived in unbridled license.

I am personally convinced as I look at my own life, and as I think back on literally hundreds of people I have counseled, that there is nothing Christians find harder than to live a disciplined life. We are legalistically careful not to do some things, but there are huge areas of life where our operating principle is "Whatever is pleasing in our own eyes."

Samson's great area of undiscipline was sex. It was easy for a man of his physique to attract willing Philistine girls. And Samson saw no reason to curb his desires. As we look at our modern world, we cannot help but recognize that sexual immorality is a very common reason why Christians lose their effectiveness for Jesus Christ. I can think of an alarming number of men who lost their ministry because they lost their sexual purity. But sex is not the only problem area of self-discipline. There are as many different problem areas as there are people.

If I do not discipline my life, I can quickly dissipate my power. That was Paul's great desire—to discipline his body so that he would be mastered by nothing apart from the Lord Jesus. Almost anything can begin to take His place— from our sexual drives, to our interest in sports, to a love for great music. Things which may be beautiful and good in their place can cause great damage when the dams of self-discipline are broken down. Samson never achieved what he could have, because he did not live a disciplined life.

Donald Gray Barnhouse tells about a friend who raised strawberry plants and once sent him a shipment of a thousand plants. Barnhouse gave them to a farmer, who was working his land on shares, to plant. About the beginning of

June, Barnhouse was delighted to look at the patch and see thousands of blossoms; his mouth watered in anticipation. The next day, around noon, he asked the farmer what he had been doing that morning. The farmer replied, "I have been picking the blossoms off the strawberry plants." Barnhouse just about had a heart attack. Then the farmer said, "If you have strawberries the first year, the strength goes into the berries and the plants become weak, and they will never produce much in the future. But if you let the strength go into the plants the first year, you will have magnificent berries."

I am afraid to use illustrations like that, because often someone misses the point and says, "Well, now I know what was wrong with my strawberries." I will not vouch for the horticulture, but the spiritual application is very true. God takes nothing good from my life that He will not give back either in a more perfect form, or for which He will provide a greater substitute. There is nothing wrong with strawberries, but, for the sake of something better, there is a time to do without them. Self-discipline is not denying our drives and desires; it is submitting them to the will of God and to the timing of God. Samson's mistake was not in being attracted to that woman, but in failing to submit his sexual drives to the Lord's control. His purpose is to produce rich fruit in my life, and that comes as I refuse to walk in the flesh, and, instead, put myself under the control of His Spirit. In His time, there is a wonderfully satisfying harvest.

THE PROVIDENCE OF GOD

When Samson disobeyed God, one result was personal tragedy in his life, the tragedy of unfulfilled desire and bitter disappointment. Samson never did get the woman he wanted, but the greater tragedy was that he never became the man God planned.

Despite Samson's disobedience, God's purpose was fulfilled. As verse 4 indicates, "[God] was seeking an occasion against the Philistines." God did not direct Samson into disobedience, but, at the same time, God did not abandon His program because of Samson's sin. In fact, the failures of Samson led to opportunities against the Philistines. We are responsible and accountable for our sins, and we cannot excuse them. But in the providence of God, His purposes triumph.

Samson's sin started him on the downward path. One act of disobedience led to another. Normally, a marriage would be held in the groom's home, and the bride would move there. Not in this case. Apparently, Manoah would have nothing to do with the normal arrangement, and, therefore, Samson entered into a marriage which involved visiting his wife at Timnah, rather than living with her.

There are four steps in Samson's spiritual decline:

1. *The downward journey* (vv. 7-9). When we read that Samson went *down* to Timnah, it is more than a geographical description. It was a downward journey spiritually. On one of those journeys he stopped to eat honey from the lion's carcass. That seemed to involve a clear violation of his Nazirite vow which forbade contact with death. Realizing that, Samson would not tell his parents the source of the food. He was consciously guilty.

2. *The drunken party* (v. 10). A second part of the vow vanished in Timnah. When we read in verse 10 that Samson made a feast, the word indicated a drinking bout, a drunken celebration. There is no suggestion that Samson was a sober abstainer, drinking Cokes while the others imbibed. So he broke that part of his vow which repudiated strong drink.

3. *The drunken riddle* (vv. 11-14). In the middle of the feast, apparently well into his cups and surrounded by his enemies, Samson proposed a wager. "I will bet each of you a linen garment and a change of clothes, that you can not guess my riddle." The clothes Samson describes are the epitome of Middle Eastern fashion, garments which were very expensive. It is hardly the proposal of a Spirit-controlled man.

4. *The downfall of compromise* (vv. 15-20). The Philistines were bad losers. They intimidated the woman into betraying Samson, and, as a result, Samson learned two bitter lessons. He learned that when you marry a woman, you marry her relatives, and, also, that it is hard to resist a woman's tears. Finally, his wife rusted away his resistance with her tears, and too late Samson realized that he had lost his bet, his honor, and his wife.

Only a few years after Samson died, another man became the judge of Israel. In many ways Samuel was like Samson. His hair also was uncut, because he, too, was born under a vow. He also was born to godly parents by the direct intervention of God. He too was the leader of Israel at a time when the Philistines totally dominated the Israelites, and the people were in deep apostasy.

But there the similarity ends. Samson fought a few personal battles against the Philistines, but he neither liberated his people nor turned their hearts to God. On the other hand, Samuel changed the course of Israel's history. Every area of life in Israel was touched for good through the life and ministry of Samuel. When he died, the whole nation mourned for him.

Why? What was the difference? It is found in Samuel's words to Saul, a man who, like Samson, had great potential but never realized it. Read Samuel's words in 1 Samuel 15:22-23.

> Has the LORD as much delight in burnt offerings and
> sacrifices
>   as in obeying the voice of the LORD?
> Behold to obey is better than sacrifice
>   and to heed than the fat of rams.
> For rebellion is as the sin of divination,
>   and insubordination is as iniquity and idolatry.
> Because you have rejected the word of the LORD,
>   He has rejected you from being king.

Samuel was self-disciplined and submissive to God's Word

in his life. Samson had never learned that lesson. As a result, he squandered his immense God-given resources.

Are you living a "Garbage Mary" Christian life? God has provided every resource you need to live an abundant, Spirit-filled life. But you will never know that life apart from a consistent commitment to God's authority and a self-discipline that brings all of life under the lordship of Jesus Christ.

EIGHTEEN

God's Freedom Fighter

In the spring of 1977, a television program and a book suddenly triggered a social phenomenon. Everyone was talking about Alex Haley's *Roots*, and a record-smashing 80 million people set aside other things to watch the final episode of the series. That was only the beginning. The publishers raced to keep an adequate supply of the book; magazine articles abounded, and people of all ethnic origins set out to discover their own "roots." One major magazine called *Roots* "a potentially important bench mark in U.S. race relations."

Roots begins with the story of an African named Kunta Kinte. In the eighteenth century, at the age of seventeen, he was kidnapped by slave traders from his Mandinka homeland in Africa and shipped, under the most degrading conditions, to a life of slavery in Virginia. But Kunta was a man with a passion for freedom. After months in chains, with his health broken, he was released for only a moment, and, instantly, he tried to escape. Dogs hunted him down, and, when he was recaptured, he was first beaten, then chained and hobbled for months on end.

All around him, Kunta saw other blacks broken and defeated by their slavery, having given in to the hopelessness of their condition. Kunta refused to give up his hope. Finally, the day came when his hobbles were taken off, and he ran away again. Since he could not go fast on an infected ankle, he was quickly recaptured, but he refused to give up. One day he stole a weapon, and he fled again. Unfortunately, it was snowing; once again he was quickly hunted down, because of his tracks in the snow. He was bound and whipped and returned to a life in shackles.

By now, the other blacks wanted nothing to do with Kunta. They treated him as if he were a kind of wild animal, and Kunta simply could not understand them. How could they be at peace with the white man when they were his slaves? Death would be better than slavery; so he tried to escape one more time. He planned his escape very carefully, and, when an opportunity came, he hid in a wagon and rode off to freedom. But this time, he was hunted down by a pair of ruthless slave-catchers, and, in a sadistic act, they cut off most of his foot with an axe.

Kunta Kinte could no longer run, but he did not lose his passion for freedom. As you read or watch his story, you cannot help but admire and sympathize with his agonizing desire to live and die a free man.

Samson was a man who had many flaws in his life, but he had one great virtue. He was a man with a passion for freedom in the middle of a society committed to compromise. With all his failures, he was the only man of his day to recognize that there can be no compromise with the enemy. The Jews were committed to appeasement, but Samson was committed to be God's freedom fighter.

Not long ago, there was a news story about 300 whales who were found marooned on a beach. Scientists could only explain the mystery by speculating that the whales had been chasing sardines and became trapped in shallow water when the tide went out.

For most of his life, Samson was like a whale chasing sardines—a great power pursuing small goals. He was finally beached by his pursuit of the sardine of sexual pleasure. But in Judges 15, we have Samson at the spiritual pinnacle of his life, except for the time of his death. We see the enormous power of the man when he trusted God, and we realize how much he could have accomplished if only he had lived consistently for God.

SAMSON'S PERSONAL REVENGE—15:1-8

But after a while, in the time of wheat harvest, it came about that Samson visited his wife with a young goat; and said, "I will go in to my wife in her room." But her father did not let him enter. And her father said, "I really thought that you hated her intensely; so I gave her to your companion. Is not her younger sister more beautiful than she? Please let her be yours instead." Samson then said to them, "This time I shall be blameless in regard to the Philistines when I do them harm." And Samson went and caught three hundred foxes, and took torches, and turned the foxes tail to tail, and put one torch in the middle between two tails. When he had set fire to the torches, he released the foxes into the standing grain of the Philistines, thus burning up both the shocks and the standing grain, along with the vineyards and groves. Then the Philistines said, "Who did this?" And they said, "Samson, the son-in-law of the Timnite, because he took his wife and gave her to his companion." So the Philistines came up and burned her and her father with fire. And Samson said to them, "Since you act like this, I will surely take revenge on you, but after that I will quit." And he struck them ruthlessly with a great slaughter; and he went down and lived in the cleft of the rock of Etam.

The episode began when Samson suddenly discovered that he had been the victim of terrible injustice, and he was not the kind of man who was committed to turning the other cheek. He had fallen in love with a Philistine girl and arranged to marry her, despite his father's wishes and the clear teaching of God's Word. Then, at a drunken marriage, Samson had thrown out a challenge over a riddle and been betrayed by his own wife. Filled with fury at the Philistines, he had killed thirty men in Ashkelon, paid off his debt, and stalked home. It is the sad story of a man of great power defeated by a lack of self-discipline.

But Samson still wanted that Philistine girl, and he believed that she was his legal wife. He did not know that it had been a terrible disgrace for the marriage not to have been consummated; so her father had immediately arranged a marriage to Samson's best man. Therefore, when his anger burned itself out, Samson headed to Timnah to spend a weekend with his bride. He carried with him a kid as a gift, apparently the equivalent of a box of candy or four dozen roses! Then the shocking truth hit him. He was not a bridegroom at all. The marriage had been annulled. Fearfully, his father-in-law told him that his "bride" was married, but he could marry her much prettier younger sister if he wanted to.

Samson would have nothing to do with a substitute. If he had been angry before, he was furious now, and he determined to get revenge. Rather than focusing on the immediate problem of his stolen bride, he attacked the real enemy. It was not the girl or the father who had caused the problem, but the Philistines who had blackmailed the girl into betraying him. So he turned his fury upon them and hit them where it hurt—in the stomach.

Somehow, he captured 300 jackals. The Hebrew word can mean either foxes or jackals, and since jackals run in packs, it is more likely that this was the animal he captured. He tied those jackals in pairs, put a torch between their tails, and set them loose in the middle of the Philistines' standing corn. The fire spread until it had destroyed a major part of the Philistines' crop. That would be a devastating blow to an agricultural people.

Samson was not simply getting personal revenge. If he had wanted that, he would have carried off his wife by force or attacked her and her family directly. But he used his personal problem as the basis of a declaration of war against the Philistines. "This time I shall be blameless in regard to the Philistines" (v. 3). He was taking seriously the call of God in his life and moving beyond personal revenge to fulfill his divine calling.

If Samson wanted to stir up the Philistines, he succeeded. When he had killed thirty of them in Ashkelon, we do not read of anything the Philistines did in retaliation. But when their harvest went up in flames, everybody was directly affected. In anger, the Philistines went up to Timnah and burned the woman and her father alive in their house.

The woman had betrayed Samson because the Philistines threatened to burn her alive in her house. When she caved in under that threat, she ended up being burned alive—by the Philistines. Satan is a very hard taskmaster, and he feels absolutely no need to keep his promises.

One of the terrible things about violence as a method is that there is no way to stop it, and, when we get on the treadmill of personal revenge and retaliation, it becomes very hard to get off. That is exactly what happened now. Samson's fury turned to rage. "If you've done something like this, I will surely avenge myself on you, and afterwards I'll cease." Well, he was wrong about the last part, but Samson did get his revenge. We are not given any details about the battle, but somewhere Samson confronted a Philistine army and singlehandedly slaughtered them. Then, knowing retaliation would come, he hid in a mountain area.

Up until now, the story seems to be no more than an account of the sad results of compromise in the life of Samson. It is true that if he had been what God wanted him to be in a consistent way, he never would have experienced this kind of personal tragedy in his own life. It is the lengthened shadow of his disobedience, a reminder that we can choose to sin, but we cannot choose the consequences of our sin. The harvest is inevitable when we sow disobedience. But the story does not end here, and, in verses 9-17, we move beyond a story of personal revenge to a display of Samson's faith and God's power.

VICTORIOUS THROUGH FAITH—15:9-17

Then the Philistines went up and camped in Judah, and spread out in Lehi. And the men of Judah said, "Why have you come up against us?" And they said, "We have come up to bind Samson in order to do to him as he did to us." Then

3,000 men of Judah went down to the cleft of the rock of Etam and said to Samson, "Do you not know that the Philistines are rulers over us? What then is this that you have done to us?" And he said to them, "As they did to me, so I have done to them." And they said to him, "We have come down to bind you so that we may give you into the hands of the Philistines." And Samson said to them, "Swear to me that you will not kill me." So they said to him, "No, but we will bind you fast and give you into their hands; yet surely we will not kill you." Then they bound him with two new ropes and brought him up from the rock. When he came to Lehi, the Philistines shouted as they met him. And the Spirit of the LORD came upon him mightily so that the ropes that were on his arms were as flax that is burned with fire, and his bonds dropped from his hands. And he found a fresh jawbone of a donkey, so he reached out and took it and killed a thousand men with it. Then Samson said, "With the jawbone of a donkey, heaps upon heaps, with the jawbone of a donkey I have killed a thousand men." And it came about when he had finished speaking, that he threw the jawbone from his hand; and he named that place Ramath-lehi.

The Philistines obviously realized that the only solution to their problem was a search and destroy mission directed against Samson; so they moved into Judah with one great purpose—to capture and kill Israel's strong man. They had no quarrel with the rest of the Israelites, and when their army invaded Judah, they met absolutely no resistance. We do not know how many Philistines there were, but we do learn that Samson killed 1,000 of them, and Judah raised a force of 3,000 to deal with Samson. We would be safe in assuming that there were at least 3,000 to 5,000 Philistines who came to deal with one man.

Perhaps the most striking thing this passage reveals to us is the spiritual condition of the people of Judah. They sent a delegation to the enemy and asked them, "What are you doing here? What is the problem?" When the Philistines told them that they had come to capture and kill Samson, not only did the Israelites not protect him, but they also sent a force of 3,000 of their own men to bring him back to his death.

Three significant things stand out, in verses 10-12, as we try to understand Samson and think through the implications of what it means to be a follower of Jesus Christ in a hostile world. In these Jews of the eleventh century before Christ, we have a vivid picture of the consequences of compromise in the twentieth century after Christ.

1. *The people had become thoroughly accommodated to the spiritual status quo* (v. 11). They could not imagine why the Philistines would have any quarrel with them, and they were filled with anger because Samson had been rocking the boat. Look at verse 11. "Do you not know that the Philistines are rulers over us? What then is this that you have done to us?"

Those questions vividly illustrate that it is possible for believers to get to the place where they prefer slavery to freedom, where compromise is more comfortable than commitment to the calling of God. Judah had never had a better opportunity to be free from the Philistines. They had a leader of amazing power and strength; they had an army of 3,000 men, and they had a God who had promised to give them victory. If they had recognized God's man and rallied around him, they could have thrown off the enemy and been free.

But the people had become so degraded by compromise that, instead of supporting Samson, they accused him of being a troublemaker. They had made peace in their hearts with a status of defeat. There is a moving passage in *Roots* where Bell, Kunta's wife, blurted out what Kunta had been afraid to even think. "Don' care how good de massa is, I gits to feelin' like if you an' me was younger'n we is, I believes I'd be ready to leave 'way from here tonight. . . . Reckon I'se got to be too old and scairt now."[1]

For Bell and Kunta, it was an awful moment of self-realization, and, of course, they were powerless to be free. But Judah was not, and neither are we. Yet we can get to the place where we have so accommodated ourselves to the world's life-style and to the presence of sins in our lives, that we just accept them and give up the fight. We do not really believe things will change, so we give in.

Another insight that emerges from the accommodation of Judah to the status quo is the recognition that compromisers have no time for the committed. Samson was a living embarrassment to Judah, and they would have rather seen him dead at the hands of the Philistines than change. It is a sad fact of Christian experience that if you are a Christian committed to growing and maturing in Jesus Christ, you will often be hindered the most by other Christians who have become accustomed and accommodated to an anemic, wishy-washy spiritual life.

2. *The people were ignored by the enemy* (v. 10). The Philistines had no quarrel with them, because they represented no threat. Satan lost no sleep over Judah. It is only when a Christian commits himself to serving God wholeheartedly and battling on the front lines that Satan works to sidetrack him. If you are encountering opposition in your life, thank God, because it shows that you are making Satan sit up and take notice. A man came up to a preacher with the comment, "What is all this talk about Satan? I have never met him in my life."

Quick as a flash, the answer came back. "Of course not. You never meet someone when you are going the same way he is. But if you turn around and start going the other way, you will meet him soon enough."

3. *The people were doing the enemy's work for them* (v. 12). The men of Judah were fighting the Philistines' battles. There are no noncombatants in spiritual warfare. There is no Switzerland where we can sit out the battle, in benign neutrality. If we are not actively involved in a positive way for the Lord Jesus, we can become positive hindrances to the cause of Jesus Christ.

THE FAITH OF SAMSON

Samson's faith shone its brightest against the background of this kind of spiritual compromise. It would be a long time before he reached this height again, but, on this day, Samson was a man trusting God. His faith was manifested in three ways.

1. *His treatment of the Jews.* Samson was remarkably gentle with his people. He would have had every right to be absolutely furious with those traitors. Instead, he did everything to keep from attacking his own people. That is why he made them promise not to kill him, but he submitted to the ultimate degradation of having them tie him up and lead him to the Philistines. Only a deep-seated commitment to God's purpose in his life could have made Samson deal so kindly with people who were mistreating him so badly. It was a great moment in Samson's life.

2. *His approach to the enemy.* The second great evidence of Samson's faith is found in his approach to the enemy. Picture the scene for a minute. There was Samson, bound by two ropes and surrounded by 3,000 Jews, walking right into the teeth of thousands of bloodthirsty Philistines. When they saw him coming, they broke out into a shout of triumph.

If you can imagine what was involved in those first words of verse 14, you will know why Samson was included in the roll call of faith. Only faith in God produces that calm courage. Samson had many failings, but no one can accuse him of being a coward. He knew his God, and that faith gave him strength.

3. *His victory of faith.* The third great evidence is found in the victory of Samson. God's Spirit came upon him in power. He snapped the ropes like weak threads, and picked up a jawbone that was lying on the ground. It was still fresh and strong, with all its teeth in place, and in the hand of Samson, it became a terrible weapon. At the end of that battle, 1,000 Philistines lay dead.

What a great evidence of what Samson could do and be, when he trusted God. He had been delivered bound into the hands of the enemy, and he had not only escaped, he had given his people a great victory. As we read verse 20, we get the impression that Samson's victory gave Israel twenty years of stability, even though the Philistines still dominated them. Compromise meant only defeat—in Samson's own life or in the life of the nation. But when Samson trusted God and committed himself to deal with the enemy, God gave him a great victory.

THE PROVISION OF GOD—15:18-20

Then he became very thirsty, and he called to the LORD and said, "Thou hast given this great deliverance by the hand of Thy servant, and now shall I die of thirst and fall into the hands of the uncircumcised?" But God split the hollow place that is in Lehi so that water came out of it. When he drank, his strength returned and he revived. Therefore, he named it En-hakkore, which is in Lehi to this day. So he judged Israel twenty years in the days of the Philistines.

SAMSON'S PRAYER

In verse 18, we see Samson praying. This unusual prayer is the only one recorded in Samson's life, prior to his death prayer. It was both the spiritual pinnacle of Samson's life and a low point of despair.

Look first at the way in which this prayer was the highpoint in Samson's life. He was fully conscious that his victory was due to God. His words revealed how he felt: "You have given into the hand of Your servant this great deliverance." He knew that his power was due to his fellowship with God. Next, he was conscious that he was God's servant, and that the Lord had called him to deal with the enemy. Obviously, he had taken seriously the words of the Lord before his birth. This event was the one great occasion where Samson was conscious of living up to God's calling.

When Queen Victoria was a little girl, she was shielded from the fact that she was going to be queen one day, even though she was being trained for that position. There was a fear that the knowledge would spoil her. As a result, she did not take her training very seriously. Finally, her teachers decided it was necessary to let her discover her future position. Her immediate response was, "Then I will be good." Her behavior was controlled by her position.

The simple principle is that when we really understand our position before God, that understanding must affect our practice. Samson may have known his position before, but this was the one time he acted on the basis of his relationship with God. Exactly the same thing applies to us. Spiritual victory comes when we live on the basis of our position in Christ.

Samson was also fully aware of the dangers represented by the enemy. Earlier, when Manoah, Samson's father, called the Philistines "the uncircumcised," and warned him to leave them alone, Samson ignored his warning. Now he had come to see the enemy for what they were. Obviously, until a Christian faces the fact that he has three enemies—the world, the flesh, and the devil—committed to keeping him from living a spiritual life, and he takes those enemies seriously, he cannot overcome them.

But while this prayer revealed real spiritual growth in Samson's life, it was also a cry of despair. "Now I will surely die of thirst and I will fall into the hand of the uncircumcised." It was an amazing cry from a man who had walked fearlessly into a horde of Philistines, now terrified of dying by thirst.

Samson's experience is not unique. Victory often makes us vulnerable to defeat. It is a short journey from the mountain peak of excitement to the bottom of the valley of depression. We must be careful that, in the middle of victory, we do not lose fellowship with the Lord Jesus. We also need to learn to protect ourselves against the inevitable letdown which follows great emotional experiences.

There is a close connection between our physical and our spiritual condition. We are whole people, and what Samson needed was not a Bible conference but a drink of water. Often we ignore some very simple facts about our spiritual condition, and we neglect to look after our bodies. An improper diet, lack of sleep, poor physical conditioning, illness—all of these can affect us spiritually. Sometimes the best thing we can do for our spiritual lives is to get a good night's sleep. It is important, when we are physically drained, to recognize how that can upset our relationship with the Lord.

GOD'S ANSWER

The Lord answered Samson's prayer in two ways. First, He supplied water. I am glad that I have a God who is concerned about my physical needs as well as my spiritual ones. In Samson's case, the Lord split open the holes in the rocks in that area and made a fountain, not only for Samson's benefit but for future generations as well. That spring became a constant reminder that God is a God who answers prayer.

The second thing the Lord did was to establish Samson's judgeship. We have no details of Samson's ongoing work as a judge. Between Judges 15 and 16, there is a gap of twenty silent years. But the available information suggests that the Lord used Samson during that time to lead and guide His people in a limited way. Before this victory, the Jews had been willing to betray him to the Philistines. Now, because he had trusted God, they were willing to follow his leadership.

With all his shortcomings, we must never forget that Samson stood almost alone for his God in Israel. In a nation committed to the status quo, Samson was committed to freedom under God. Because he dared to believe God, God was able to use Samson.

Do you have that passion for God's victory in and through your life? Are you committed to serving your generation in the will of God, whatever the cost of radical discipleship may be?

NINETEEN

Toying with Temptation

When I was a boy, my bedroom resembled an athletic shrine. My walls were papered with the pictures of my athletic heroes, and my mind was filled with facts about their achievements. Even now, my brain is cluttered with the names of obscure heroes and forgotten moments of glory. Occasionally, one of those names resurfaces in an article or a book devoted to nostalgia, telling sports buffs of the present lives of the stars of the past. Many of them have gone on to success in other realms. Others have melted into the great American middle class, living the good life of suburbia. Sometimes, however, the story is a very sad one. A man whose name was once a household word, whose skills brought him fame and fortune, has become a criminal or a broken man, whose current life bears no resemblance to his past glory. How could a man fall so far so fast?

Judges 16 is a story like that, a chapter which could almost be entitled, "Didn't you used to be Samson?" It is hard to believe that this helpless slave with his feet chained, his head shaved, his eyes gouged out, stumbling his way through a woman's work, is the legendary Samson, the proud and powerful man who singlehandedly held back the Philistines. It is a story over which are written two of Scripture's great warnings: "Pride goes before a fall and a haughty spirit before stumbling" (Prov. 16:18); and, "Let him who thinks he stands take heed lest he fall" (1 Cor. 10:12).

The story of Samson's downfall at the hands of Delilah is one of the most famous stories of the Bible. Its blend of love, sex, violence, and treachery gives it all the dimensions of classical tragedy; therefore, it has been told and retold down through the ages. But Samson's tragedy is not unique. His experience was more dramatic than most, but there are countless Christians who have lost their spiritual strength for exactly the same reason as Samson. If I am honest, I must confess that I also have a tendency to toy with temptation rather than to resist it, to trifle with sin rather than to flee from it. It is so easy to play with the Delilah of sin; all of us know the pull of her persuasive powers.

Temptation is a constant part of the Christian life. Because we face a threefold enemy—the world, the flesh, and the devil—temptation comes in a variety of ways. Nevertheless, we can learn some basic lessons for twentieth-century living from the ancient story of Samson's downfall.

SAMSON AND THE PROSTITUTE AT GAZA—16:1-3

Now Samson went to Gaza and saw a harlot there, and went in to her. When it was told to the Gazites, saying, "Samson has come here," they surrounded the place and lay in wait for him all night at the gate of the city. And they kept silent all night, saying, "Let us wait until the morning light, then we will kill him." Now Samson lay until midnight, and at midnight he arose and took hold of the doors of the city gate and the two posts and pulled them up along with the bars; then he put them on his shoulders and carried them up to the top of the mountain which is opposite Hebron.

Oscar Wilde once wrote, "I can resist anything ... except temptation." That seems to be an accurate analysis of Samson's attitude here, in Judges 16. But if ever there was an illustration of the truth of 1 Corinthians 10:13, it is found here. "No temptation has overtaken you but such as is common to man; and God is faithful, who will not allow you to be tempted beyond what you are able, but with the temptation will provide the way of escape also, that you may be able to endure it." Samson did not fail because the temptation was too strong, and he did not fail because the temptation was inescapable; he failed because he toyed and trifled with sin, until, finally, he gave in. Ambrose, an early Christian writer, put it like this:

> Samson, when brave, strangled a lion; but he could not strangle his own love. He burst the fetters of his foes; but not the cords of his own lusts. He burned the crops of others, and lost the fruit of his own virtue when burning with the flame enkindled by a single woman.

The first part of Samson's downfall is not very well known. But in the episode with the prostitute in Gaza, we discover all the seeds of his future destruction. What he sowed in Gaza, he reaped in Sorek with Delilah; so this first episode bears careful study.

There is no way of knowing when this sad event occurred. It could have been anytime in the twenty years Samson acted as judge, but probably it occurred toward the end of that period. Why Samson went down to Gaza we are not told, but we do know that Gaza was one of the five major cities of the Philistines. It was a stronghold of the Philistines, a place in which Samson was not about to win any popularity contests. They hated him in Gaza!

This is extremely significant, because it reveals a great weakness in Samson's life. He deliberately exposed himself to the enemy with a self-confidence that bordered on carelessness in the spiritual as well as the physical realm. While he was there, he saw a prostitute to whom he was immediately attracted and with whom he became involved in sin.

There can be no doubt that Samson, at this point in his life, was totally out of fellowship with God. He was very confident, but it was a confidence based entirely on the flesh, and he was deliberately ordering his life in conflict with the will of God. Apparently, he had learned absolutely nothing from the results of his sin of lust, as recorded in chapters 14 and 15. It was that carnal self-confidence, that belief in his invincibility, that would make Samson pliable dough in the hands of Delilah.

When his enemies discovered that Samson was in the city, they laid plans to trap him inside the walls. They posted a guard by the house and set an ambush by the city gates. The massive city gates were studded with nails and covered with metal to make them fireproof. Once they were locked, there was no way out of the city. Secure in that knowledge and certain that there was no way out of the city until morning, the guard either grew careless or fell asleep.

They had not reckoned on the enormous strength of their enemy. In the middle of the night, Samson left the prostitute's house, put his arms around the gateposts, which would be driven deep into the earth, tore out the gates—posts and all—and carried them on his shoulders "to the top of the mountain which is opposite Hebron." That phrase could mean that he carried them to "a hill in the direction of Hebron," or to Hebron itself, an uphill journey of thirty-eight miles. The latter seems to be what is meant, but either way it was an incredible feat of strength. No wonder the Philistines did not attack him! They were paralyzed with fright.

As a feat of strength, this is one of the greatest exploits in human history. Imagine the shame of the Gazites in having their city gates stolen! If Samson were to appear in the twentieth century, he would require a special category in the Olympics! But that only makes his tragedy greater. Samson had power without purity, strength without self-control, and because he did not know holiness, he would know a crushing defeat.

For twenty years, Samson had experienced the thrill of victory. Not once had he felt the agony of defeat. That ought to have left him very thankful to God. Instead, it produced a deadly complacency about his spiritual life. He was a Nazirite, set apart to God, but that meant very little to him. He had broken each vow he had made, except the one relating to his hair, and God was still looking after him. He had sinned sexually, and, arising from the bed of sin, he had displayed power of awesome proportions. He had been drunk, he had defiled himself with dead bodies, but God had not intervened. There had been no voice from heaven, no sudden disasters, not even any minor defeats! The more he sinned, the more of God's grace he experienced. To Paul's question, "Should we continue in sin so that grace might abound?" Samson would have given a ringing answer, "Yes! God is not concerned about petty details like sexual sin and broken vows."

Samson probably never verbalized his attitudes quite so clearly. Yet these were apparently his feelings, and they led him to become involved with a woman named Delilah. In that relationship, Samson harvested the crops he had sown so freely in the past. There are two stages to his experiences, the first of which we see revealed in verses 4-14.

The Process of Temptation—16:4-14

After this it came about that he loved a woman in the valley of Sorek, whose name was Delilah. And the lords of the Philistines came up to her, and said to her, "Entice him, and see where his great strength lies and how we may overpower him that we may bind him to afflict him. Then we will each give you eleven hundred pieces of silver." So Delilah said to Samson, "Please tell me where your great strength is and how you may be bound to afflict you." And Samson said to her, "If they bind me with seven fresh cords that have not been dried, then I shall become weak and be like any other man." Then the lords of the Philistines brought up to her seven fresh cords that had not been dried, and she bound him with them. Now she had men lying in wait in an inner room. And she said to him, "The Philistines are upon you, Samson!" But he snapped the cords as a string of tow snaps when it touches fire. So his strength was not discovered. Then Delilah said to Samson, "Behold, you have deceived me and told me lies; now please tell me, how you may be bound." And he said to her, "If they bind me tightly with new ropes which have not been used, then I shall become weak and be like any other man." So Delilah took new ropes and bound him with them and said to him. "The Philistines are upon you, Samson!" For the men were lying in wait in the inner room. But he snapped the ropes from his arms like a thread. Then Delilah said to Samson, "Up to now you have deceived me and told me lies; tell me how you may be bound." And he said to her, "If you weave the seven locks of my hair with the web and fasten it with a pin, then I shall become weak and be like any other man." So while he slept, Delilah took the seven locks of his hair and wove them into the web. And she fastened it with the pin, and said to him, "The Philistines are upon you, Samson!" But he awoke from his sleep and pulled out the pin of the loom and the web.

THE SOURCE OF TEMPTATION

First, we need to look at Delilah. Actually, we know very little about her except that she was sexually attractive to Samson, and he entered into an affair with her. There is no suggestion that they were husband and wife, and we cannot even be sure what her nationality was. Her name was Semitic, not Philistine, but from the story, she seems to have been a Philistine who had Hebrew blood in her family.

By now, Samson had become a national problem for the Philistines, and the leaders of the Philistines were determined to be rid of him once and for all. The Philistines had five major cities, each ruled over by a tyrant (1 Sam. 6:4), and those five lords came to Delilah with a proposal. They were convinced that there was a secret to Samson's strength, and they offered Delilah about $5,000 to discover what it was. They apparently thought in terms of some magic Samson used. That was a great deal of money, and Delilah immediately agreed to sell the man who loved her.

We should not pass over this too quickly. There are, in fact, three very important principles about temptation which are embodied in the person of Delilah. These principles lie at the heart of why we succumb to temptation when it enters our lives.

1. *Moral compromise always makes us vulnerable.* If Samson had not had a sinful relationship with Delilah, he would never have been open to this temptation. In Samson's case, the moral compromise was an obvious one. In our lives, it is often much more subtle. It relates to the kind of material we read, the kind of programs we watch, the kind of values we accept. We do not fall off a cliff morally; we go down a toboggan slope, until finally we are going so fast we cannot stop. In many ways, the crucial issue is not what happens at the bottom of a toboggan run or even halfway down. Once we start down, we can only bail out by drastic action. It is the first steps which are determinative. That is why personal purity is such a crucial issue for Christians. To compromise, even in our thought lives, makes us very vulnerable.

2. *Temptation comes to us in attractive packages.* The Philistines didn't hire Tugboat Annie; they hired a beauty queen. Delilah was a beautiful, attractive woman, and Samson wanted her very much. And so it is with us. When sin comes, it will not come as something ugly and destructive, but as something desirable, good, and fulfilling. It was only later that Delilah was revealed for what she really was.

Not long ago, I was talking to a girl about her involvement with a man in a relationship that the Bible clearly forbids. She said, "But I want it so much. It is so attractive to me." I had to tell her, "Of course it is. Do you think you would be interested if Satan came right out and said, 'I want to destroy your effectiveness as a Christian. I want to rob you of your joy. Are you interested?' Of course you would not be. So Satan puts his poison in the middle of a sirloin steak and invites you out for dinner." That is exactly what is going on here.

The third principle is going to sound very moralistic and old-fashioned, but let me assure you that it is thoroughly biblical.

3. *Temptation comes when we choose the wrong company.* Samson had an unfailing ability to choose the wrong

kind of girl. First, he was attracted to the Philistine woman from Timnah, then the prostitute from Gaza, and then Delilah. It was those women, with whom Samson chose to spend his time, who helped destroy his character.

There is nothing that shapes our character more than the people with whom we *choose* to spend our time. That is a truth the Bible teaches. First Corinthians 15:33 says, "Do not be deceived: bad company corrupts good morals." As I see my children in school, struggling with what it means to live in a pagan society, I have come to realize that one of the most important things I need to help them learn is how to say "No"—to be distinctively different, to stand alone with grace and strength. That golden word "No" becomes even more urgent and difficult to pronounce as life goes on.

God is not calling us to an isolationism that retreats into a holy huddle. But we need to look very carefully at our friendships to discover whether those associations are drawing us away from Jesus Christ. I have no hesitation in saying that some of us will never grow up in Jesus Christ until we break off those relationships that are dragging us down. Samson had no right to have this illegitimate association with Delilah. What about you? Are there any Delilahs in your life that you need to deal with?

THE PROCESS OF TEMPTATION

Delilah now went to work with all her seductive charm. She asked Samson to tell her the secret of his strength. Samson should have immediately sensed the danger, refused to answer, and gone home. But he did not. He played with her and told her, "If you tie me with seven fresh, undried bowstrings, I will be helpless." So Delilah waited until he was asleep, had him tied, then shouted, "Samson, the Philistines are coming." Immediately he jumped up, snapped the cords, and rushed out to discover that there were no Philistines in sight.

Delilah tried again. This time he told her to use fresh

ropes, which had never been used. When she called him, he broke the ropes as easily as he broke the bowstrings.

She tried again. This time, because of what he said, when he was asleep (the boy was quite a sleeper!), she took seven locks of his hair—which had never been cut and must have been very long—and wove them into some cloth she already had on the loom. Then she fastened the weaving with a pin. The posts of that loom were planted right in the ground. Her preparation done, she shouted a thiid time, "Samson, the Philistines are here." Samson immediately jumped up. As he rushed out, he pulled the pin and the weaving off of the loom and rushed outside with it hanging from his hair!

THE PRINCIPLES OF TEMPTATION

Now I can not think of anything more ridiculous than to see a man walking around with weaving hanging from his head! It must have been quite a job to untangle all that mess. You would think that by now Samson would begin to get a little bit suspicious. It would seem to me that, if every time I woke up, I was tied up in cords or wrapped with ropes or woven into a loom, I might guess that something fishy was going on.

Let me point out two other principles about dealing with temptation from this part of Samson's story.

1. *When we toy with temptation, it traps us.* The New Testament does not ask us to fight this kind of temptation; it tells us to run away from it. "Flee sexual immorality" (1 Cor. 6:18). "Flee from idolatry" (1 Cor. 10:14), which is involved with immorality. "But you, man of God, flee these things" (1 Tim. 6:11), talking primarily of materialism. "Now flee . . . youthful lusts" (1 Tim. 2:22).

Fleeing is not easy. It would have been difficult for Samson. He had a real affection for Delilah. He chose not to flee, and he lost his character. There may be things in your life that you need to deal with in a drastic way if you are going to live wholeheartedly for Jesus Christ. There may be major areas of your life that need to be changed if you are going to preserve your character. Your life-style or your leisure activities or even your job may be involved. But God calls you to flee temptation and find your character. Fleeing is hard, but it is essential.

2. *Self-confidence blinds us to reality.* I remember speaking to a friend about things that were having a dangerous effect on his life. He said to me, in effect, "Gary, don't worry. I can handle it." Today, that friend is a world away from Jesus Christ. Samson thought playing with De-lilah was a game. It turned to be Russian roulette, and he bought the bullet. You cannot trifle with sin in your life. If you are like Samson, flirting with a Delilah, believing that you can keep sin in bounds, let me warn you that you are playing with a lion. You may stick your head in its mouth once and get away with it, even twice and three times. Samson did. But, one of these times, that lion will shut its mouth, and you will lose your head, once for all.

THE DOWNFALL OF SAMSON—16:15-22

Then she said to him, "How can you say, 'I love you,' when your heart is not with me? You have deceived me these three times and have not told me where your great strength is." And it came about when she pressed him daily with her words and urged him, that his soul was annoyed to death. So he told her all that was in his heart and said to her, "A razor has never come on my head, for I have been a Nazirite to God from my mother's womb. If I am shaved, then my strength will leave me and I shall become weak and be like any other man." When Delilah saw that he had told her all that was in his heart, she sent and called the lords of the Philistines saying, "Come up once more, for he had told me all that is in his heart." Then the lords of the Philistines came up to her, and brought the money in their hands. And she made him sleep on her knees, and called for a man and had him shave off the seven locks of his hair. Then she began to afflict him, and his strength left him. And she said, "The Philistines are upon you, Samson!" And he awoke from his sleep and said, "I will go out as at other times and shake myself free." But he did not know that the LORD had departed from him. Then the Philistines seized him and gouged out his eyes; and they brought him down to Gaza and bound him with bronze chains, and he was a grinder in the prison. However, the hair of his head began to grow again after it was shaved off.

Delilah was a very persistent woman. Her stubbornness is a good reminder that Satan does not give up easily. If he took three shots at the Lord Jesus, you can be sure that he is not going to give up easily on us. So, Delilah pulled out all the stops. She knew the power of a woman's tears. You can almost taste the salt when you read verse 15. "How can you say you love me. You have tricked me three times." She kept at him and at him; until, finally, she rusted away his resistance, just as her Philistine predecessor had in chapter 14.

At last, Samson had had enough. But he did not solve his problem by rejecting Delilah. It was too late for that. Instead, he blurted out the most important fact about his life to a woman, who, he must have known was committed to destroy him. If you have ever been to a slaughterhouse and seen cattle lining up to be slaughtered, you have a vivid picture of Samson here. What a fool sin makes of us!

But listen to Samson, "A razor has never come on my head, for I have been a Nazirite to God from my mother's womb. If I am shaved, then my strength will leave me, and I shall become weak and be like any other man. Forty years, Samson had kept one part of his vow. He had broken all the other parts, but he had kept his hair unshaven, as a sign of his commitment to God. He had not made a very strong commitment or felt a deep faith, but he had trusted God at least in this. There was no magic in his hair. It was only a symbol of his separation to God. But if his hair was shaved, Samson's feeble dedication would crumble completely.

It is pathetic to read verses 18-21. How could Samson ever go to sleep in the lap of a woman like Delilah? He must have known what she was going to do. But sleep he did, and, suddenly, in the midst of his sleep, he heard the same old shout, "The Philistines are upon you, Samson!" This time he jumped up, but he was bald. And not only his hair had gone. The last phrase of verse 20 is one of the saddest statements of the Bible. "But he did not know that the LORD had departed from him." In verse 17, he said, "If you cut my hair, my strength will go." It was worse than that. He had lost touch with God.

In verse 21, we see the awful results of Samson's sin. This was the mighty man who had stalked off with the gates of Gaza in an amazing display of physical strength. Now he was blind, his eyes gouged out by his enemies. He was reduced to doing the work of a slave woman, shackled in chains. God had not failed Samson. It was Samson's pride and self-indulgence that had devastated his life.

God does not want us to miss the picture of Samson in 16:21. With all of our potential, strength, and accomplishments, we can end up like Samson, if we do not learn that we cannot toy with temptation.

But I do not want to leave Samson at that point. Because, even in prison, a total failure, God had not abandoned him. Look at verse 22. "However, the hair of his head began to grow again after it was shaved off." That is a beautiful verse! Even in the midst of the worst kind of failure, God was present, working to restore Samson. In my mind, there is no doubt that Samson genuinely repented of his sin, and God refused to give up on him.

It may be that you know all too well what it is to fail as Samson failed. You have fallen under temptation, and you would be ashamed if anyone knew the details of it. There is a bumper sticker that puts it beautifully. "Christians aren't perfect; they're forgiven." The hair can grow again. God will use you again. Even in your failure, He will not abandon you. So when you fail (and fail you will), come to Him, claim His forgiveness, and He will work His healing grace in your life.

TWENTY

The Restoration of a Failure

The British navy was involved in some peacetime maneuvers at sea, involving a column of cruisers. They were steaming along in formation, when a signal was given to execute a 90-degree turn. The maneuver went off flawlessly, except for one cruiser, whose captain missed the signal. The ship almost collided with the one in front, and, when it swerved to avoid a collision, the whole convoy was thrown into confusion. Only some very skillful seamanship by the other captains prevented a serious accident.

When some order had been regained, the admiral on the flagship sent a message to the captain who had caused all the trouble, "Captain, what are your intentions?" Immediately the reply came back, "Sir, I plan to buy a farm." He knew without being told that one missed signal had terminated his naval career. Failure meant drydock.

Failure is one of the realities of life, especially the Christian life. There is not a single Christian, even the most mature and saintly, who does not experience significant failure in his walk with the Lord Jesus. As one man said, "I do not fail often, but when I do, it's a beaut!" Anyone who thinks that does not apply to him is badly self-deceived. Christians fail. But what happens when we do? Does God sentence us to a kind of spiritual drydock, where we spend the rest of our lives rusting away, while we observe others doing what we no longer can do?

The best answer to that question is found in the Word of God, written in the lives of people who knew what it was to fail. You do not have to look very far for examples. In fact,

Hebrews 11, often celebrated as "God's Hall of Faith," could equally well be entitled, "God's Hall of Reclaimed Failures." There is scarcely an individual in that chapter without a serious blemish in his life, which, by human standards, could have landed him in spiritual drydock. But God is in the business of restoring failures. Human failures become God's heroes of faith. That is a great principle of God's grace. The spiritually successful Christian is not the person who never fails, but the believer who learns how to accept God's remedy for failure.

One of the gems of God's restoring grace is Samson. Few have fallen so far, but he did not fall outside the grace of God. There is beautiful encouragement for us, as we examine God's restoration of Samson at the end of his life, as recorded in Judges 16:21-31.

> Then the Philistines seized him and gouged out his eyes; and they brought him down to Gaza and bound him with bronze chains, and he was a grinder in the prison. However, the hair of his head began to grow again after it was shaved off. Now the lords of the Philistines assembled to offer a great sacrifice to Dagon their god, and to rejoice, for they said, "Our god has given Samson our enemy into our hands." When the people saw him, they praised their god, for they said, "Our god has given our enemy into our hands, even the destroyer of our country, who has slain many of us." It so happened when they were in high spirits, that they said, "Call for Samson, that he may amuse us." So they called for Samson from the prison, and he entertained them. And they made him stand between the pillars. Then Samson said to the boy who was holding his hand, "Let me feel the pillars on which the house rests, that I may lean against them." Now the house was full of men and women, and all the lords of the Philistines were there. And about 3,000 men and women were on the roof looking on while Samson was amusing them. Then Samson called to the LORD and said, "O Lord GOD, please remember me and please strengthen me just this time, O God, that I may at once be avenged of the Philistines for my two eyes." And Samson grasped the two middle pillars on which the house

rested, and braced himself against them, the one with his right hand and the other with his left. And Samson said, "Let me die with the Philistines!" And he bent with all his might so that the house fell on the lords and all the people who were in it. So the dead whom he killed at his death were more than those whom he killed in his life. Then his brothers and all his father's household came down, took him, brought him up, and buried him between Zorah and Eshtaol in the tomb of Manoah has father. Thus he had judged Israel twenty years.

When Thomas Edison was working on one of his inventions, he would try experiment after experiment. He reputedly performed 50,000 experiments before he developed the storage battery. But, inevitably, after one of his failures, he would come to the dinner table and say, with great enthusiasm, "I had good results today. Now I know one more way it can't be done."

The crucial issue in life is not whether we fail, but how we fail. There is such a thing as "failing forward," learning from what we have done wrong and laying hold of the forgiveness of God. On the other hand, if, in the midst of our failure, we wallow in guilt and remorse, or if we turn to self-pity, excuse-making and accusations, we will be overwhelmed by our failure. The person who lives life blithely unaware of his failures is in the saddest position of all. You cannot learn from what you will not admit.

GOD'S DISCIPLINE OF SAMSON

Samson had lived like that. He had failed over and over again, but he had never learned from his failures. I doubt that he had ever thought of himself as a failure. But he was. He had broken the law of God; he had toyed with the vow of God under which he was born, and he had dissipated his enormous God-given potential. Judged by what he could have been, and by what God wanted him to be, Samson was a desperate failure. God's law was not abdicated, just because it was Samson. "Do not be deceived; God is not mocked; for whatever a man sows, this he will also reap. For the one who sows to his own flesh shall from the flesh reap corruption" (Gal. 6:7-8).

At the end of verse 20, we see Samson reaping the corruption of the flesh. God had put His Holy Spirit within him, but Samson had chosen to live in the flesh. Two things operated in Samson's life—the stubborn self-confidence of the flesh within him and the seduction of Delilah outside. It is impossible to exaggerate the stupidity of Samson, but that is exactly what sin does to all of us. When Samson awakened, his hair was gone, his strength had vanished, and his fellowship with God was broken. What makes it even sadder is that Samson had no idea that he had lost his spiritual power. It is bad to be weak because of sin, but it is tragic not even to know it.

Notice how Samson's sins boomerang upon him, in verse 21. He had done what was right in his own eyes, and followed the lusts of his eyes; now the Philistines gouged them out. He had refused to discipline his own life; now he became a slave and prisoner of his enemies. He had visited a prostitute in Gaza and escaped without harm; now he was a prisoner in Gaza. He had pursued Philistine women; now the strong man was reduced to doing a woman's work for the Philistines. Samson was learning the reality of God's discipline in his life. And so will every wayward son, as Hebrews 12:4-11 promises.

If that shame was not deep enough, Samson was degraded even more. The only reason the Philistines did not kill Samson immediately was because they wanted to have a great celebration with Samson as their chief entertainment. So we are told, in verses 23-25, that the rulers of the Philistines ordered a grand occasion to honor Dagon, their god. They held it in the stadium at Gaza, and, from all we can tell, this was a massive building. There was a covered portion, supported by pillars set on stone bases, looking out on a courtyard, with the dignitaries sitting under cover, and the general public up on the roof.

The liquor flowed freely, and finally, the chant built to a crescendo: "We want Samson, we want Samson, we want Samson." So Samson was led, blind, chained, and broken, onto the arena floor. You can imagine the glee of thousands of Philistines, when they saw the hated and feared Samson led in like an animal on a chain, a broken, defeated man. How sweet their revenge! They toyed with him, playing cruel, sadistic tricks on a helpless man, while the mob shouted their approval and urged them on. He entertained them, not by his strength, but by the degrading acts they made him perform.

We need to realize that none of this is happening by accident. It is part of God's grace in the life of Samson. It may not seem very much like grace, but sometimes God must strip away everything from our lives that keeps us from trusting in Him. It may be a very painful process, but, if we will not listen when God whispers in love, God will make us listen when He shouts in discipline. His purpose is not to destroy us; it is to build us up and teach us to trust in Him. God's purpose is never to break us; it is always to refine us. And what God did in the life of Samson, He may have to do in our lives, if we persist in walking in the flesh—in carnal self-confidence and rebellion against Him.

But God's discipline is never isolated from His restoration. God never punishes the believer; He always disciplines him. The difference is very important. Punishment is designed to satisfy justice, but discipline is designed to produce maturity and to restore to usefulness. We see that fact magnificently displayed in the life of Samson.

God's Restoration of Samson

We have already noticed the statement of verse 22, "However, the hair of his head began to grow again after it was shaved off." That verse fascinates those of us whose foreheads are growing higher every year, but, unfortunately, the Hebrew text gives us no clues we can turn into a

cure for baldness. Actually, the verse is not so much concerned with what was happening *naturally* on Samson's
head as with what was occurring *spiritually* in his relationship with God, because his growing hair was a visible
indicator that his fellowship with God was restored and
growing.

Verse 22 is, therefore, a small verse with enormous
implications. In the first place, it reminds us that no matter
how far we fall in our spiritual experience, we never fall
beyond the possibility of God's forgiveness. In his absolute
weakness, Samson began to reach out to the Lord, and the
Lord unreservedly accepted him. It happened to David, a
man who not only committed adultery with Bathsheba but
had her husband killed. It was a horrible act of sin, but
when David called upon God for forgiveness and restoration, immediately, he knew the happiness of God's forgiveness (Psalm 32: 1-2). It happened to Peter. He denied the
Lord Jesus three times at the time of the Lord's greatest
need, right after he had loudly trumpeted that others might
fail the Lord, but he never would. But the Lord Jesus not
only forgave Peter, He established him as an apostle, the
leading evangelist in the early church.

There was a very capable evangelist whom God used in
a significant way in the British Isles. But he lost his interest
in spiritual things and drifted into a life of sin, for a number
of months. Some of his sin was done in secret but ultimately, it became public knowledge and even made the
headlines. At first, all he could think of was that he had
been ruined for life, but, finally, he realized what a fool he
had been, and he came back to God like the prodigal from
the pigpen.

He found exactly the same thing the prodigal did. The
Lord welcomed him with open arms and began to
strengthen him and bless him. Finally, after a period of
waiting, he felt pressed back into a public ministry for the
Lord. He was afraid that his sin would be found out and
brought up all over again, but, after he felt sure it was

hidden and tucked away in the past, he went back to preaching, rejoicing in the forgiveness of God.

One night, when he was in Aberdeen, he was given a sealed letter. Just before the service began, he read the unsigned letter. It described a shameful series of events he had been engaged in. His stomach churned as he read it. The letter said, "If you have the gall to preach tonight, I'll stand and expose you."

He took that letter and went to his knees. A few minutes later, he was in the pulpit. He began his message by reading the letter, from start to finish. Then he said, "I want to make it clear that this letter is perfectly true. I'm ashamed of what I've read, and what I've done. I come tonight, not as one who is perfect, but âs one who is forgiven." God used that letter and the rest of his ministry as a magnet to draw people to Jesus Christ.

God is a God who is in the business of restoring failures who trust Him. Forgiveness is not just a nice word, it is a blessed reality for anyone who claims the promise of 1 John 1:9: "If we confess our sins, He is faithful and righteous to forgive us our sins and to cleanse us from all unrighteousness." By virtue of the finished work of Christ on the cross, we stand unconditionally accepted before God. Our sin has already been paid for, and, in the Lord Jesus, we are free.

But forgiveness needs to be understood, and Samson's experience shows us a second thing. While forgiveness is immediate, restoration is gradual. It took time to grow the hair. The very instant I turn to the Lord on the basis of 1 John 1:9, I am forgiven, but the process of restoration takes time. There is an important reason for that. When a significant failure occurs in our life, it is not the product of a moment. Nearly always, it is the result of sinful habits in our life which are the accumulation of years of disobedience. Those habits must not only be unlearned, new habits must replace them, and that process of dehabituation and rehabituation takes time. The Lord's purpose is not just to forgive our past, but to guarantee our future, and that kind of restoration does not occur overnight.

A third thing which Samson's gradually growing hair shows us is that the consequences of sin are not erased. Samson grew new hair, but he did not receive new eyes. When we finally repent of our sins, God does not automatically obliterate the past. No amount of repenting will undo the birth of an illegitimate child. David's repentance did not bring Uriah back to life, and David paid for his sin in his family life for years afterwards. His guilt was gone, but he dealt with the ramifications of his sin until his death.

We must face this fact squarely. It is a great truth of Scripture that God restores failures. But we are not necessarily restored to our original usefulness for the Lord. Samson was blind. He would never again be able to do what he could have done if he had not sinned. But he was truly and completely forgiven, and the Lord had a great ministry for him. We must not minimize the seriousness of sin and its consequences. On the other hand, we must not miss the reality of God's forgiveness. God did not give Samson his eyes back, but He did use Samson's blindness to enable him to do what he could never have done if he were sighted. The amazing truth is that our God is able to turn the consequences of our sin into instruments for His glory.

In verse 28, we gain an insight into Samson's heart. This is only the second time we hear him pray. The first time was a cry of faith in the midst of discouragement. This time it is a prayer of faith from a man who had been through God's refining fire. Surrounded by 3,000 drunken, screaming Philistines, Samson prays, "O Lord GOD, please remember me and please strengthen me just this time, O God, that I may at once be avenged of the Philistines for my two eyes."

Notice three things in that prayer:

1. *Samson had accepted God's forgiveness.* He was not remorseful over the past, saying "Oh, Lord, I know I blew it before. I know I am unworthy. . . ." I am convinced that Samson had prayed like that, but not now. God had forgiven him. His sin had been dealt with, and it was part of the past.

Someone has well said, "Christians are notorious for

forgetting what they should remember and remembering what they should forget." One of the hardest things many of us have to do is to accept the forgiveness of sin. We keep digging up the past over and over, replaying our sins in slow motion, mining them for every last ounce of guilt. We become chained with regret. There is a deadly variety of spiritual masochism which insists that we must continually punish ourselves for our sin, if we want to please God.

The greatest mistake we, as Christians, make does not take place when we sin. It takes place when we do not immediately come to Calvary and claim the value of what the Lord Jesus did for us there. The cross is God's way of repairing the irreparable, of forgiving the unforgivable. Our sin has not just been forgiven, it has been dealt with, for all eternity, by the blood of Jesus Christ. Do not forget what you should remember. Your forgiveness rests on nothing less than the Word of God and the blood of Jesus Christ. Do not keep remembering and replaying your sin. Forget what God tells you to forget, and remember what He calls you to remember.

2. *Samson was trusting wholeheartedly in God.* He did not say, "If I try hard, I can do it." He did not rely upon the fact that his hair was growing. No, Samson had become totally dependent upon God. In verse 28, he used three different names for God to emphasize his complete dependence: "My Lord Yahweh, remember me and strengthen me, just this once, oh God." That was a new Samson talking, a man relying upon his Lord, and not on himself.

3. *Samson was committed unreservedly to God.* Samson's prayer was not a pious religious act performed in private. It was a prayer raised in the middle of a blood-thirsty mob, and it called for an action which would mean his death. Samson could have been absolutely paralyzed by remorse, fear, and disgrace. Instead, he viewed his situation as an opportunity to do battle for God and to win a victory for the people of Israel. I do not think Samson ever had a clearer understanding of what God wanted him to do with

his life than he did when he prayed that prayer. It was much more than an act of personal vindication, though it was that. It was not the act of a suicide, convinced that there was no reason to live. This was the prayer of a martyr, a man committed to pay the price of death, if that was the cost of victory.

Samson had gone through the discipline of God, and this prayer is the result. If only he had learned this lesson before. This Samson was a new man, trusting in God and deriving his strength and energy directly from God, rather than from himself. This is the only time we ever read of Samson praying before he used his strength. Now his strength was disciplined by faith, but it took failure to teach him this response.

GOD'S VICTORY THROUGH SAMSON—16:29-31

As Samson began to pray, he asked the young man who was his keeper to let him feel the pillars. That boy was leading Samson around like a dog on a leash, and he did not think anything of Samson's request. After all, he was an ordinary, blind man, no threat to anyone. Besides, he needed something to hold onto, so that he would not become dizzy and fall over.

Do you see what is going on here? If Samson had had his sight, the Philistines would not have allowed him anywhere near those pillars. The whole structure rested on them, and if they were pushed off their base, the entire building would collapse. But nobody was worried about blind Samson. He was a failure.

The grace of God took the very results of Samson's failure and used his apparent weakness and his blindness to win a great victory. Because Samson was prepared to trust God even though he had failed, even though he had no right to claim anything from God, the Lord answered his prayer in a supernatural way.

As Samson pulled on those pillars, and God worked through him, he became a living embodiment of the truth that God is a God of grace. Restoration is not based on performance, and yet Satan tempts us to believe that it is. I convince myself that I must earn God's favor, that I have to achieve before I am loved and used by God. Samson had not performed because he could not. When he had physical capacity, he had proven to be a miserable failure. Now his powers were gone. He had no claims on God. But in his distress, he called on the Lord, and the Lord met his need. In the goodness of God, He can use even blinded, broken, *forgiven* sinners. He can even use the blindness which is the product of our failures. Do not miss this, because it is a truth about God you need for your life on a daily basis. In the Lord Jesus, we find a limitless ocean of grace upon grace.

The results of Samson's prayer were both immediate and spectacular. In faith, he pulled on those two pillars, and the stadium collapsed in dust and death. In a few moments, 3,000 Philistines and Samson lay dead. In some ways, verse 30 is a very sad verse: "So the dead whom he killed at his death were more than those whom he killed in his life." It is a reminder of the tragic way in which he traded God-given power and potential for a carnal pursuit of pleasure. If only he had followed the Lord with all his heart, how much he could have done! But at the same time, it is a verse that is full of the grace of God. His death was not a defeat; it was a victory. Samson, the failure, died as a hero!

At the darkest point of World War II, when Europe had been overrun, and the Nazis were raining tons of bombs every night on the city of London, Winston Churchill aroused the British people with some very significant words. "This is not the end. It is not even the beginning of the end. But it is perhaps the end of the beginning." Militarily speaking, the Allies had failed, but Churchill was right. It was not the end. In fact, because they learned from their initial defeats, it was the first stage of victory.

By God's grace, failure, properly dealt with, can be a giant step forward in our growth to Christlikeness. We have a God who restores failures. The hair can grow again. God does not drydock failures; He refits them.

Are you a failure? Of course you are. There is no such thing as a perfect Christian. "Then we shall be what we should be," as the hymn writer says, but not now. Have you learned how to deal with failure?

1. *Admit it.* See yourself for what you are—blind, shaven, and enchained. You are not a spiritual superstar.

2. *Accept God's forgiveness.* First John 1:9 is not just a text to be memorized; it is a truth to be lived. Live at Calvary and luxuriate in the benefits of Christ's death on the cross.

3. *Be patient.* Restoration takes time. The Lord wants to build habits in your life which will enable you to become a godly Christian. The psalmist puts it like this, in Psalm 119:67, "Before I was afflicted I went astray, but now I keep Your Word." He wants to build habits in your life that will keep you in the Word.

4. *Trust God to use you.* Ask him to show you how even the scars left by your sin can become instruments to display His glory. He will!

TWENTY-ONE

Spiritual Junk Food

The vista from the top of Sulphur Mountain, just outside the town of Banff, is one of the most picturesque views in the Canadian Rockies. A gondola takes you to the top of the mountain where you stand looking at peak after peak, stretching off into the distance in a virtual sea of mountains. When the sun is shining, and the snow is glistening, it is a breathtaking scene.

On top of the mountain, there is a tea house, as well as a herd of about thirty mountain sheep. They have become very tame and have taken to begging handouts from tourists. They love anything salty, and that is the problem. Those sheep are actually starving to death on a diet of peanuts, potato chips, popcorn, hamburger, licorice, and even salty plastic bags. As a result, the herd has been neglecting its normal grass diet, and, consequently, the animals are losing weight, and the females no longer produce enough high quality milk to nourish their lambs. One of the park wardens said, "Sheep develop a taste for this kind of junk. It is pathetic to see, but there is really very little we can do about it. I wish people would realize their 'kindness' amounts to cruelty." Those sheep have actually become "junk-food junkies."

It is not only four-legged sheep who have that nutritional problem. Many of God's spiritual sheep are addicted to junk food, only it is the kind which produces spiritual malnourishment. They have become spiritual junk-food junkies.

Junk food is fascinating stuff. The problem with it is

not that it tastes bad. It nearly always tastes good. Nor is it that it immediately destroys us. It never does. The problem is that it has little or no nutritional value, and it spoils our appetites. So it is with spiritual junk food. When it spoils our appetite for God's solid food and addicts us to what is only superficially satisfying, the result is spiritual starvation in our own lives and danger to the lives of those who depend upon us.

The passage of Judges we want to explore in this chapter presents us with three brands of spiritual junk food. At first glance, they may not seem especially relevant to our situation, but, as we probe a little deeper, we will discover that, although the labelling and packaging may have changed over the last 3,500 years, the basic product remains the same. In fact, I am convinced that there is not a single modern Christian who is not enticed by at least one of these forms of spiritual junk food which we discover in Judges 17 and 18.

SPIRITUAL ANARCHY

For sixteen chapters in the book of Judges, we have seen the people of Israel go around and around the same downward spiral of sin, servitude, supplication, salvation, and repeated sin. No matter how often God warned them, or how many miraculous interventions He made on their behalf, or how many times they knew defeat, they refused to learn the lesson of wholehearted obedience to God.

In those chapters, the focus was upon the deliverers whom God raised up, especially the major judges: Othniel, Ehud, Deborah, Gideon, Jephthah, and Samson. In the last five chapters, the emphasis changes. Two stories are recounted, which are designed to give us an insight into the moral condition of the times. In terms of chronology, they do not follow the career of Samson, but rather are flashbacks to an early stage of the period, not long after Joshua's death. The stories are related for a very specific reason—to teach us what happens when we turn away from the authority of

God's Word to religious and moral anarchy. A verse, which is repeated twice in these chapters, is the key, not only to this section but to the entire period of the judges. It is first found in Judges 17:6, "In those days there was no king in Israel; every man did what was right in his own eyes." In 21:25, the last verse of the book, we read virtually the same thing.

There is an extremely important and very contemporary insight in those verses. The Israelites did not do what was wrong in their own eyes. On the contrary, they were convinced that they were doing what was right. It was a society filled with violence, idolatry, gross immorality—utterly pagan—and yet these people thought that what they did was right. Their value systems, moral standards, religious doctrines, and practices had lost all touch with reality and absolute truth. As a result, only the swamp of relativism was left. That is what makes Judges so practical to twentieth-century Christians; for we, too, live in a society that has no standards. The basic life philosophy of the modern man is, "If it is right to you (i.e. in your own eyes), do it."

The two stories which conclude Judges stand in a cause-effect relationship. The first is a story of spiritual and religious anarchy; the second (chapters 19 to 21), a shocking picture of moral collapse. The two go hand in hand, and usually in that order. When spiritual anarchy prevails, moral collapse is inevitable. Religious apostasy leads directly to moral confusion.

The first story presents us with three brands of spiritual junk food. The first is found in Judges 17:1-6.

THE JUNK FOOD OF SELF-MADE RELIGION—17:1-6

Now there was a man of the hill country of Ephraim whose name was Micah. And he said to his mother, "The eleven hundred pieces of silver which were taken from you, about which you uttered a curse in my hearing, behold, the silver is with me; I took it." And his mother said, "Blessed be my son by the LORD." He then returned the eleven hundred pieces of silver to his mother, and his mother said, "I wholly dedicate the silver from my hand to the LORD for my son to make a graven image and a molten image; now therefore, I will return them to you." So when he returned the silver to his mother, his mother took two hundred pieces of silver and gave them to the silversmith who made them into a graven image and a molten idol, and they were in the house of Micah. And the man Micah had a shrine and he made an ephod and household idols and consecrated one of his sons, that he might become his priest. In those days there was no king in Israel; every man did what was right in his own eyes.

Right from the start, the story is a pathetic one. There was a man living in the hill country of Ephraim, obviously from a very wealthy family, whose name was Micah. It is a great name, which means "who is like the Lord," but in Micah's case, it was in contradiction to his character. He was a thief, who had stolen 1,100 pieces of silver from his mother. The value of that amount is indicated by the fact that, in verse 10, the Levite was delighted to get a job which paid him ten pieces of silver a year. So Micah had stolen a considerable fortune.

But Micah was also a very superstitious man. He heard his mother cursing the thief in the name of God, and he was terrified. Therefore, he brought the money back, explained why, and his mother responded with a blessing. "Blessed is my son to Yahweh. He is a thief but at least he is an honest one." Probably, the blessing was to cancel out the effect of the curse, but this mother never condemned her son. There was a good reason for that—she was a thief too. Look at what she said in verse 3. "I wholly dedicate the silver . . . to the LORD . . . to make a graven image and a molten image; now therefore, I will return them to you." But then, in verse 4, we read that she paid out 200 silver pieces for the idols and gave them to Micah. What happened to the other 900 pieces that she had promised to the Lord?

One of the saddest phenomena of our time is the

number of parents who have no true values to communicate to their children. Their children steal even from them, but they receive no discipline and no correction. Talk to almost any Christian public school teacher. The major problem is not a lack of school discipline but a lack of home discipline. In fact, if a teacher tries to punish an open, undeniable wrongdoing, he will often receive nothing but opposition and animosity from the child's parents.

Not only did Micah's mother not correct him, but she actually led him into idolatry. He established a full-fledged shrine in his home, complete with a priestly garment (the ephod), a molten image (an idol of poured silver), a graven image (a carved idol coated with silver), and a number of portable household gods, called teraphim. He went one step further and ordained one of his sons as a priest. At this point, God's Word declares this an act of spiritual anarchy. Micah represented the mood of the times. He was "doing what is right in his own eyes."

The list is growing, so we need to catalog Micah's sins. He began as a thief. He has advanced to become an idolater in plain contradiction of the third commandment which reads, "You shall not make for yourself an idol, or any likeness of what is in heaven above or on the earth beneath or in the water under the earth. You shall not worship them or serve them" (Exod. 20:4-5). In addition, he had set up a shrine, in direct contradiction to God's command that worship was only to be carried out at the tabernacle, the place appointed by God (Deut. 12:4, 14; 16:1-7). Furthermore, he had established a false priesthood, again in direct disobedience to God's Word.

Micah's shrine may have been very beautiful. It may well have been a tourist attraction. But God hated it. It was the homemade worship of a man-made god.

At this point, we need to think about why God hates idolatry and so strongly forbids it. It is important to notice that Micah was not worshiping Baal or a false god. He was trying to worship the true God, and Lord, by his idols. That is very clear, in verse 13. "Now I know that the LORD [Yahweh] will prosper me." When God condemns idolatry, He not only forbids the worship of false gods, He forbids the worship of the true God by images. Such false worship robs God of His glory.

No one likes a bad picture of himself being circulated. We have a wedding picture mounted in a conspicuous place in our house. That is my wife's idea. If you ask me, I was a pretty spiffy-looking bridegroom of the class of '66, but that picture always incites some less than complimentary remarks from my college friends ("Look at his hair cut!"); so I am not very fond of it.

None of us likes a picture which is less than flattering. Often that is simply due to our pride. But no picture and no image can properly honor God. No likeness of any created thing, no matter how skillfully made, can possibly reflect the nature of God. We may admire the artist, but we can never admire the God of glory by a hand-tooled likeness. In fact, such images hide and deface the majesty and greatness of our God. Calvin was right when he said, "A true image of God is not to be found in all the world and hence His glory is defiled, and His truth corrupted by the lie, whenever He is set before our eyes in visible form. Therefore to devise any image of God is itself impious: because by this corruption His majesty is adulterated and He is figured to be other than He is."[1]

It is bad enough to have an unflattering picture of yourself around. It is worse yet to have a poster circulating with your name and someone else's picture. It is even more intolerable if someone takes your picture or name and puts it to something totally contrary to all that you are. I would not be delighted if my picture appeared on a wanted poster by mistake, nor would I be very happy if the paper printed Adolf Hitler's picture with my name under it. That is why God detests images. They mislead men. They give false views of God, and nothing is more destructive than that.

But our problem is not carved idols, but mental idols.

We form mental pictures of God. People constantly say, "I like to think of God as the great Father in the skies. I do not like to think of Him as a judge." But, our desires have nothing to do with God's true character. I shudder when I hear the way some people speak of God. Quite frankly, it does not make the slightest bit of difference what I prefer to think of God. God is who He is and what He is, and that is why any false image of God of any sort is forbidden by Him. Man's concepts of God are irrelevant. God has revealed Himself, and He demands that we take our understanding of Him from His Word.

Micah was guilty of a self-made religion, a homemade god. At least he was aware of it. He says, in 18:24, "You have taken away my gods which I made." How foolish! Imagine fighting over a god you can make, and a god you can steal! I am reminded of Isaiah's delightful sarcasm about the stupidity of idolatry in Isaiah 44:9-20. But Micah knew he was an idolater. Our society does not worship before a molten idol, but it does worship a man-made god. Our generation knows almost nothing of the living God who has spoken in Scripture. The great danger is that we, as Christians, begin to bow down and worship false gods as well. So it is essential that every Christian engage in a study of the attributes of God.

There is one final thing to notice about Micah's idol. In Judges 18:31, we are told, "So they set up for themselves Micah's graven image which he had made, all the time that the house of God was at Shiloh." The tabernacle was at Shiloh. A quick look at a map reveals the fact that Shiloh was in the hill country of Ephraim, only a short journey from Micah's house. Micah's idolatry had nothing to do with the unavailability of God's house. It had everything to do with his refusal to follow God's Word.

Martin Luther once said, "Anything that one imagines of God apart from Christ is only useless thinking and vain idolatry." We can add to that. Anything in our lives to which we attach the worth and importance that belongs only to God becomes an idol in our lives. Idolatry is not a relic of the past; it is a constant problem for every believer. That is why we need to pray with the hymn writer,

> The dearest idol I have known
> Whate'er that idol be
> Help me to tear it from its throne
> And worship only Thee.

That is the first danger point in the portrayal of spiritual anarchy. It is religion without revelation, religious practice without God's truth. How committed are you to the truth of Scripture? How biblical is your view of God? Or is your God a twentieth-century god, molded by the philosophies of the age?

THE JUNK FOOD OF SELF-SEEKING SERVICE—17:7-13

Now there was a young man from Bethlehem in Judah, of the family of Judah, who was a Levite; and he was staying there. Then the man departed from the city, from Bethlehem in Judah, to stay wherever he might find a place; and as he made his journey, he came to the hill country of Ephraim to the house of Micah. And Micah said to him, "Where do you come from?" And he said to him, "I am a Levite from Bethlehem in Judah, and I am going to stay wherever I may find a place." Micah then said to him, "Dwell with me and be a father and a priest to me, and I will give you ten pieces of silver a year, a suit of clothes, and your maintenance." So the Levite went in. And the Levite agreed to live with the man; and the young man became to him like one of his sons. So Micah consecrated the Levite, and the young man became his priest and lived in the house of Micah. Then Micah said, "Now I know that the LORD will prosper me, seeing I have a Levite as priest."

One phrase, repeated twice, tells us a great deal about the wandering Levite. It appears first in verse 8: "He departed from Bethlehem in Judah, to stay wherever he might find a place." In other words, he set out from Bethlehem looking for a place to better himself. That was a perfectly natural ambition; except that in this case, it was totally contrary to the will of God. The man was a Levite. Levites were men who had the call of God upon their lives. They were not to be opportunists moving from place to place, looking for a job. They had been assigned specific cities in which to live, and that is where they were to reside and serve God. As a matter of fact, this man probably should not have been in Bethlehem in the first place, since it was not a Levitical city.

Here was a man who refused to be satisfied with God's arrangements for his life. God had given him an area of service, and, had he lived faithfully within the sphere of his divine calling, the Lord would have extended his area of ministry. But he was committed to self-promotion and to personal betterment.

One of Satan's most subtle devices is to get a Christian dissatisfied with the life-circumstances and the area of service God has given him. "I should be better known." "I should be in public more." "I should be paid more." "I should receive more praise." It is very subtle, but far too often Christians will not do a job because they think it is beneath them; or they will leave a church because no one pays enough attention to them; or they will pout because someone else is more important than they are.

The next stage in the Levite's career occurred when he met Micah. Observe what happened when two men who had no principles got together. Micah wanted a proper Levitical priest, and the Levite wanted a job; so, suddenly, the Levite is an ordained member of the clergy. It was not God's clergy but man's. Once again there was a direct denial of God's Word. In Numbers 16, when an ordinary Levite named Korah tried to act as a priest, God intervened by causing the ground to open up and swallow him.

The Levite had refused to be satisfied with God's arrangements for his service, but now he had made his own, and he was satisfied. At least for awhile. Then in chapter 18, we have the third stage in his career. One day five spies, sent out by the tribe of Dan, happened on Micah's house. They heard the Levite speak and instantly recognized him as a southerner. Perhaps he greeted them with, "Shalom, y'all!" But when they recognized that he was a Levite, they asked him for a blessing, and he obliged.

The contact bore fruit for the upwardly mobile Levite a short time later when the tribe of Dan moved north. Along the way, they decided to steal Micah's idols; so they surrounded the house and carried off Micah's shrine. At first, the Levite tried to stop them, but then Dan made him an offer he could not refuse. "And they said to him, 'Be silent, put your hand over your mouth and come with us, and be to us a father and a priest. Is it better for you to be a priest to the house of one man, or to be priest to a tribe and a family in Israel?" (18:19) The biblical answer, of course, was that it was better for a Levite not to be a priest at all. That carried little weight. "The priest's heart was glad, and he . . . went among the people" (18:20).

If this was not so sad, we might laugh. The Levite was getting a promotion. He was climbing the spiritual ladder.

There is an old story about a preacher who had received a call from a larger church. But was it God's will? Somebody from his present smaller church called to talk about it, and he was met at the door by the pastor's little girl. "Where are your mom and dad, dear?"

"Oh, dad's upstairs praying about the move, and mom's downstairs packing!" To be honest, usually the preacher packs, and the wife prays.

The self-promoting upward mobility of the priest was only taking him deeper and deeper into apostasy and sin. He had begun as a dissatisfied individual. Now he had become the apostate priest of an entire tribe, responsible for leading the tribe into idolatry. His life was a parody of the Word of God. "Ungodliness is a means of great worldly gain, if it is accompanied by discontent." (See 1 Tim. 6:6.)

There is a sad note when we finally learn the identity of the Levite. In Judges 18:30, he is called "Jonathan, the son of

Gershom, the son of Manasseh." However, *Manasseh* is a scribal attempt to avoid the embarrassment of what the Hebrew text really says. The text reveals that Jonathan was a descendant of the great Moses. To cover the fact that such a godly man could have so worthless a descendant, the scribes altered his name. But it is a stark reminder that it does not do any good to have a godly ancestor if you do not know God yourself. Godliness is not genetic.

Jonathan is an extreme example of self-promoting service, but it is a danger from which none of us is exempt. What is your attitude to service for Jesus Christ? Are you looking for a place, or are you seeking God's place? Are you content to be what God wants you to be, where He wants you? Or are you a Jonathan, climbing the ladder of Christian promotion, wanting prominence, wanting attention, wanting praise? You do not have to be in vocational Christian work to develop a professional attitude toward the Lord's work. Who are you serving—yourself? Your church? Your organization? Or are you serving the Lord Christ? The lesson of Jonathan's life is the necessity of godly contentment with God's arrangements for our lives. Jonathan's apparent gain brought eternal loss. "But godliness actually is a means of great gain, when accompanied by contentment" (1 Tim. 6:6).

THE JUNK FOOD OF EASY LIVING—18:1-10, 27-31

In those days there was no king of Israel; and in those days the tribe of the Danites was seeking an inheritance for themselves to live in, for until that day an inheritance had not been allotted to them as a possession among the tribes of Israel. So the sons of Dan sent from their family five men out of their whole number, valiant men from Zorah and Eshtaol, to spy out the land and to search it; and they said to them, "Go, search the land." And they came to the hill country of Ephraim, to the house of Micah, and lodged there. When they were near the house of Micah, they recognized the voice of the young man, the Levite; and they turned aside there, and said to him, "Who brought you here? And what are you doing in this place? And what do you have here?" And he said to them, "Thus and so has Micah done to me, and he has hired me, and I have become his priest." And they said to him, "Inquire of God, please, that we may know whether our way on which we are going will be prosperous." And the priest said to them, "Go in peace; your way in which you are going has the LORD'S approval." Then the five men departed and came to Laish and saw the people who were in it living in security, after the manner of the Sidonians, quiet and secure; for there was no ruler humiliating them for anything in the land, and they were far from the Sidonians and had no dealings with anyone. When they came back to their brothers at Zorah and Eshtaol, their brothers said to them, "What do you report?" And they said, "Arise, and let us go up against them; for we have seen the land, and behold, it is very good. And will you sit still? Do not delay to go, to enter, to possess the land. When you enter, you shall come to a secure people with a spacious land; for God has given it into your hand, a place where there is no lack of anything that is on the earth."

Then they took what Micah had made and the priest who had belonged to him, and came to Laish, to a people quiet and secure, and struck them with the edge of the sword; and they burned the city with fire. And there was no one to deliver them, because it was far from Sidon and they had no dealings with anyone, and it was in the valley which is near Beth-rehob. And they rebuilt the city and lived in it. And they called the name of the city Dan, after the name of Dan their father who was born in Israel; however, the name of the city formerly was Laish. And the sons of Dan set up for themselves the graven image; and Jonathan, the son of Gershom, the son of Manasseh, he and his sons were priests to the tribe of the Danites until the day of the captivity of the land. So they set up for themselves Micah's graven image which he had made, all the time that the house of God was at Shiloh.

Judges 18:1 states that the tribe of Dan "was seeking an inheritance for themselves to live in, for until that day an inheritance had not been allotted to them as a possession among the tribes of Israel." We are not to understand from that statement that Dan had been omitted when Joshua divided up the land. Joshua 19 makes it clear that their assigned portion was between Ephraim and Judah, stretching out to the Mediterranean. Dan had refused to trust God by driving out the Amorites. As a result, Judges 1:34 indicates that Dan was forced into the hills and reduced to living in two towns.

Dan was left with two choices. As a tribe, they could repent of their unbelief and trust God to keep His Word as they entered into battle against their enemies. That was God's will. Or they could look for a new area, a comfortable place where the natives were unprepared, undefended, and vulnerable to a sneak attack.

Dan chose the easy place and the easy way. They found it far to the north in Laish, a quiet area colonized by some Phoenicians, who were isolated from any allies. God had called Israel to war, and Dan had refused to fight His battle. But it was not because they were committed to peace. They were dedicated to ease. Why fight Philistines when you can blitz Laish? Why stand when you can run?

Dan's love of ease went hand in hand with their turning to idols. The five spies did not go to Shiloh to discover the will of God. They went to Micah's shrine and hired a priest. They knew what the living God wanted, but they wanted a man-made god who would fit their life-style without making any demands. That is why, before they ever attacked Laish, they seized Micah's idols and set up Jonathan to be their priest.

There is no greater danger faced by North American Christians than the love of ease. It is so tempting to carve out a Laish for ourselves—a quiet little island of peace where we can live in affluence and forget all about the needy world outside, and the enemies of the gospel, and the radical claims of Jesus Christ on our lives. Why fight when we can sleep? Why sacrifice when we can settle down?

One thing is obvious. If you want to live in Laish, you must become an idol-worshiper. No consistent New Testament Christian can live a life of ease. No lover of the cross can retire from God's mission in the world. If you want to settle down into life as a comfortable Christian, casually unconcerned about the need of men and women and the call of God, you are going to have to serve an idol.

We need to see the outcome of Dan's commitment to easy living. In their immediate crusade, they were very successful. In verses 27-31, we see them overwhelming the people of Laish, burning the city and rebuilding a new city. Then they live a life of ease in northern Israel with their own priesthood and their own idolatrous shrine.

It looked like everything had worked out beautifully for Dan. However, you do not always reap the harvest of your sins immediately. There are two things we need to know. In the book of 1 Chronicles, when the list of the tribes and families in Israel is given, Dan is the only tribe which is totally ignored.[2] They had vanished into obscurity, probably because of intermarriage with the Philistines.[3] Dan did not take what God had given to them, and they took what God had not given them. In the process, they lost all that they had.

We can take the process one step further. In Revelation 7, we are introduced to the 144,000 Hebrew believers who will carry out a special ministry for God in the Tribulation, after the rapture of the church. In that list of tribes, Dan is not mentioned. They refused to follow God's mission for them in the land of Israel, and they chose the easy way Therefore, God refused to give them this special ministry of blessing for Him in the future.

Thus, in Judges 17-18, we have seen three kinds of spiritual junk food which ultimately lead to destruction. It is exactly as God's Word says, "There is a way which seems right to a man, but its end is the way of death" (Prov. 14:12). It does not matter how good junk food tastes, it is still junk, and, if it becomes more important to us than the pure milk and food of the Word, it will destroy us.

Do you have any junk food in your spiritual diet? It

may be Micah's food of self-made religion, a man-made comfortable god. Perhaps you are addicted to Jonathan's product—self-seeking service. Or you may have the Danites' taste—a love for easy living. It could be a combination of all three. Be careful—you are what you eat.

TWENTY-TWO

Steering Through the Moral Fog

Up until April 3, 1977, few people knew anything about a place called Tenerife. In fact, most of us probably were not very sure of the location of the Canary Islands. But, on that day, at a little airport, two 747s collided on the runway. That accident left 575 people dead, thousands mourning, and Tenerife at the focal point of world attention.

There are some questions about that tragedy which will never be answered, although the chief facts are clear. The airport was crowded because the main airport at Los Palmas had been closed due to a bombing. As a result, the 747s had to taxi on the runway rather than on the taxiway. It was a foggy day, and the two pilots could not see one another, but, for some inexplicable reason, the Dutch pilot began his takeoff without clearance from the control tower. Obviously, he thought he was doing the right thing, but he was not. The other plane was in the way, and he was unable to avoid it. As a result, hundreds of people were killed.

Every pilot is taught one very basic lesson at the beginning of his training. In an air traffic control zone, you do not do what seems best in your eyes; you do what the control tower tells you to do. That is always true, but it is especially true when the visibility is bad. The reason is, of course, very simple. The controller knows things that you do not know. He has better information and a better perspective to guide a pilot safely to his destination. To act on your own causes disasters.

That is an obvious principle of aviation, but it is also an important principle of life. We live at a time when a thick moral fog has settled upon our society. The old moral landmarks have been obliterated, and no one seems to know the difference between right and wrong. Ethically and morally, the visibility is nil, and people are groping for anything that will help them find their directions. It is very tempting, at such a time, to fly by the seat of your pants, living by your own standards, doing whatever is right in your own eyes. The passage of Scripture we are going to study gives us a vivid picture of what happens when we follow that method.

The other alternative is to be guided by Someone who can see what we cannot see and who knows what we do not know. The great promise of God's Word is that, if we commit ourselves to doing what is right in God's eyes, we will be directed safely through the moral fog. The Lord is not a controller who makes mistakes. He is the omniscient, loving Father who wants only the best for His children.

In many ways the last section of Judges is the sewer of Scripture. It holds the dubious distinction of being the most disgusting and degraded story in the Bible, unredeemed by an admirable character or a noble act. To read these chapters is to be repelled by them, and you cannot help feeling rather dirty. It is almost as bad as reading a newspaper today. That is not an exaggeration, but a reminder that the awful degradation that blotched Israel's history is an everyday occurrence in our society. Perhaps that is why God allowed this story to be recorded. After all, the Spirit who inspired Scripture is the *Holy* Spirit. He did not give us this story to shock our sensibilities but to teach us truth.

It would be helpful to take a Bible and read these three chapters before you go further. The following is a selection of verses which reveals the main flow of the action.

> Then all the sons of Israel from Dan to Beersheba, including the land of Gilead, came out, and the congregation assembled as one man to the LORD at Mizpah. And the chiefs of all the people, even of all the tribes of Israel, took their stand in the assembly of the people of God, 400,000 foot soldiers who

drew the sword. (Now the sons of Benjamin heard that the sons of Israel had gone up to Mizpah.) And the sons of Israel said, "Tell us, how did this wickedness take place?" So the Levite, the husband of the woman who was murdered, answered and said, "I came with my concubine to spend the night at Gibeah which belongs to Benjamin. But the men of Gibeah rose up against me and surrounded the house at night because of me. They intended to kill me; instead, they ravished my concubine so that she died. And I took hold of my concubine and cut her in pieces and sent her throughout the land of Israel's inheritance; for they have committed a lewd and disgraceful act in Israel. Behold, all you sons of Israel, give your advice and counsel here." Then all the people arose as one man, saying, "Not one of us will go to his tent, nor will any of us return to his house. But now this is the thing which we will do to Gibeah; we will go up against it by lot. And we will take 10 men out of 100 throughout the tribes of Israel, and 100 out of 1,000, and 1,000 out of 10,000 to supply food for the people, that when they come to Gibeah of Benjamin, they may punish them for all the disgraceful acts that they have committed in Israel." Thus all the men of Israel were gathered against the city, united as one man. Then the tribes of Israel sent men through the entire tribe of Benjamin, saying, "What is this wickedness that has taken place among you? Now then, deliver up the men, the worthless fellows in Gibeah, that we may put them to death and remove this wickedness from Israel." But the sons of Benjamin would not listen to the voice of their brothers, the sons of Israel. And the sons of Benjamin gathered from the cities to Gibeah, to go out to battle against the sons of Israel (20:1-14).

Now the men of Israel had sworn in Mizpah, saying, "None of us shall give his daughter to Benjamin in marriage." So the people came to Bethel and sat there before God until evening, and lifted up their voices and wept bitterly. And they said, "Why, O LORD, God of Israel, has this come about in Israel, so that one tribe should be missing today in Israel?" And it came about the next day that the people arose early and built an altar there, and offered burnt offerings and peace offerings. Then the sons of Israel said, "Who is there among all the tribes of Israel who did not come up in the assembly to the LORD?" For they had taken a great oath concerning him who did not come up to the LORD at Mizpah, saying, "He shall surely be put to death." And the sons of Israel were sorry for their brother Benjamin and said, "One tribe is cut off from Israel today. What shall we do for wives for those who are left, since we have sworn by the LORD not to give them any of our daughters in marriage?" And they said, "What one is there of the tribes of Israel who did not come up to the LORD at Mizpah?" And behold, no one had come to the camp from Jabesh-gilead to the assembly. For when the people were numbered, behold, not one of the inhabitants of Jabesh-gilead was there. And the congregation sent 12,000 of the valiant warriors there, and commanded them, saying, "Go and strike the inhabitants of Jabesh-gilead with the edge of the sword, with the woman and the little ones. And this is the thing that you shall do: you shall utterly destroy every man and every woman who has lain with a man." And they found among the inhabitants of Jabesh-gilead 400 young virgins who had not known a man by lying with him; and they brought them to the camp at Shiloh, which is in the land of Canaan. Then the whole congregation sent word and spoke to the sons of Benjamin who were at the rock of Rimmon, and proclaimed peace to them. And Benjamin returned at that time, and they gave them the women whom they had kept alive from the women of Jabesh-gilead; yet they were not enough for them. And the people were sorry for Benjamin because the LORD had made a breach in the tribes of Israel (21:1-15).

And the sons of Benjamin did so, and took wives according to their number from those who danced, whom they carried away. And they went and returned to their inheritance, and rebuilt the cities and lived in them. And the sons of Israel departed from there at that time, every man to his tribe and family, and each one of them went out from there to his inheritance. In those days there was no king in Israel; everyone did what was right in his own eyes (21:23-25).

After the My Lai massacre was uncovered, and Lieutenant William Calley was imprisoned for his part in it, one news report depicted him sitting in his cell, shaking his head and saying, "It couldn't be wrong or I'd feel remorse about it."

It is hard to imagine how a man could be involved in such a brutal act and not know that it was wrong, but the book of Judges tells us that it is possible. We saw when we looked at Judges 17 and 18, that the last five chapters of Judges contain two stories held together by a common theme which is stated twice, in 17:6 and 21:25, "In those days there was no king in Israel; every man did what was right in his own eyes." In chapters 17-18, we have a story of spiritual anarchy; in 19-21, of moral anarchy. But in both those passages men are doing evil, gross evil, because it is right in their eyes.

We see that all around us. Our society is filled with gross immorality, defended by suave, articulate, attractive spokespersons. You can scarcely find a perversion that someone is not willing to defend as essential to human freedom. I am reminded of the man who summarized his life in these words: "I have spent the best years of my life giving people the lighter pleasures and all I get is abuse and the existence of a hunted man." Who was that poor, persecuted, misunderstood humanitarian? Al Capone, the gangster.

When God goes, everything and anything goes. That is the lesson of Scripture and history, and it is presented in vivid detail here in the book of Judges. It is a story of "3 Rs," only they are not "reading, 'riting, and 'rithmetic" but "rape, revenge, and reaping."

THE SORDID SAGA OF GIBEAH

THE RAPE OF THE CONCUBINE

The story begins with an unnamed Levite living with his concubine in the hill country of Ephraim. A concubine was a kind of second-class wife, who was either a slave or a woman without a dowry. The concubine was unfaithful to the Levite, and, finally, she deserted him and went back to her father's home in Bethlehem. After four months, her husband realized she was not coming back, and he set out to convince her that he cared for her.

The woman's father was delighted to see him. After all, his daughter had done a disgraceful thing in deserting her husband. So he held a great feast to celebrate their reunion. There was lots of food and drink, and the celebration lasted for three days. On the fourth day, the man tried to leave, but his father-in-law persuaded him to stay. The next day, he did the same thing, but, early in the afternoon, the man finally pulled himself away and went off with his concubine and his servant.

After they had gone about six miles, it began to get dark. His servant wanted to spend the night in Jerusalem, but that was a Gentile city. It would not be safe. So they pressed on for another five miles to a town in Benjamin called Gibeah. There was no Holiday Inn there; so the custom was to go to the town square, and the citizens would give travellers a place to stay. But no one did. It was a terrible breach of Eastern hospitality, but, finally, an old man—a farmer from Ephraim—came along and offered his house.

At this point, the story turns very sordid. In the midst of the celebration in the old man's house, they heard a pounding on the walls of the house. The men of the city almost knocked down the doors. "Send out the man who came to you so that we can homosexually attack him." The man and his host were horrified and terrified. It was Sodom and Gomorrah all over again. The old man was shocked into speaking. "No. It is wicked and godless. Here is my daughter and the concubine. Do whatever is good in your eyes to them." But the men kept pounding on the doors, until, with despicable cowardice, the man pushed his concubine out the door, and the evil Benjaminites raped her all night long.

The next morning, the man came out the door, saw the woman lying on the ground, and callously said, "Come on, get up. We have to get out of here." Of course, she was dead. He picked up her body, carried it home, where he cut it into twelve parts and sent the pieces throughout Israel to show the despicable thing that had happened.

THE REVENGE OF ISRAEL (20)

When the nation saw the bloody evidence of this horrible act, they were moved to revenge. Revenge is deadly business. In the old Amos 'n Andy show, Andy was being terrorized by a big man who would slap him on the chest. Finally, Andy had taken all he could, and he said to Amos, "I'm fixed for him. I put a stick of dynamite in my vest pocket and the next time he slaps me, he's going to get his hand blown off!" Sure, but at the same time Andy's own heart will be blown out. That almost happened to Israel, as 400,000 men gathered at Mizpah, determined to deal with this injustice.

There was never a time in Israel's history when they more desperately needed God's guidance. The whole tribe of Benjamin was absent, and civil war was at hand. But they did not turn to God for the answers. Instead, they did what was right in their own eyes. They took three vows.

1. No one will go home until Gibeah is attacked and destroyed.
2. Anyone who does not join against Gibeah will be killed.
3. No one will allow his daughter to marry a Benjaminite.

They then sent a messenger to Benjamin, demanding that they turn over the men of Gibeah. Benjamin not only refused to punish the guilty, they were willing to defend them with their lives. Benjamin was morally very sick, and, therefore, they gathered an army to defend themselves.

It does not seem like a very fair battle—26,000 Benjaminites against 400,000 Israelites. But Benjamin was hilly country, easier to defend than to attack, and, on the first day, 22,000 Israelites were killed and only a handful of Benjaminites. The next battle resulted in the death of 18,000 Israelites. Finally, with 40,000 men dead, the Israelites turned to God for direction, and, in the next battle, all but

600 Benjaminites were killed, and those 600 ended up hiding at the rock of Rimmon.

REAPING THE RESULTS (21)

That brings us to the third part of the story. All of a sudden, the people woke up to what was going on. They were about to wipe out one of their tribes and leave a permanent gap in the nation. In a typical way, they turned around and blamed God. "Why, O LORD, God of Israel, has this come about in Israel?" (v. 3). It was rather late to be turning to God, and this was hardly a prayer of repentance. The Israelites determined not to kill the last 600 Benjaminites, but now they had another problem. They had made a vow not to give any of their daughters to the men of Benjamin. How could the tribe continue without children? They could not marry Gentiles.

Rather than admit they had made a sinful and willful vow, they solved their problem in a typically cruel way. First, they discovered that the remote northern area of Jabesh-Gilead had not sent any soldiers. They did not ask why. They just sent an army of 12,000 to kill everyone in the place, except unmarried girls. That provided 400 wives, but 200 more were needed. Then they decided that their vow was not to *give* daughters to Benjamin. If the Benjaminites kidnapped their wives, they would be legally acceptable. So they told Benjamin how to kidnap wives at the festival at Shiloh. With that business done, they went home.

A recent Oscar-winning film advertized its delights in the following way: "Moviegoers: If violence, madness, rape, larceny, and bloodshed appeal to you, then see the best." Millions did. Nothing could more eloquently illustrate the deep sickness of our society. It is disgusting that Israel practiced such perversions. It is infinitely worse that we not only practice them, we celebrate them in movies and flock to see them for pleasure! We are entertained by immorality and titillated by godlessness. Gibeah has nothing on the Western world!

Judges 19-21 gives us the ugliest story in the Bible. The key to it is that, at every stage, men were acting on the basis of what was right in their own eyes. As far as the men of Gibeah were concerned, rape was all right. To the former and the Levite in the house, homosexual rape was unthinkable, but other rape was acceptable. The men of Benjamin thought it was right to overlook sin and to defend evil men. To Israel, revenge and retaliation could be justified, and to solve their problems about marriage for the Benjaminites, the massacre of innocent people and kidnapping could be condoned.

The interesting thing is that none of this had anything to do with idolatry or Baal worship. It began with individuals ignoring the law of God, doing what was right in their own eyes, and it led a whole nation into moral collapse.

THE ORGANIC NATURE OF SIN

There is an important truth about sin in this story. In our naiveté, we tend to think of sins as isolated acts, individual events which have no relationship one to another. However, the Bible views sin organically. There is a vast cause and effect link which, if it is not dealt with, leads a whole society into moral collapse. No sin was ever committed which affects one person alone. There is no such thing as victimless sin. Any sin sends ripples into all of society.

There is an old story of a ship that was traveling across the Mediterranean, and one of the passengers cut a hole through the side of the ship. The sailors came to him and demanded to know what he was doing. "What difference does it make to you?" he asked. "The hole's under my own bunk."

If you understand the absurdity of that story, you have gained an important insight into the biblical view of the effects of sin. Men go around shouting, "Do your own thing," and demanding the freedom to do what they please, when they please, where they please. Then we wonder why the boat is filling up with water, and we are beginning to go under. We do not live to ourselves, and we do not sin to ourselves.

The interrelatedness of sin is vividly illustrated here. Where did Israel go wrong? Where did the problem begin? The answer is not immediately apparent, but notice Judges 20:27-28. It describes *spiritual sin.* "The Ark of the Covenant of God was at Bethel in those days." If you are not careful, you will miss the significance of that statement. From Joshua, Judges, and 1 Samuel, we know that the tabernacle was in Shiloh, and the Ark of the Covenant belonged in the Holy of Holies of the tabernacle in Shiloh. The ark was intensely holy, and no one was to view it, except the high priest once a year. But the holiness of God had been so cheapened that the high priest had allowed it to be taken out of the tabernacle and transported to Bethel, in direct disobedience to God. What makes this doubly sad is that the priest was Phinehas, a man who once stood powerfully for God (see Num. 25).

That is the root of all sin—a weak conception of the holiness of God. That is where Israel went astray.

That leads directly to *sexual sin*—the adultery of the concubine, and the homosexuality and rape in Gibeah. At first, it seems that sexual sin is the most private of sins. Over and over we hear it said, "It is no one's business what two consenting adults do. It affects no one but themselves." That is sheer nonsense. Not only are other people almost always involved, but our view of sex is one of the most determinative things about us. Hand in hand with sexual sin goes a cheapened view of the value of people and life. Sexual immorality brutalizes and dehumanizes us. It touches our "self" more deeply than any other sin.

It is worth noting that at the heart of Gibeah's sin was homosexuality. It was the desire of the men of the city for the Levite, not his concubine, which triggered the devastation. Paul indicates in Romans 1 that widespread acceptance of homosexuality is an evidence that a people have rejected the truth of God, and, in turn, have been given up by Him to "dishonorable passion." Sodom and Gibeah are symbols of this, and it is a frightening commentary on our own society, that something the Bible calls unnatural and shameful (Rom. 1:26-27) has become increasingly accepted.

Related to sexual sin, intriguingly, there is often another step downward—a *cheapened view of life* and a loss of human dignity and worth. It is expressed in the rape at Gibeah, the desecration of a woman's body, the slaughter of Benjamin, the massacre at Jabesh-Gilead, and the kidnapping at Shiloh.

There are many other sins, but I wonder if you notice the downward flow. We lose our sense of the holiness and greatness of God, and soon we find ourselves engaged in sexual sin, the sin Paul says is against our own body. Then we lose our self-worth, and we are plunged into the lowest level when we view people as things and treat them as commodities. Sin devastates our *spirit* in our relationship to God, distorts our *soul*—our sense of self, and reduces us to little more than animals, living as mere *bodies,* with our humanity almost erased. That is the process of Judges 19-21, and it is the process of the twentieth century.

PRINCIPLES TO PONDER

I want to draw some important principles out of all this. Ugly as Judges 19-21 is, it is a passage uncomfortably close to what is going on all around us. In fact, it reads like the plot of a modern movie. Therefore, we need to learn five important lessons from God's Word to enable us to survive morally and spiritually in a society without standards

1. *The basis of moral behavior is of critical impor-tance.* Why you do what you do is as important as what you do. That point may not be immediately apparent, so let me try to clarify it. For years, many people said that premarital sex was wrong because of the possibility of a child out of wedlock. But now two things have changed that argument—birth control and a new acceptance of casual

relationships. If the only reason for sexual purity is a fear of unwanted pregnancy, obviously sexual immorality is now entirely appropriate. Technology has done away with the problem.

The point is this: If your moral behavior is not grounded on the moral absolutes of God's Word, you will end up doing what is right in your own eyes. You may get your ethical guidelines from an ethical theory of nominalism, utilitarianism, or situationism. It may be based on your parents' teachings or peer pressure or religious tradition. It may be based on the life-style of rock musicians or Hollywood stars. Whatever it is, if it is not based on God's Word, it is empty.

The great question is, "Why is something right or wrong, moral or immoral?" The way you answer that question will determine a great deal about your future moral behavior, and for a believer there can be no answer which does not begin with God's Word.

2. *Ethical relativism is degrading and dehumanizing.* It does not take a genius to recognize that we are terribly confused as a society, ethically and morally. We have lost any basis of judging right and wrong. The current motivation is, "Do your own thing," and, in modern music, or television, in movies and literature, there is a concerted effort to prove that the old standards and values no longer have any meaning.

I cannot help but think of 2 Peter 2:19 when I hear all this talk about personal freedom and doing your own thing. Speaking about the people who preach this philosophy, Peter says, "[They promise] them freedom while they themselves are slaves of corruption; for by what a man is overcome, by this he is enslaved." There is a tragically long trail of broken lives and shattered dreams in the wake of the new morality, and it is those who shout "freedom" loudest who are the most enslaved. Because a man believes something to be right does not make it right, and, if Judges 19-21 tells us anything, it tells us that moral anarchy breeds disaster. The so-called new morality is not only a refined form of the old immorality; it is a moral cancer which spreads rapidly and destroys painfully.

3. *Theology and morality cannot be separated.* The only certain basis for morality is the character of God and the Word of God. Right and wrong are not what men think they are, but what God says they are. Quite frankly, I do not care what all the psychologists, sociologists, pornographic publishers, Hollywood producers, and rock musicians in the world say about right and wrong. One million words by them does not carry the authority of one word from God. Men can no more decide what is moral than they can decide whether the earth will rotate on its axis. Those issues are determined by a holy and righteous God. To go back to our opening illustration, a unanimous vote taken by the passengers of a 747 that it is safe to take off does not make it safe, if the control tower says that it is not. Everyone in the cockpit of that Dutch 747 believed he was doing the right thing. Everyone was wrong.

There are three facts that ought to guide every Christian through the moral fog.

- Our God is a holy God, who has absolute standards of right and wrong. He is also our Father, who loves His children and wants the very best for us.
- God has revealed Himself in the Lord Jesus. Apart from Him, we cannot know eternal life or life now. He is the Way, the Truth, and the Life, and nothing makes sense apart from Him.
- God has spoken in His Word. Scripture is absolutely and unconditionally reliable, and as we order our lives by it, we will be completely equipped for every good work.

Apart from those three facts, there is no morality.

4. *The alternative to the moral fog is not legalism or asceticism, but a personal dynamic faith in the Lord Jesus.* Many Christians have given people the impression that the Christian faith is a pleasure-denying, life-negating, joyless, legalistic kind of life. The truth is exactly the opposite. To

live in the will of God is both life-affirming and joy-producing. No one ever accused the Lord Jesus of being a monastic recluse or an ascetic. The path upon which He leads us through life is not only safe, it is good. To follow His values is to find life.

5. *We must not only know God's answers, we must internalize His values.* The only safe procedure in our time is to have the values of God so much a part of us that we instinctively turn to them, when moral visibility is suddenly obliterated. One of the most important ways to do that is by the environment in which we live. We learn from what we see in the lives of other believers, and it is at this point the fellowship of other Christians becomes extremely important. If we are constantly bombarded by false values, it is hard to be unaffected. That is why we need fellowship with other Christians whom we can observe and with whom we can honestly discuss our moral struggles.

We need to be deeply in the Word of God. Reality is life as God sees it, and, as we read His Word, He dispels the fog from the moral horizon.

We need constantly to go beyond instruction to application. My children need more than right answers. They need right attitudes, and they must internalize truth by applying it to their lives. They must see those values in me. It is valuable to ask them, not only, "What did you learn in Sunday school today?" but also, "What difference should that make this week?" I need to ask myself that question as well.

We are living in the middle of a thick moral fog. Millions around us are committed to doing what is right in their own eyes. That is the path of personal and social disaster. God has called us to listen to His direction. The path to safety is the converse of Judges 21:25. Not "Everyone did what was right in his own eyes," but "Everyone did what was right in His eyes." When men in the time of the judges lived by that standard, God used them to bring freedom and victory to His people. The lesson

is one put most profoundly in the book of Hebrews: "Therefore . . . having laid aside every weight and the sin which so
easily entangles us, let us run with endurance the race that
is set before us, looking away from all else unto Jesus, the
Leader and Completer of faith" (Heb. 12:1-2, literal translation). The sin which trips us up is the sin of unbelief, and
the danger that we constantly face is a lack of endurance
and commitment. Endurance is difficult in a time such as
ours, especially if we get our eyes fixed on ourselves or our
circumstances. So the gaze of our hearts must be on the
Lord Jesus. I am inspired and encouraged when I study the
lives of significant Christians, although I am usually disap-
pointed as well. But when I look away to Jesus, I am not
only inspired; I am empowered and enabled. That is the
only way to run!

Conclusion

There is a three-thousand-year-wide gulf between the times of the judges and our times. Modern technology makes that gulf look even larger, and we wonder how we can learn anything relevant from such a different world. Yet as we look more closely, the gulf begins to shrink. We see the people of God locked in a deadly conflict over their values and spiritual convictions, as their society turns its back on the living God and is overrun by the very contemporary evils of moral relativism, sexual libertinism, and religious anarchy. "Everyone did what was right in his own eyes" is our motto, and, in the book of Judges, we see graphically portrayed the seductive appeal and inevitable disaster of such a life-style.

We could write Paul's words over the book: "Now these things happened as examples for us, that we should not crave evil things, as they also craved. . . . Nor let us act immorally. . . . Nor let us try the Lord. . . . Nor grumble. . . . and they were written for our instruction, upon whom the ends of the ages have come" (1 Cor. 10:6-11). One of the levels on which Judges speaks to us is a solemn warning of the seriousness of sin. No matter how great our past accomplishments for the Lord, we can fall into great sin if we take our eyes off the Lord Jesus. Every believer has feet of clay, and when he tries to stand on his own in a society without standards, he will quickly crumble into failure. That is the lesson of a Gideon, a Jephthah, or a Samson. "Therefore let him who thinks he stands take heed lest he fall" (1 Cor. 10:12).

But the book of Judges is also written "for our instruction, that through perseverance and the encouragement of the Scriptures we might have hope" (Rom. 15:4). If Judges tells of strong men made weak by self-confidence, it also eloquently describes weak men made strong through faith in God and by His work in their lives. Judges is the great Old Testament book on the Holy Spirit, and it describes the transforming work of the Spirit in making His people adequate servants of the Old Covenant. If there is hope in seeing how the Lord gave weak men hearts of iron then, it is reinforced by the glorious truth that the Holy Spirit works in the life of the humblest believer today in a way far surpassing anything Old Covenant believers knew. We serve a crucified, risen Savior. We live by the power of His indwelling Spirit. We hold in our hands the complete, inerrant Word of God. Our resources in Christ far outstrip anything the judges knew, and our potential for spiritual victory is far greater than theirs. But, at heart, the issue remains the same. There can be no victory apart from a dynamic, obedient fellowship with the Lord Jesus. A distinctive positive life in a difficult secular age is not the product of proper techniques but of a daily walk of faith.

The Apostle Paul was a man whose spiritual achievements and experiences set him apart from the common herd of believers. But because the Lord was aware of the danger of self-exaltation and self-confidence, He gave him a physical disability that he might learn this truth of the spiritual life. "When I am weak, then I am strong" (2 Cor. 12:10). God's strength does not remove human weakness, it transforms it; so that men with fearful hearts and feet of clay become men with hearts of iron to serve their God. That and that alone is the pathway to a spiritually powerful life in a secular and seductive age.

Hudson Taylor once spelled out what the Lord had taught him about the life of faith in words that aptly summarize the book of Judges:

Want of trust is at the root of almost all our sins and our

weaknesses; and how shall we escape it but by looking to Him and observing His faithfulness? The man who holds God's faithfulness will not be foolhardy or reckless, but he will be ready for every emergency. The man who holds God's faithfulness will dare to obey Him, however impolitic it may appear. Abraham held God's faithfulness and offered up Isaac, "accounting that God was able to raise him . . . from the dead." Moses held God's faithfulness and led the millions of Israel into the waste, howling wilderness. "And what shall I more say? for the time would fail me to tell" of those who, holding God's faithfulness, had faith, and by it "subdued kingdoms, wrought righteousness, obtained promises . . . out of weakness were made strong, waxed valiant in fight, turned to flight the armies of the aliens."

Satan, too, has his creed: Doubt God's faithfulness. "Hath God said? Are you not mistaken as to His commands? He could not really mean just that. You take an extreme view, give too literal a meaning to the words." How constantly, and alas, how successfully are such arguments used to prevent wholehearted trust in God, wholehearted consecration to God! How many estimate difficulties in the light of their own resources, and thus attempt little and often fail in the little they attempt! All God's giants have been weak men, who did great things for God because they reckoned on His being with them.[1]

Notes

Chapter 2

1. John W. Gardner, *Self-Renewal* (New York: Harper & Row, 1964), p. xv.

Chapter 4

1. Ray Stedman, *Death of a Nation* (Waco, Texas; Word, 1976), p. 17.
2. Joni Eareckson and Joe Musser, *Joni* (Grand Rapids: Zondervan, 1974).

Chapter 5

1. Cited by Ted W. Engstrom, *The Making of a Christian Leader* (Grand Rapids: Zondervan, 1976), p. 12.
2. G. Campbell Morgan, *Living Messages of the Books of the Bible* (Westwood, N. J.: Revell, 1912), pp. 125-26.
3. Two factors indicate it was the dry season. First, Sisera would not be so foolish as to use his chariots in the rainy season. He definitely did not expect rain. Second, the Lord's intervention was seen as an unexpected, supernatural one (cf. 5:20-21).

Chapter 8

1 Alexander Whyte, *Bible Characters: Old Testament*, Vol. 1 (London: Marshall, Morgan & Scott, 1972), p. 182.

Chapter 12

1. This concept of the New Testament doctrine of the church is developed in more detail in my book *Life in His Body* (Wheaton, Ill.: Harold Shaw, 1975).
2. Ray Stedman, "Should the Pastor Play Pope?" *Moody Monthly* (July-August 1976), p. 42.
3. Donald Gray Barnhouse, *Let Me Illustrate* (Old Tappan, N. J.: Revell, 1967), p. 71.

Chapter 13

1. Charles H. Spurgeon, *Autobiography: The Early Years 1834-1859*, Vol. 1. (Edinburgh: Banner of Truth Trust, 1962), p. 100.
2 David C. K. Watson, *God's Freedom Fighters* (Croydon, England: Movement Books, 1972), pp. 40-41.
3. Ibid., p. 45.
4. James Montgomery Boice, *The Gospel of John: An Expositional Commentary*, Vol. 1 (Grand Rapids: Zondervan, 1975), p. 251.

Chapter 15

1. James Packer, *Knowing God* (Downers Grove, Ill.: Inter-Varsity, 1973), pp. 14-15.
2. The *New American Standard Bible* text reads, "or I will offer it up," with "and" found in the margin. However, the Hebrew text clearly says "and," as all other translations recognize, and the translation is unfortunate.
3 *Targum of Jonathan*, cited by F. W. Farrar, "The Book of Judges" in C. J. Ellicott, ed., *The Layman's Handy Bible Commentary Series* (Grand Rapids: Zondervan, 1961), p. 150.

Chapter 18

1. Alex Haley, *Roots* (Garden City, N. Y.: Doubleday, 1976), p. 335.

Chapter 21

1. Cited by James Packer, *Knowing God* (Downers Grove, Ill.: Inter-Varsity, 1973), p. 40.
2. Zebulun's genealogy is also not chronicled, but it is mentioned elsewhere (1 Chron. 6:63, 77; 12:33, 40). Dan appears only as a geographical name, not as a tribe.
3. E.g., 2 Chron. 2:14.

Conclusion

1. Dr. and Mrs. Howard Taylor, *Biography of James Hudson Taylor* (London: Hodder & Stoughton, 1965), pp. 348-49.

Moody Press, a ministry of the Moody Bible Institute, is designed for education, evangelization, and edification. If we may assist you in knowing more about Christ and the Christian life, please write us without obligation: Moody Press, c/o MLM, Chicago, Illinois 60610.